Identity, Interest, and Ideology

Identity, Interest, and Ideology

An Introduction to Politics

MARTIN C. NEEDLER

Westport, Connecticut
London

Library of Congress Cataloging-in-Publication Data

Needler, Martin C.
    Identity, interest, and ideology : an introduction to politics /
    Martin C. Needler.
        p.   cm.
    Includes bibliographical references and index.
    ISBN 0–275–95440–4 (alk. paper). — ISBN 0–275–95441–2 (pbk. :
alk. paper)
    1. Politics, practical.   2. Political culture.   3. International
    relations.   I. Title.
    JF2051.N394 1996
    320—dc20   95–50731

British Library Cataloguing in Publication Data is available.

Library of Congress Catalog Card Number: 95–50731
ISBN: 0–275–95440–4
        0–275–95441–2 (pbk.)

First published in 1996

Praeger Publishers, 88 Post Road West, Westport, CT 06881
An imprint of Greenwood Publishing Group, Inc.

Printed in the United States of America

The paper used in this book complies with the
Permanent Paper Standard issued by the National
Information Standards Organization (Z39.48–1984).

10 9 8 7 6 5 4 3 2 1

*To the students and faculty of the
School of International Studies
University of the Pacific*

Contents

III. INTERNATIONAL POLITICS

Preface

This is the space in which one should acknowledge, thank, disclaim, and perhaps even apologize. Let me first thank my wife, Jan Knippers Black, whose benign influence is notable at many points in this book. I need also to acknowledge an intellectual debt to my professors of long ago at Harvard, particularly Carl J. Friedrich, Samuel H. Beer, Samuel P. Huntington, and Herbert J. Spiro. Mary Boughton and Arlene Whittle are especially to be thanked for their work on the manuscript, as are Cathy Tanner, Ruth Merz, and Lani Leberman.

Thanks are also due to my compatriot, coeval, coreligionary, and near neighbor, Ashleigh Brilliant, for permission to use his "Pot Shots," which are more usually to be found decorating T-shirts and postcards. The Pot Shots are individually copyrighted and are not to be reproduced without the permission of Mr. Brilliant.

This book is deliberately conceptualized as an introduction to politics and not to political science, so let me apologize to all my professional colleagues who have done clever things that are not discussed here.

Monterey and Stockton, California
June 1995

INTRODUCTION

© ASHLEIGH BRILLIANT 1983

POT-SHOTS NO. 3101.

THE UNIVERSE
SEEMS WONDERFUL
IN THEORY,

BUT
IN PRACTICE
I DON'T
THINK
IT WILL
EVER
WORK.

Ashleigh Brilliant

To understand human behavior in any general way, we should start with the acknowledgment that nature has programmed humans, like other animals, as individuals, as members of a family, and as members of the species. The complex of motives built into our DNA includes not only those to assure survival of the individual and the family—that is, economic activity that will provide immediate and future food and shelter—but also the survival of our DNA through the procreation of new generations of descendants and close relatives. This not only entails the search for appropriate marriage partners, sexual jealousy, and dynastic politics, but may also provide the basis for ethnic chauvinism and racism.

The range of motivations implanted means that conflicting courses of action are indicated in specific situations, thus providing the raw material for tragic drama. Some predispositions give humans the capacity to bind with each other in solidarity to achieve common purposes, while others motivate deadly competition for resources and for the ranking in status hierarchies which gives priority access to resources.

Civilized social living has consisted of the establishment of institutions and accepted patterns of political behavior that partly recognize and accept the powerful motivational drives encoded in our genetic makeup, and partly restrain and try to bring them under control in the interest of the optimal functioning of the social unit. Thus, for example, a hierarchy of status may be recognized for certain purposes, such as the wielding of political power by officeholders, but denied in other instances in which all people are held to have equal rights. Sexual jealousy in its relation to procreation may be given a certain legitimacy, as when divorce is allowed on grounds of adultery, but may stop short of accepting a husband's killing of his wife and her lover caught in the act. For the requirements for successful living in civilized society, nature has oversupplied its implanted purposes with motivational power, but it has also provided a reasoning ability that can be used, up to a certain point, to resolve the problems presented.

Individual structures of motivation, thus, include the primary drives serving the purposes of survival, self-assertion, and perpetuation of the genes; behavior inculcated by society in the attempt to make civilized social living possible; and the psychodynamic structure developed by the individual child to find a way to survive and prosper in the long transition from helpless dependence in a particular family setting to mature self-assertion. Complicated, yes; but, one hopes, not too complicated to be understandable.

POLITICAL SCIENCE

This book is an introduction to politics not, like so many basic texts, an introduction to political science. That is, our focus will be on the substance of politics, not on how it is studied by scholars. I will not be footnoting the work of colleagues, and will deal with current differences among schools of thought only occasionally in passing. It is nevertheless worthwhile to outline how the academic discipline of political science is organized so that the student can have some idea of what it is that political scientists do.

A variety of ways of organizing the field of political science are defensible, but probably the most commonly used in the United States is that which establishes a series of four subfields. One of these is *the history of political thought*, sometimes called "political theory," the study of the ideas of major political thinkers through history. Although of great importance to the discipline of political science, courses in the history of political thought can sometimes be found also in departments of philosophy.

The second subfield is the study of *international relations*. This is obviously an integral part of political science, although some institutions have separate departments for international relations, which also integrate subjects like international economics and diplomatic history along with studies of international politics.

Comparative politics is the study of actually existing political institutions and practices in different countries. It includes studies of legislatures, court systems, political parties, and interest groups.

Logically, American politics should simply be a subdivision of comparative politics, but because a majority of the world's professional political scientists are Americans and a colossal body of material having to do with U.S. politics exists, *American politics* is in the United States treated as a separate field, and further subdivided into subfields such as U.S. national government, state and local government, parties and political behavior, public law, and public policy and administration. Because public administration is not just an academic field of study but also a technical specialty training future practitioners, it is very often established as a separate academic program.

BASIC PRINCIPLES

CHAPTER 1

Politics and Power

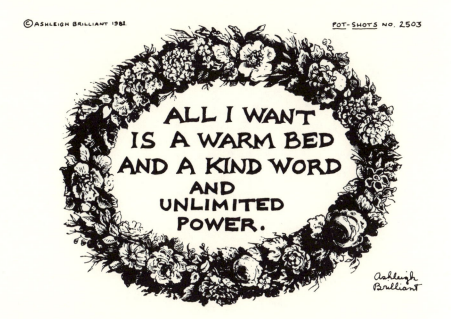

© ASHLEIGH BRILLIANT 1981   POT-SHOTS NO. 2503

ALL I WANT
IS A WARM BED
AND A KIND WORD
AND
UNLIMITED
POWER.

Ashleigh
Brilliant

THE PURSUIT OF INTEREST

Fundamental to the study of politics is the concept of *interest*. Now quite clearly human individuals are self-interested—that is, concerned to promote their own well-being. This is necessarily so, after all, since otherwise the human species would have died out long ago. If human animals were indifferent to their own requirements for food and shelter, then clearly humankind would never have been able to survive.

Nor would it have survived if parents were indifferent to the nurturance of their young. Human babies are defenseless and incompetent. They have to be sheltered, nursed, and fed. Thus the human animal which has survived to the present day is necessarily one that promotes not only his own interests, but also those of his juvenile dependents.

To put it another way: human beings create for themselves an identity that extends beyond single individuals and encompasses one's family; but this capacity to identify with other humans beyond the immediate biological self, necessary if helpless infants are to survive, can also extend to larger collectivities—the extended family, the tribe, the nation; even a company, a government agency, a fraternity or an athletic team. In fact, it can and does extend to all of humankind.

Often the pursuit of self-interest is taken to be opposed to altruistic behavior; one is said to be either selfish or unselfish. In fact, however, what we are dealing with here is not a polarity but rather a continuum. The character of self-interested behavior depends on the nature of the "self" in question. Different individuals conceptualize their identities differently. To some the national or racial group to which they belong is a very important source of conceptualizations of their own identities; for others, the identification with all of humankind is stronger than with that of the ethnic or language group into which they happen to be born.

THE SELF

Even with respect to the individual, the concept of self is problematic. "Two souls," writes the poet, "are at war within my breast." To the great Greek philosopher Plato, the individual was a battlefield between the forces of reason, emotion, and appetite. Is it in your self-interest to take the money when no one is looking? Or is it in your self-interest instead to develop a just character of which you can be proud?

Am I being self-interested if I vote for lax enforcement of local tax collection laws? Sure, because I identify myself as one who can get away with underpaying his taxes. But am I being self-interested if I vote for stricter enforcement? Yes again, because then I am concerned that the county be adequately supplied with the revenue to provide the services from which I benefit.

The individual's capacity to extend his or her ego to include a variety of social collectivities can be seized on and exploited by the leadership of various kinds of social formations. Cheerleaders promote enthusiastic identification with a sports team, which raises its morale and thus improves its chances of winning. Leaders of nation-states try to arouse patriotic feeling through indoctrination in schools, which prepares people to respond to symbols such as anthems and flags.

EMPATHY

It has been generally accepted that the fundamental principle of morality is the Golden Rule: "Do unto others as you would have them do unto you." There have been many ways of formulating this principle (the work of the late-eighteenth-century philosopher Immanuel Kant is particularly notable) but the basic premise is clear: that, being of equal moral worth, human beings are entitled to be treated with equal consideration.

If, instead of asking the question in terms of logic and rights, however, we instead look for the basis for moral behavior in human emotions and psychology, we get an interesting answer. Psychological experiments suggest that the basis for moral behavior toward others is the capacity to empathize with them, the capacity to be aware that others feel the same kind of pain as oneself. Those found guilty of crimes of brutality frequently lack this capacity to empathize, perhaps as a result of some inherent biological defect, perhaps as a result of a cold and alienating upbringing as children.

Morality thus has emotional as well as logical roots. In fact, one of the early formulations of the Golden Rule, by the first-century rabbi, Akiva, was "Love your neighbor as yourself."

To Walter, his regional *identity* is all-important: he is first and foremost a Southerner, regarding Yankees as an alien and suspect race; Mary identifies primarily with women and the handicapped; while José thinks of himself as a Catholic and a self-employed businessman. These varying identities affect the political interests each will try to promote: how they will vote, what organizations they will join and support, what they will write to their congressmen. The shape of each individual's identity profile is different and therefore the values that each person seeks to promote and the strategies each pursues are different. Thus the resulting range of behaviors can vary a great deal, without changing the basic point that a person's political activity generally consists of the promotion of interests, variously conceptualized and defined, which reflect that person's self-identification.

SOME BASIC CONCEPTS

Interests are promoted in dealings with other people by means of techniques of both conflict and cooperation—fighting or voting on the one hand, forming alliances and organizations on the other. This is the activity we call *politics*. These techniques of politics are similar whether the purposes of political activity are the establishment of policies in the general public interest, the promotion of the interests of an economic or ethnic group, or simply the advancement of an individual career.

Another key term used in discussions of politics is *power*. Briefly put, power is the ability to influence others to do what one wants. There are thus several possible sources of power: physical coercion, legal authority, emotional attachment, and economic leverage, for example. Although normally we speak of politics when referring to activities in the public sphere, related to the state and its authority, politics takes place everywhere—in the family, in the university, in the courts of justice—and power, in its various forms, is used in these arenas. A mother may have power over her children because of their emotional attachment to her; an employer has power over his workers by virtue of his control of their wages; a television broadcaster may have power because of his or her influence on the viewers' attitudes and beliefs.

Legal authority is a specific kind of power, the power assigned to individuals by the law to act on behalf of the organized community. A political constitution establishes the allocation of powers for the government it sets up. Holders of office under that constitution then have legal authority to act in the name of all of the members of the polity.

This polity, or politically organized community, is called the *state*. This is not "state" in the sense of a constituent unit in a federal system, fifty of which together constitute the United States; the more general meaning of "state" refers to the political aspect of an organized human community.

Today the term normally used is "nation-state," signifying that the political boundaries drawn among mankind are in principle approximately the same boundary lines that distinguish between people of different nations—that is, different languages and ethnic identities. Reality often deviates from this norm, however, as we shall see in Chapter 12. A *state* is thus an organized body of people, located in a specific extension of territory and under the authority of a single government.

SOVEREIGNTY

The state is often said to enjoy *sovereignty*. The doctrine of sovereignty, as this was developed in the early modern period in Europe—for example, by writers such as the sixteenth-century French jurist Jean Bodin—is that within any jurisdiction there can be only a single authoritative source of law. The logic of the principle of sovereignty is this: a French peasant, let us say, living in Normandy, may be subject to the authority of the duke of Normandy, of the king of France, and of the local bishop. It is quite likely, however, that in this situation the duke may require the peasant to do something opposed to what he has been required to do by the bishop. The duke says "To get this castle built on time, I want you to work seven days a week." The bishop says "Don't work on Sunday. I want you in church." In this case of conflicting sources of law, the peasant can follow only one set of requirements; the source of whichever body of law the peasant actually follows in case of conflict is the sovereign. (The king of France is appealed to by the duke, while the bishop appeals to the pope, who confirms that no one should work on Sunday. But the king says, "Of course I have the greatest respect for the pope, and I like to follow his edicts where possible. Normally, people should observe the Sabbath. However, I rule that in cases of military emergency, as decided by local lords, people can be required to work on Sunday.") A single source of law is thus necessary to avoid the problem of conflicting requirements placed on the citizen. If, for example, the king of France is sovereign in the sense that his laws override those of other authorities when they are in conflict, then the king may permit other jurisdictions—the municipality, the province, or the bishopric—to make regulations within a sphere defined as their own. Nevertheless, he has the authority to overrule them if he thinks it is necessary. The sovereign is thus that source of law which has the last word in cases of conflict.

Needless to say, this doctrine was a very handy one for kings to use in the early modern period, when all across Europe monarchs were trying to establish their absolute authority at the expense of loyalties owed to the pope and the Catholic Church, or to local notables and landowning aristocrats. There had been a confusion of overlapping and shifting authority in Europe since the gradual decay of the Roman Empire.

In fact, however, the doctrine of sovereignty oversimplifies and thus distorts the real situation. Thus, for example, what person or body is the sovereign in a constitutional democratic system? A good parlor game could be organized around that question. Where does sovereignty lie in the United States? In U.S. political oratory, state governments are frequently referred to as "sovereign," but that is only a rhetorical flourish. Is Congress sovereign at the national level? No, Congress cannot be regarded as the wielder of sovereign power since its acts can be vetoed by the president or nullified by the Supreme Court. Presidential acts can also be set aside by the Court. But the president appoints the members of the Supreme Court, with the advice and consent of the Senate, which may impeach and remove them from office.

Thus there appears not to be a determinate "sovereign" in the U.S. system. But why should this be surprising? After all, the whole point of a constitutional system is to divide and allocate powers so that no individual or agency of government becomes too powerful. One could say that the whole purpose of a democratic constitution is to eliminate the existence of a single sovereign power as too dangerous to individual liberty. The checks and balances in the U.S. Constitution serve to ensure that no single individual or body of individuals has "the last word," except perhaps the electorate itself.

Although it was developed for its usefulness in cases of domestic clashes of jurisdiction, the doctrine of sovereignty finds its greatest application today in international relations. The premise that governments of nation-states are sovereign implies that a government cannot interfere in matters solely within the domestic jurisdiction of another state.

Thus sovereignty remains the basic organizing principle in international relations. In practice, however, although legally they have full sovereignty, most governments in the world today do not have complete control over their own affairs. The world is so interdependent economically that sometimes a small state may be completely at the mercy of a larger trading partner. Moreover, a large and powerful state has a variety of techniques it can use to dominate its neighbors. We will return to this theme in Chapter 12, where we will discuss imperialism and hegemony.

THE STATE AND SOCIETY

The state, as we have seen, is the organized political community. Another way of putting this is to say that it is the grouping together of the political functions needed in any organized society. Some societies do not have a state in this sense. In these less-developed societies, political functions are not separated from other social functions; decisions about matters we think of as political may be made by the same community elders as make religious or cultural decisions, or by the same tribal councils or assemblies.

ARISTOTLE (384–322 B.C.)

A student at Plato's Academy in Athens, Aristotle served as tutor to the boy who would become Alexander the Great before returning to Athens to found his own school, the Lyceum. Although his early writings are close to Plato's dialogues in style and content, the major works of Aristotle's that survive are substantial texts based on his mature thought and the extensive research carried on by Aristotle himself and by younger colleagues and students at the Lyceum, apparently compiled by later editors from Aristotle's lectures at the school. These are extraordinary in the range of subjects covered, from logic and ethics to poetry and rhetoric to physics and biology; and for the wide-ranging empirical research on which they are based. In many fields, Aristotle's work was not surpassed until the nineteenth or twentieth centuries; in some, it is still the best work that has been done.

In his writing on politics, Aristotle classified the different kinds of constitution and wrote that while monarchy or aristocracy would be fine if their rulers, king or elite, remained virtuous and public-spirited, it was most likely that they would be corrupted and become, respectively, the degenerate forms of tyranny or oligarchy. Democracy was also likely to become corrupt—although in its corrupt form it would be less harmful than tyranny or oligarchy—so that the most desirable and stable political system in practice would be a mixed one, a constitutional system in which different institutions represented different interests. Such a system is most likely to be led by people of moderate wealth, who are less likely to follow extreme policies than either the rich or the poor. This kind of mixed system, which combines the virtues of freedom and stability, is the most likely to provide an environment in which individuals and families can grow in knowledge, virtue, and wisdom.

Although Aristotle seemed to have considered that the classic city-state provided the appropriate size for a political system, it is likely that he would recognize the constitutional democracies of today as the kind of mixed political system he advocated.

The great Greek political scientist, Aristotle, is often quoted as saying that man is by nature a political animal—in other words, that the state is a natural and inevitable accompaniment of human existence. Man is certainly naturally a social animal—which is probably closer to Aristotle's meaning—in the sense that without society man would not be man as we know him. A distinctive feature of human animals, for example, is their ability to think; but complex thinking is hardly possible without language, and language is a structure that develops only through living in society. Although some people, who are called *anarchists*, believe that government does more harm than good and people would be better off without it, most people would say that some kind of government is necessary in society, that the common life of society requires a decision-making mechanism, and that the decisions made must bind all the members of the society, and not just those that agree with them.

SOCIAL CONTRACT THEORY

It is certainly true that the existence of government creates a paradoxical situation. Since government establishes rules and enforces them, even against the wishes of individuals in specific cases, it is in effect saying "Yes, you are being forced to do something you don't want to do. Government forces you to do what you don't want to do, but government nevertheless exists for your own good." In his *Social Contract*, Jean-Jacques Rousseau heightened the paradox, writing that under government, which alone made it possible for people to enjoy freedom, man would be "forced to be free." "Man is born free," wrote Rousseau, "but he is everywhere in chains." In his dramatic way, Rousseau was asking "Why should human freedom be restricted?"

JEAN-JACQUES ROUSSEAU (1712–78)

A philosopher of Protestant origins from Geneva writing in French, Rousseau was an influential figure in the development of the ideas of the Enlightenment that contributed to the French Revolution, but also in the Romantic reaction against the Enlightenment which set in during the nineteenth century. His writing, which extended to novels and opera as well as to works of philosophy, had as its theme that man was by nature good but was corrupted by society.

The answer had already been given in an earlier version of the "social contract" that Rousseau described. In his *Leviathan*, published in 1651, Thomas Hobbes wrote that the fundamental problem of human life was that anyone could kill anyone else. The first problem of existence, therefore, was to assure public safety; government thus begins with a police force. Instead of being able to rely only on an unsure self-defense, people constitute a state that will provide them security through collective defense. Because the threat to security is so pervasive, so permanent, and so great, the state that guarantees security must be all-powerful, even despotic.

Writing after Hobbes, John Locke thought that this view went too far. The state was indeed necessary only to assure law and order. But Hobbes was wrong: most people do not pose any threat to their neighbors. A state that exists primarily to provide a minimal police force may need some other minor powers, but does not need to have power to regulate the economy, transfer the ownership of land, or fight foreign wars. Government

---

THOMAS HOBBES (1588–1697)

Influenced by contemporary developments in the natural sciences, Hobbes attempted to construct an all-embracing philosophy, which would include biology and theology, in a rigorous deductive manner like that of mathematics. While this approach gives clarity and power to his work, it forces him to overlook subtleties and nuances that a more complex treatment would require. In Hobbes's theory, a state with absolute power is necessary to provide security, and law is simply the command of the sovereign. The utilitarianism of his political theory made conservative monarchists as uncomfortable as it did liberals.

---

should be limited in what it does, leaving to individuals as much freedom as possible. This was a doctrine taken up enthusiastically by Thomas Jefferson, who embodied it in the American Declaration of Independence.

Social contract theory supplies a logical explanation of why the state exists. It answers the question "Why would people create the state?" But *log-*

JOHN LOCKE (1632–1704)

Although Locke's writings on epistemology (theory of knowledge) and politics are somewhat lacking in consistency and rigor, they led to conclusions consistent with what people of his time wanted to believe. He advocated toleration of religious views, at least among the various Protestant sects (that is, he excluded Catholics and atheists from toleration) and he urged limited government, arguing that an implicit social contract only authorized government to do what men could not do for themselves. If government exceeded its appropriate limits, the people had a right of rebellion.

This political philosophy seems primarily a justification of the "Glorious Revolution" of 1688, which removed James II and placed William and Mary on the throne of Britain; and of the desire of the emerging capitalist class to be free of archaic government-imposed obstacles to free trade. This combination of political and economic liberalism was particularly well received in the American colonies and Locke was in great favor with the theorists of American independence such as Thomas Jefferson.

---

ical explanation of a human institution is only one of the alternatives. The other is *genetic explanation*—that is, an explanation in terms of the institution's genesis, or historical origins, which answers the question "How did that institution actually arise?" This distinction between logical and genetic explanation is an important one, since people are perhaps too prone to assume that something exists for a good reason, whereas in fact it may exist as the outcome of a process of historical accidents, or for reasons not immediately apparent.

THE ORIGINS OF STATES

If we look at the actual historical processes involved in the creation of states, we find some examples of an actual social contract being made, but they are very few. (One such actual social contract, for example, is the so-called Mayflower Compact, drawn up by those sailing from England on the *Mayflower* in 1620, agreeing to establish a new colony and specifying the extent and organization of government power in it.) In a sense, every new written constitution is in effect a social contract, but in a limited sense only, since the society already exists, as does the state structure and the system's laws, so that in fact a new constitution introduces changes that may be only marginal in the life of the polity. A constitution is most likely to approximate the social contract discussed by the philosophers when individuals coming from different societies settle new lands, carving out a new jurisdiction in previously unsettled territory.

The lives of most political systems, however, had other origins. Most typically, the state seems to have developed as the third stage of the evolution of a society that had originated as an extended family, and then became a tribe; or out of the conquest of one such group by another. The Bible, for example, contains an account of how the ancient Israelites decided to give themselves a government "like the other nations." A persuasive account of the origins of ancient political systems as they evolved from extended families can be found in *The Ancient City* of Numa Denis Foustel de Coulanges, first published in 1864. In this model, the senior male of the family, the patriarch, decides major issues. As the family grows through natural increase, through marriages to members of other families, the purchase of slaves, and the contracting of indentured servants, the family may become a small tribe. The patriarch may need to become a leader in war. He probably also has religious functions, perhaps leading in the veneration of ancestors. Tribal leadership of this kind can still be found in Africa or in Papua New Guinea, coexisting uneasily with modern state structures. Until quite recently, vestiges of this system could still be found in places like the Scottish highlands or the hills of East Tennessee. Only rarely has a modern state structure been able to accommodate preexisting tribal organization. A case exists today in the Republic of Western Samoa, in the South Pacific, where only the *mataes*, the heads of extended families, can vote in elections for the legislature. Thus sometimes the state originates in a situation of conquest and must coexist with a preexisting tribal structure, whereas in the ancient world a tribal society might itself generate a state structure.

The contact of tribal political units within a common territory results in a structure of intertribal relations in which we can discern in primitive form many of the features of the system of relations among modern states. In the absence of an effective structure of international government, as we shall see in Chapter 11, states rely on mechanisms of reciprocity and retaliation to enforce compliance with the rules by which they live. That is, states extend to other states the treatment they wish accorded to themselves and take punitive action against states that violate their rights commensurate with the magnitude of the offense.

A similar system of retaliation for the violation of the rules of intertribal conduct can be seen in systems where the effectiveness of the modern state is limited, even today. For example, in Papua New Guinea, the tribal units (called, in pidgin, *wontok*, because they share "one talk," or a single common language) take direct action against members of a *wontok* that has injured theirs in a direct and commensurate manner. If a member of one tribe kills a member of another, the injured *wontok* is justified then in killing a member of the other tribe. This is a system of deterrence by retaliation, which is after all an early form of the system of deterrence by threat of punishment generally characteristic of contemporary legal codes. Retaliation may, under certain circumstances, be avoided by the *wontok* inflicting the injury if it instead offers compensation that the injured group finds acceptable. In fact, in present-day Papua New Guinea a great deal of time is taken up in negotiation and litigation among tribal groups to establish acceptable amounts of compensation for injury.

An intermediate system existed in early Anglo-Saxon Britain where a tariff of amounts of compensation for specific injuries to specific categories of people was established. The amount to be paid to the family of somebody killed was called the person's *wergeld*, and varied according to the person's social rank.

When John Locke wrote his *Second Treatise on Government*, in which he laid out his social contract theory, he was in fact attempting to refute the argument of an Anglican bishop named Filmer, who had derived the powers of the king from a patriarchal model of the polity: the king was said to stand in the place of the father of an extended family and therefore had natural authority deriving from that role. Locke argued, by contrast, that the king only had power because it was convenient for members of society to give up a small part of their own natural power to one person, who would have a limited police function to perform.

In fact, although they may subsequently have been given a contractual character by the adoption of a written constitution, almost all present-day states trace their historical origins to acts of force—either the conquest of one group by another or the seizure of power by an insurgent revolutionary group from a ruling class or foreign state; although sometimes a colonial power may not wait for the colonial insurgency to take place, but may read the writing on the wall and give up control without a struggle. In ancient and medieval times, slavery based on conquest was generally thought reasonable and acceptable; that is, a conquering army could have killed people on the defeated side, but instead their lives were spared in return for their labor, which seemed a reasonable bargain on both sides. An account even exists of how the Mongol conqueror, Genghis Khan, who hitherto had simply plundered and killed those he defeated in battle, was persuaded instead to spare Chinese provinces and take annual tribute instead of plunder. A one-time capital gain was converted, as it were, into a source of perpetual income.

Optimism, and a certain faith in the rightness of the way things are, seem to be necessary for man to survive and function. It is certainly a lot easier to rule over subjects who accept the situation willingly, rather than over the recalcitrant and the rebellious. In this way, what was originally money forcibly extorted becomes instead taxes given in return for protection—security, after all, as we learned from Hobbes, being the primary concern of the state. Tribute demanded by the conqueror on pain of dispossession becomes instead reconceptualized as rent.

This kind of transformation can readily be seen in the history of Europe. For example, the state of Germany owes its origin to the unification of the various German states in 1870. This was carried out by conquest, persuasion, and coercion by the dominant state at the time, the kingdom of Prussia. Prussia itself consisted of territories put together mostly by conquest, originating with the conquest of Brandenburg by the Teutonic Order of Knights. An order of knights, we might say without much exaggeration, was the medieval equivalent of a motorcycle gang. There is even a hint of the parallel in the name given the military caste that established itself as overlords over the primarily Polish peasants that constituted the first population of the Prussian lands. They were called "Junkers," which seems a contemporary word for juveniles.

Throughout the history of Prussia, the landowning Junker class was primarily military in character, and its character as a military caste determined the nature of the Prussian, and later the Imperial German, state. Prussia was not a state that had an army, as one wit put it, but an army that had a state. When asked what limits there were to Germany's territorial ambitions, Otto von Bismarck, the first chancellor of Imperial Germany and the moving force in putting together the German Empire from his position as prime minister of Prussia, is said to have replied: "That is easy to answer. The limits of Germany's territorial ambitions are determined by the size of the German army, and the size of the German army is determined by the number of Junkers I have to serve as officers."

The English state originated in the conquest of England by William of Normandy in 1066. The French state was put together out of the conquests of the House of Bourbon. Spain was finally unified in 1492 by the military exploits of the troops of Ferdinand and Isabella. The vast Russian Empire, likewise, was put together by the steady accretion of conquests.

Although the United States was founded by a constitutional act that brought together preexisting colonies at Philadelphia, the present-day

United States is also the fruit of conquest—the taking of land from Native American tribes, from Mexico, and from the kingdom of Hawaii—together with some purchases of land from the Russians (Alaska) and the French (Louisiana).

The development of legitimacy—the process by which a title to rule originating in an act of force becomes over the years transmuted into a legitimate claim to govern—will be examined in Chapter 4.

KEY TERMS

interest	sovereignty
identity	anarchists
politics	social contract theory
power	logical explanation
legal authority	genetic explanation
state	

CHAPTER 2

Democracy, Authoritarianism, and Political Culture

©ASHLEIGH BRILLIANT 1979.   POT-SHOTS NO. 1448.

LET'S RESPECT EACH OTHER'S VIEWS,

NO MATTER HOW WRONG YOURS MAY BE.

DEMOCRACY: ANCIENT AND MODERN

Of course the term *democracy*, meaning "government of the people," originated in ancient Greece. The democracies of ancient Greece were limited ones, in the sense that slaves, women, and resident aliens did not vote, but in other respects the power of the assembly was greater than that of a modern legislature. There was no separation of church and state, so that the assembly voted on religious questions; nor was there a clearly separate judicial system, so the assembly could vote punishments on specific individuals.

THE POLIS

The *polis*, or city-state, was the standard political unit in ancient Greece. It consisted of the city itself and its rural hinterland. Aristotle wrote that the ideal maximum size for a state was one whose body of citizens could all gather within the sound of an orator's voice. The city-states of ancient Greece were numerous enough and various enough, in their political regimes, to provide a rich source of data for the study of comparative politics. The polis reached its cultural heights in Athens of the fifth century B.C., with achievements in sculpture, architecture, philosophy, drama, and politics that were extraordinary.

Even in the "democracy" of Athens, however, it should be remembered that slavery existed and women did not vote or hold office. Moreover, there were no limits such as those provided by bills of rights to the power of the Athenian assembly, which legislated on matters of religion and rendered judicial verdicts extending to the death penalty—even in matters that would be protected by freedom of speech provisions in modern constitutions. Most notably, the great philosopher Socrates was condemned to death by the Athenian Assembly for corrupting the morals of the young by teaching them to think for themselves.

Democracy today is *representative democracy*, in that people vote for representatives who will legislate for them. It is also *constitutional democracy*, in that the power of the legislature is limited with respect to the matters it can deal with. As we shall see in subsequent chapters, almost all states of the world today have written constitutions that allocate powers among different organs of government and specify what can and cannot be done by legislatures; and indeed what cannot be done by *any* organ of government, in the sense that individuals have reserved rights. This is the area generally known as "civil liberties," the rights people have to be free of government control and regulation with respect to their speech, writing, organization, and worship.

ARGUMENTS FOR DEMOCRACY

Arguments in favor of democracy can be regarded as either absolute or relative: absolute arguments justify democracy in terms of its own merits; relative ones, by comparison with the merits of competing systems. One absolutist argument sometimes made by convinced democrats, for example, is that the masses, on average, on the whole, have good judgment. The common person, so to speak, has common sense. William F. Buckley once said he would prefer to be governed by the first thousand people listed in the Boston telephone directory rather than the thousand members of the Harvard faculty.

In support of this approach, it can be argued, for example, that the traditional common-law jury of twelve people chosen at random from the community make sounder judgments on the guilt or innocence of an accused person than would a judge sitting alone. It is indeed true that the results of the jury system have generally been satisfactory, and that sometimes a jury will return a carefully balanced and solidly based judgment clearly sounder than the judge's remarks in summing up. But the trial jury is an unusual situation. Chosen from those without previous opinion or knowledge relative to the case, it is systematically presented with a great deal of information about the case organized by opponents and proponents of a specific hypothesis, and sequestered from other influences for the duration of the trial.

This is clearly not the case with a democratic electorate, so it is difficult to draw conclusions from the success of the jury system that would be applicable to democratic politics. Indeed, we have a great deal of evidence that a democratic electorate differs from a jury precisely in the ways that give the jury its characteristic strengths in making fair and unprejudiced decisions. That is, voters start out with all kinds of biases and prejudices. The electorate does not need to pay systematic attention to the salient issues. People are swayed by deliberately misleading campaign propaganda put out by the candidates; in fact in some recent U.S. presidential elections the advantage lay with the candidate least scrupulous in allowing misleading advertising on his behalf. Newspapers are unbalanced and superficial in their coverage of events; and particular candidates start with heavy advantages over their opponents because they are incumbents whose names are already well-known, or because they have superior financial resources to put across their message or a favorable view of their personal characteristics.

It might well be argued that these defects are not those of democracy itself but of the way it is institutionalized in specific countries today and that legislation that would remedy some of these defects is possible. This view may certainly suggest to each of us what new legislation we ought as citizens to be supporting; perhaps, as has sometimes been said, they constitute arguments for more democracy rather than less; but if such defects are widespread, they have to be accepted as characterizing democratic systems as these actually exist and as they are likely to continue to exist.

The case for democracy need not be based on the quality of democratic decision-making, however. Potent arguments can also be based on the values and practices that democratic systems promote. One of the greatest of modern political philosophers, John Stuart Mill, argued that the important contribution made by democracy to human welfare was that it provided individuals with an incentive to become informed and to form their own political opinions, thus contributing to that personal development of individual faculties which is one of the major human goals.

A similar argument on the basis of the collateral benefits that a democratic system can bring is that the system of regular competitive elections required by a system of representative democracy—whether or not it results in the best people being elected or the best decisions being made— requires that there be guarantees of freedom of speech, freedom of the press, and freedom to organize politically: in other words, the whole range of civil liberties. Moreover, in giving the vote to the poorer classes of society, representative democracy gives them a claim to have their economic and social needs considered. In seeking votes in a competitive system, rival elites must appeal to those who have votes. This creates an incentive for government to attend to the needs of people who might otherwise be ignored.

These advantages appear all the stronger when they are contrasted with what occurs under nondemocratic political systems. After all, since *some* kind of government is going to exist, democracy has to be evaluated not simply on the basis of its own claims, but relatively, by comparison with alternative available systems. As the British statesman Winston Churchill once put it, "Democracy is the worst political system, except for all the others."

What alternatives are there to democracy? Well, they all involve government by some kind of *elite*, a limited set of people with some claim to being "better" than the nonelite. Many critics of democracy, including the great Athenian philosopher Plato, have argued that instead of being governed by the masses, it is self-evidently better to be ruled by only "the best" elements of society: the enlightened, the educated, or the virtuous. Of course, in practice, actual systems of elite rule, even where the elite claim to be the most virtuous or the most able, generally find themselves with rulers who have merely inherited their position, or else who have come to it by force or treachery of some kind. In fact, actually ruling elites would be hard put to persuade anybody they represented the "best" elements in their societies.

For purposes of argument it is instructive to consider a hypothetical case. Even if it were somehow possible to choose the most able members of society and install them in power, the republic of Platonic idealists would not result. Even the most virtuous among us would soon become corrupted by the temptations of power into assuming privileges. The rulers would become isolated from the masses and lose awareness of their needs. Not required to listen continuously to mass opinion because they did not have to face periodic elections, they would overlook the drawbacks of some course of action and follow lines of policy that ended in disaster. Without democratic forms of election, the means of choosing leaders from within the elite would become corrupted so that the unscrupulous would rise to the top. Fearful of being displaced by another schemer like himself, the ruler who rises to power undemocratically would become jealous, fearful, and even paranoid in crushing opposition, so that what was to have been the rule of an incorruptible and public-spirited elite becomes arbitrary totalitarianism.

PLATO (427–347 B.C.)

The great Greek philosopher of the fifth century B.C., Plato was the founder of the Academy—so called because the school met in the Grove of Academe—and worked at first under the inspiration of his own teacher and friend Socrates. He also conveyed his teachings through a series of published dialogues, many of which survive today, in most of which Socrates is represented as helping others form clear ideas of right thought and behavior through persistently asking them questions. In the lengthy dialogue *The Republic*, Plato conveys most of his views on government, justice, and human psychology, among other matters. The charm of his writing, and his love of justice and of learning, have made Plato a strong influence intermittently from his day to our own, despite the fact that his political views are elitist and often unrealistic—as his own pupil Aristotle pointed out long ago.

None of this is hypothetical. This describes the typical course of events in postrevolutionary systems, which begin with revolutions by the pure in heart, wishing to put right the mistakes of the past, to end exploitation and oppression, only to end with different versions of the same thing. Such was the history of the most famous of modern revolutions, the Russian and the French. Sometimes, rarely, a country is lucky and the revolutionary leadership stays more or less benign. But one should not count on the lucky circumstance where matters of such importance are concerned. Democracy may not be able to produce rapid results; it may not put into the hands of the just and virtuous the power to put through drastic reforms that the society needs. Instead, it provides moderate amounts of power to people who will mostly be mediocre, preferring not to take the risks involved in having powerful but nonresponsible governments. It is a sort of "minimax" solution to the problem of government, attempting to minimize risks while maximizing benefits—a moderate and undramatic, but prudent, solution to the problem of power.

POLITICAL CULTURE

To what extent do cultural factors peculiar to a particular society predispose it to democracy or authoritarianism? Political science has attempted to borrow the concept of culture from anthropology and incorporate it into the study of politics, understanding by the concept "political culture" the values, attitudes, and beliefs of a particular society, passed on through the processes of socialization, which influence political behavior. Clearly, there is merit in the concept of political culture, but it is also a dangerous tool to use. It can easily degenerate into racial stereotyping, or give rise to ethnic snobbery.

There are some tendencies of this kind in the most well-known book that uses the concept of political culture, *The Civic Culture*, by Gabriel Almond and Sidney Verba.[1] The premise of *The Civic Culture*, derived from the concept of political development, was the entirely reasonable one that a particular culture, or set of attitudes, was appropriate to each different stage of the process of political development. In a completely "developed" society—that is, a modern constitutional democracy—one could expect to find attitudes appropriate to the institutions of such a political system. For example, one would expect people to believe that they would be treated fairly by an honest public service, and that government policies would by and large reflect the opinions of the voters. In "less developed" societies, beliefs such as these would be held less frequently.

This approach reflected a whole series of assumptions, some of them questionable. One was that the attitudes embodied in the "civic culture" had a causal role to play in maintaining the institutions of a democratic polity, rather than being a dependent variable, the effect of the existence of that system. In fact, it is quite unclear what is cause and what effect in the relation of attitudes to behavior and to institutions. Then the question arises of how much culture reflects a country's state of development and thus changes, and how much is it constant in a given country through time. For example, *The Civic Culture* found that West Germany had attitudes appropriate to a developed democratic polity, in the sense that people expected bureaucrats to be fair and honest, the police to be impartial and effective, and so on. However, those attitudes may not reflect only the current democratic stage in German development, but have probably characterized German society since the Prussian state was established in the eighteenth century, through many different types of political systems, and would no doubt have been found in the authoritarian imperial regime that ruled prior to World War I, for example.

DEMOCRACY AND EDUCATION

Both Plato and Aristotle believed that one of the defects of democracies was that people unwarrantedly extended the principle of political equality on which democracies are based to fields outside of politics. This would lead to refusing to accept the existence of inequality in the areas where such an acceptance was necessary, such as education, where different people could absorb educations of different calibers, depending on their ability.

Criticisms of this kind are frequently made of American education, especially by Europeans and East Asians who are surprised to find how little Americans learn during the course of a standard education in the public schools. This may be partly due to a reluctance among Americans to acknowledge differing abilities, which means that the pace of learning is set at its lowest gear; but alternatively, it may reflect American reluctance to assert authority, and a preference to operate by consensus, so that teachers shrink from insisting on arduous learning and instead opt for the easy and undemanding. The memorable activities of an American high school seem to center on sports and extracurricular events rather than learning.

In fact, most treatments of political culture regard it as specific to a given country over time rather than characteristic of a particular stage of development; that is, political culture interpretations are generally advanced to account for the permanent characteristics of a specific country's political system. The difficulty is that explaining given practices and institutions by reference to political culture can become a lazy man's explanation for anything that needs to be explained. Why does a practice exist? Because the people's culture impels them to behave that way. Why do they have these cultural traits? Well, because they've always had them. This is rather like the notorious story of a medical diagnosis in which the doctor asks the patient to describe his symptoms, and then asks, "Have you had this problem before?" The patient says yes, and the doctor replies, "Ah, well, you've got it again."

To avoid problems of this kind, the basic rule of political science should be, in the first place, that as much as possible of a country's political behavior and institutions should be explained on the premise that people are acting rationally in pursuit of their interests, under a given set of circumstances. Only if the situation is not completely explained by rational self-interested motives does it make sense to look for explanations deriving from culture. And when explanations are used that impute certain attitudes to people, every attempt should be made to demonstrate, on the basis of opinion survey data, that people actually hold such attitudes.

EXAMPLE 1: AUTHORITARIANISM IN LATIN AMERICA

A classic instance of the use of political culture explanations is the view that now seems widely accepted, that the incidence of dictatorship and other *authoritarian* practices in Latin America derives from the region's heritage from Spain. According to one textbook,

> a widely discussed determinant of Latin America is the colonial heritage, manifested in the attitudes of the Latin American people toward both the decision-making level of government and their participation in it. The strong tendency towards personalism and authoritarianism in political culture is well-known. . . . Political participation in the decision-making process means very little to average Latin Americans.[2]

Perhaps the political culture of colonial Spain was authoritarian—as was that of England, France, and everywhere else during the sixteenth century, after all—but public opinion surveys in countries of Latin America show that people today have the same prodemocratic attitudes as are general today in North America and Europe. Observers seem to assume that because Latin American countries have often had dictatorships, their people's attitudes must be favorable to dictatorship. But that doesn't follow. Dictatorships rule by force because they *don't* represent what the majority wants, after all. Since they prevent the majority from expressing its wishes through the voting process, it is more logical to look for the causes of dictatorships in the desire of a powerful minority to hold onto its privileges, power, and property. Apologists for dictatorship always come up with "cover stories" to justify them. But whenever they get the chance, people everywhere seem to prefer to choose their leaders and to want to hold them accountable.

LATIN AMERICA

The term "Latin America" is generally used to describe the twenty countries of the Western Hemisphere that secured their independence during the nineteenth century or the first decade of the twentieth century from France, Portugal, Spain, or another Spanish-speaking country: Haiti, Brazil, Mexico, the Dominican Republic, Cuba, Guatemala, El Salvador, Honduras, Nicaragua, Costa Rica, Panama, Bolivia, Colombia, Venezuela, Ecuador, Peru, Chile, Argentina, Uruguay, and Paraguay. The term "Spanish America" would not be exact, because Brazil speaks Portuguese and was originally a series of Portuguese colonies, and Haiti, which was once a colony of France, speaks French and French-based Créole. Although the geographic expression "South America" is often thought to be an equivalent, actually only ten of the twenty countries are in South America, the others being geographically in what is sometimes called "Middle America"— that is, Central America and the Caribbean, with Mexico actually in North America. Although some pedants have quibbled that "Latin America" should include French-speaking Quebec, and the Spanish-speaking areas under the U.S. flag such as Puerto Rico or New Mexico that are not usually included in "Latin America," the main terminological problem today is that many former British colonies in the Caribbean and mainland areas surrounding the Caribbean in Central America and South America have become independent during the second half of the twentieth century. For political purposes it sometimes becomes necessary to talk about them in the same category as the traditionally independent countries of Latin America, but they are predominantly not "Latin" in cultural heritage, being primarily former colonies of Britain and the Netherlands, with primarily black and mulatto populations. When the intention is to include this set of newly independent countries, the general term used today is most commonly "Latin America and the Caribbean."

Despite these problems and the cultural heterogeneity of the region, it has long been customary to deal with Latin America as a distinct region for purposes of political analysis, analogously with "Eastern Europe" or "the Middle East." During the twentieth century, the common features of Latin American politics have been the economic and political dependence of the countries despite their formal legal sovereignty; strong class differentiation, with lower classes being of indigenous American or African origin and elites primarily of European ancestry; and the dominance of the military in a political life that frequently took extraconstitutional detours, such as the military seizure of power.

Clearly, political culture exists in the sense of a complex of values and attitudes that is at least to some extent distinct from country to country. But since it is not clear how much culture influences behavior and institutions, it seems most prudent to try to explain political phenomena primarily on the basis of the rational pursuit of interest, leaving the causal role of political culture to be investigated only if the behavior in question seems not to be rational in those terms.

EXAMPLE 2: THE TWO-PARTY SYSTEM IN BRITAIN

The two principal parties in Britain between them always control more than 90 percent of the seats in the House of Commons. What accounts for this overwhelming *two-partyism* in the British political system?

BRITISH POLITICAL PARTIES

Growing originally out of aristocratic factions, British political parties extended their membership and support as the suffrage was extended by degrees during the nineteenth and twentieth centuries. Today's Conservative party still shows signs of its origins in the Tory party of supporters of the monarchy and the established Church of England, the king's party, but has broadened its appeal to include most of what in Britain is called "the middle class"—that is, nonmanual workers in offices. Today it represents primarily business interests. The bulk of the manual "working class" votes for the Labour party, founded in the early twentieth century and closely linked with labor unions and consumer organizations, whose commitment to socialism has now been attenuated to support for a mixed economy, although still with concern for the less fortunate in society.

The Whig opponents of the Tories evolved during the nineteenth century into a Liberal party that originally represented city interests as opposed to the Tory landowners. With the rise of the Labour party, the Liberal party shrank as most Liberals felt they had to choose between a Conservative party that had extended its range to include business interests or a Labour party whose progressivism was cast in a fairly doctrinaire mold. However, a much-reduced Liberal party of those who felt at home with neither the well-fed establishment types in the Conservative party nor the rough-hewn doctrinaire socialists of Labour continued to present a high-minded alternative. During the 1980s, the Liberals absorbed a social democratic party that had split from Labour and, in alliance with the Liberals, had briefly threatened to replace Labour as the second largest party, to become the Liberal Democrats. The single-member-district plurality system ensures that a third party such as the Liberals will be drastically underrepresented in the House of Commons, so that despite the loyalty of an approximate 15 percent of the electorate, it is unlikely that the Liberal Democrats could become a significant factor in the formation of governments in Britain.

Political culture explanations have been offered by various authors. For example, it has been argued that because of the predominance of lawyers in politics, politics is modeled along the lines of a legal dispute. In the English common-law legal system, disputes at law are always between two parties—for example, *Smith vs. Jones, U.S. vs. Johnson, State of Illinois vs. Kelly*. Lawyers, it is argued, have modeled the British system in a similar fashion. Alternatively, the explanation has been advanced that the English, the inventors of so many of our team sports, conceive of politics as a game that can only be played by two teams.

These explanations may seem to have a certain plausibility until one decides to look first for explanations resting on rational and interested behavior under a specific set of institutional constraints. When approached from this perspective, it becomes clear that in fact more than two political parties are active in Britain; indeed, in the general election of 1983, the third electoral force, the Alliance of Liberals and Social Democrats, polled 23 percent in the popular vote, only slightly behind the 28 percent polled by the Labour party, the country's second political force. Nevertheless, the Labour party secured ten times the number of seats in the House of Commons won by the Alliance and remained the official opposition. The secret to Britain's two-partyism, it becomes clear, is the electoral system, under which, in *single-member districts*, whichever candidate has a *plurality* is successful. The leading party may dominate the results completely. If its national margin over the second party is not great, the second party may hope, since results will not be uniform across all districts, to happen to have the plurality in some. Unless a third party appeals particularly to an ethnic group that is geographically concentrated, however, it is likely to have a plurality over the leading two parties quite rarely. Moreover, third and fourth parties are discouraged under this system. Voters are afraid that votes will be wasted if they do not choose between one of the two main contenders.

Minor parties agitate continually for a change in the electoral system to one based on proportionality, which would enable them to win representation reflecting their percentage of the vote, encourage their supporters, and enable them to conduct successful electoral campaigns. The two major parties, of course, resist any change in a system that favors them. It is a general rule of politics that the electoral system in effect reflects the interests of the party or combination of parties constituting a majority at the time it was adopted, or constituting a majority at the time when an attempt was made to change it. Clearly, national political culture has no explanatory role in all this.

NOTES

1. Gabriel Almond and Sidney Verba, *The Civic Culture* (Boston: Little, Brown, 1956).

2. Russell H. Fitzgibbon and Julio A. Fernandez, *Latin America: Political Culture and Development*, 2nd ed. (Englewood Cliffs, NJ: Prentice-Hall, 1981), pp. 4–5.

KEY TERMS

democracy	elite
representative democracy	authoritarian
constitutional democracy	two-party system
dictatorship	single-member district
political culture	plurality
civic culture	

CHAPTER 3

Ideology

POT-SHOTS NO. 826.

I HAVE ABANDONED MY SEARCH FOR TRUTH,

AND AM NOW LOOKING

FOR A GOOD FANTASY.

Ashleigh Brilliant

Ideology can be defined as a set of more or less coherent—that is, mutually consistent—beliefs about the world, including both empirical and normative elements. By *empirical* is meant descriptive, having to do with matters of fact; *normative* elements are views on what should be, what is right or wrong, what the individual ought to do. Because an ideology contains both of these elements, related to each other in a coherent way, it both makes sense of the world (interprets for the individual what is happening) and at the same time provides a guide to action and to evaluation of what is done by others.

People differ in how well worked out and how detailed their ideologies are. Even in the ideological constructions of the most politically conscious and sophisticated intellectual, there may be inconsistencies and factual misunderstandings; others may have sets of attitudes and prejudices that are tied together only by the personality and life experience of the individual, and not by any reasoning process at all. Even in such a case, however, such a set of attitudes and prejudices fulfills the function of an ideology: it serves as interpreter of the world and guide to action.

Political leaders, who are called on to articulate points of view on a wide variety of subjects, are particularly in need of explicit ideologies. Leaders who lack opinions on some significant matter, or whose views on one issue seem to contradict their views on another, may find themselves in trouble, unable to choose among alternatives or pursuing policies that neutralize each other.

EXAMPLES OF IDEOLOGY: CARTER AND REAGAN

Since the primary function an ideology discharges is to serve as a coherent interpretation of the world, the quality of an ideology depends on how consistent it is and how faithful to reality. From this point of view, it is interesting to consider the ideological structures of two recent presidents of the United States, Jimmy Carter and Ronald Reagan.

The problem with Carter's ideology in this perspective was its weakness and lack of consistency. For example, when Anastasio Somoza, the dictator of Nicaragua, was overthrown, Carter vacillated between treating this as a victory for democracy or a defeat for anti-Communism, and his policies were thus inconsistent and ineffective. Carter is reported to have made the decision on whether to proceed with building the B-1 bomber by compiling lists of the arguments pro and con, and assigning weights to each. Someone with well-developed strategic views could have seen right away whether the deployment of the B-1 was consistent with his strategic philosophy. Ironically, the ambiguity and even inconsistency of Carter's views was precisely what had made him a strong candidate for the Democratic nomination in 1976. He was able to attract the support of a wide range of the disparate interests represented in the Democratic party by identifying himself, perfectly sincerely, with the views of each, rather than being perceived as the candidate of only one faction or point of view.

A strong contrast is provided by the example of Ronald Reagan. His ideological views, at least as he expressed them, were generally consistent and strongly held. That gave clarity to his vision and power to his public appeals. At the same time, this clarity and consistency were achieved at the cost of a radical simplification of reality and an inability to acknowledge realities that would call his views into question. Thus during the 1980 election year, Reagan was able to espouse with apparent sincerity what George Bush, as a rival candidate for the Republican nomination, referred to as "voodoo economics," the position taken by Reagan that it would be possible to cut taxes, especially on the wealthy, increase military spending substantially, and balance the budget at the same time. Of course, in the event, Reagan presided over the most drastically unbalanced budgets in peacetime. The same tendency was manifested generally in Reagan's treatment of reality: typical was the illustrative anecdote that substituted for an informed appraisal, sometimes an anecdote without actual basis in fact.

This raises a crucial point of methodology, that one's attitudes and beliefs should always be open to modification in light of new data. This is the essence of the scientific method: one understands the world by formulating general principles that account for the observable data. Those scientific "laws" are always subject to modification or even abandonment as new data become available—in fact, one should search out precisely the kind of evidence that would call the law into question. Only if negative evidence is sought and not found can one have any confidence that the hypothesis formulated is in fact an adequate description of reality.

THE FUNCTIONS OF IDEOLOGY

As we've seen, an individual's interests reflect the various identities that he or she assumes—partisan, racial, national, and so on—reflecting the collectivities of which he or she is a member. The relative weight given to each of these identifications varies, individual by individual, in response to a host of social and psychological factors, some of them quite subtle. One of the most significant factors guiding the general principles by which the individual ties together his or her congeries of interests is the need for social adjustment, the pressure to be in agreement with the opinions of those with whom one comes into contact frequently: spouse, family, co-workers, and neighbors. A second significant determinant is the effect of the mass media, of newspapers, movies, radio, and television, as they provide cues as to what is acceptable or desirable in the national and world cultures of the day. A third guiding principle in the organization of ideological structures is the externalization of what is internal to the individual's personality—that is, the psychological balance of forces that has been established on the basis of his or her own heredity and life experience. Following these personality dynamics, some individuals may instinctively rebel against authority, or follow authority slavishly; they may find comfortable what is old and established, or favor what is new; they may be animated by a passion for justice and a resentment of inequality, or cynically accept injustice and inequality as inevitable and unchangeable.

One of the interesting things about ideology is that although it is based, in some sense, on the individual's interests, in any particular case it may counsel action that actually contravenes his or her interests in that case.[1] That is, one of the key functions of ideology is that it provides a handy guide to opinion and action *in general*, without the necessity of becoming intimately familiar with the details of every issue on which a position must be taken. It is clearly impossible to become totally familiar with every circumstance of every question; one needs only to see that one ideological principle or another implies a vote for or against. This is not simply a case of sacrificing one interest because another interest takes precedence, as when soldiers die fighting for their country. Sometimes the person may vote one way on the basis of economic principles that grow out of economic interests, even though in that particular case those economic interests would actually be better served by a contrary vote. A small businessman may vote for a candidate who stands for government nonintervention in business, reflecting his general ideological position, even though circumstances of the moment imply that in fact his business would be better off with government regulation of his industry. Usually, perhaps, this action against interest is unwitting; but sometimes it may occur in full consciousness of the implications of the decision. That is, somebody may take a position "on principle" against his or her own interests, in an act which may be condemned as foolish by the cynic, or applauded as honorable by the moralist.

THE LEFT-RIGHT CONTINUUM

One of the most common shorthand ways of characterizing ideologies is to place them on a continuum from left to right. It is sometimes said that positions more on the left of the scale are more progressive and those to the right more conservative, but the terms have somewhat more complex meanings than that. Perhaps they can be understood best genetically— that is, in terms of their genesis or origin. This was in the National Assembly following the French Revolution, when factions placed themselves further to the left (as this is seen from the podium; traditionally, those speaking in French assemblies face the assembled members) depending on how revolutionary they were—that is, how much they opposed the prerevolutionary order, or *ancien régime.*

THE FRENCH REVOLUTION

The French Revolution (1789) has major significance as a symbolic event that defined the terms of political discourse down to the present. France was at the time the largest country of Western Europe, culturally the most influential and militarily the most powerful. For those on the Left the Revolution represented the realization of the rational and liberal ideas of the Enlightenment, freeing men's minds of irrationality and superstition, freeing the economy of counterproductive, exploitative practices, and liberating society and politics from class-based oppression. To those on the Right, in its arrogance the Revolution swept away institutions tested by time and sanctified by religion and with its naive faith in the goodness of human nature prepared the way only for cruelty, barbarism, and tyranny.

There is truth in both views. Internal barriers to trade, aristocratic privileges, official corruption, and royal power stood in the way of the requirements of a modern capitalist and democratic system, but the violence directed against the old order became a method of rule and political differences were finally settled by massacre and the guillotine. However, many of the innovations of the Revolution, such as the reorganization of the French administrative structure, the introduction of internal free trade, and the metric system remained; other attempted reforms, such as the separation of church and state and the assertion of legislative preeminence over the executive, became the stuff of political controversy in France, as elsewhere, for another 150 years; but the revolutionary pursuit of rationality, virtue, and social solidarity—or, in its own slogan, liberty, equality, and fraternity—exhausted itself in the dictatorship of Napoleon Bonaparte (1799–1815).

The old system had three aspects: an absolute monarchy, an established Roman Catholic Church, and a particular distribution of property. Accordingly, one was more to the Left the more one wished to weaken the absolute authority of the monarch (and, under republican regimes, the authority of the executive power), the more anticlerical one was—that is, the more one wished to reduce the authority of the Catholic church—and the more one favored the redistribution of wealth. A somewhat hyperbolic extreme Left position was thus represented by Voltaire's aphorism, "Mankind will not be free until the last king is strangled with the entrails of the last priest." Extreme anticlericalism is usually hard for people to understand today, now that the church has generally been stripped of its temporal power. But in the days of the establishment of Catholicism as the only official religion (the situation is similar where other religions are "established"), it would have been illegal to practice another faith; there were stringent civil penalties for blasphemy or morally lax behavior; education was in the hands of the church and had to conform to church doctrine; books, plays, and newspapers were censored and could be prohibited if they were doctrinally unsound. Even in our own day one comes across survivals of this era, as in the prohibition of divorce in the Republic of Ireland. The author was struck to find, on a visit to Argentina, that it was illegal to give an infant a name other than the name of a Catholic saint.

The French long wrestled with the problem of what revolutionary opposition to monarchic absolutism meant after the monarchy was overthrown. Generally, it was taken to mean that power had to be lodged in the legislative assembly; and the executive power, even now that it was republican and representative, had to be kept weak. This view was reinforced when the leader who finally emerged from the turmoil of the revolution of 1789, Napoleon Bonaparte, staged a military coup and proclaimed himself emperor. It was reinforced again when the Second Republic, founded in 1848 with a constitution calling for a strong president, was overthrown by the president who had been elected—Bonaparte's nephew—who proclaimed himself Emperor Napoleon III (on the premise that his father, who had never served as Emperor, should have been Napoleon II). It wasn't until after the Fifth Republic was founded in 1958 that the traditional Left in France, then represented by the Socialist party, accepted the strong executive as a legitimate feature of a republican system. Their conversion on this point was vindicated when the Socialist leader, François Mitterrand, finally became president himself.

Elsewhere, where the question of separation of church and state has, at least in its broad outlines, long been settled, and where the general shape of the nation's constitution is no longer a matter of dispute, the Left-Right dimension centers on opinions about the proper distribution of wealth and income. To be on the Left means to favor economic redistribution in a more equal direction. For this reason a position on the Left no longer necessarily entails support for a weak executive, since a strong government may be necessary to bring about economic redistribution.

Today, of course, the arguments made by the traditional Right at the time of the French Revolution in favor of the existing unequal distribution of property are no longer politically viable: that if property was unequally distributed, it must be because God wanted it that way; that the poor were privileged in being allowed to suffer more greatly, because that would assure them of a saintly afterlife; or that people were created unequal in their rights and entitlements. Although occasionally it is half-heartedly argued that the concentration of wealth should be encouraged—for example, through favorable tax laws—so that capital for investment may be accumulated (a view sometimes mocked as "trickle-down" economics), the more common, and more convincing, argument for economic inequality is that, while it may be unfortunate, it is a necessary consequence of allowing a free economic market to flourish, and the free market is so beneficial to everyone that its requirements should be met, even at some cost. Accordingly, we now move on to consider the logic of free-market economics, why the free market is thought to be so desirable, and what establishment of a free market implies for government economic policy.

THE FREE MARKET

In the model of a perfectly free, perfectly competitive, market economy as this was laid down by its great advocate, Adam Smith, individuals pursue their self-interest but "as though guided by an invisible hand," the result is the good of all. Since they work to advance their own interests, people work hard and put out their best efforts. If the economy is competitive and consumers are free to choose, they patronize suppliers whose products are best; if products are equally good, they buy those whose price is lowest. This means that those able to produce the best-quality goods at the lowest prices flourish; inferior and higher-cost producers go out of business. Alternatively, if the quality of goods and their prices are all comparable, the most efficient producers will be able to make the largest profit. They are thus in a position to be able to expand their businesses. They will also be able to offer a higher price than their competitors for the raw materials they all need, if these should be in scarce supply. Since efficient producers earn more profit than their competitors, they will be able to pay higher rates of interest on money they borrow, or larger dividends on the capital of those who invest in their businesses.

Thus the free market not only ensures that consumers get the best goods at the lowest price, it also determines that scarce raw materials and scarce capital are directed toward the most efficient producers. Optimum production and optimum allocation of materials and capital are thus achieved through these movements in supply and demand, which are registered, regulated, and publicized through movements in prices; in a perfectly free market, shifts in price represent the resultant of movements of supply and demand as these reflect judgments of consumers, producers, and suppliers.

ADAM SMITH (1723–1790)

Although he wrote on other matters, Adam Smith is known today as the author of *An Inquiry Into the Nature and Causes of the Wealth of Nations*, which became the Bible of free-market economic theory. The book made clear the merits of the division of labor, of free trade, and of comparative advantage, and provided powerful arguments against the existing system of government regulations and controls that interfered with production. However, many free marketeers forget that Smith clearly understood and argued that some government regulation of the economy was necessary in order to maintain an honestly competitive economic system.

This model of the functioning of a free-market economy is a brilliant construct that reflects some real truths about economic relations and can provide help in understanding economic behavior and in guiding policy preferences. The primary problem in the use of the model, and the main reason why economists' recommendations based on it are frequently misguided, is that, like any model of rational human behavior, it is based on a series of assumptions that may or may not hold true in any particular case. To overlook or forget this fact is to court disaster.

What are the key assumptions that have to hold in practice if the predictions of the model are to come true? First, agreements among businesses not to compete with each other cannot be tolerated. An agreement among producers of the same commodity to fix prices, or an agreement to divide up territory and not seek to take customers away from each other, would deprive the system of the benefits of competition. Adam Smith himself pointed out this danger, which is nevertheless permitted to exist in many economic systems. The United States has "antitrust" legislation, making an agreement "in restraint of trade" illegal, although some exceptions are allowed.

An equivalent deformation of the free-market model is created by a monopoly situation, in which there is only one supplier of a particular product or service, who is thus not prevented by competition from charging whatever he or she likes for the product. In the United States, monopolies that seem unavoidable are generally subjected to regulation in the public interest, although the monopoly frequently comes to control the regulatory body—for example, a state public utilities commission—by one means or another, in violation of the intent of the law.

Second, consumers must have accurate information. If they are not aware of the differences among different producers in the price and quality of a product, they cannot make the correct decisions about what to buy. A great deal of legislation in the United States tries to protect the quality of the consumer's decision. Correct weights and measures have to be noted on the outside of packages, for example, and the ingredients of food and drug items have to be listed in the order of their relative contribution to the finished product. Demonstrably false statements cannot be made in advertising. It remains true nevertheless that a great deal of advertising effort goes into trying to confuse the consumer in the attempt to establish a preference for a particular brand on the basis of factors other than its quality and price.

Third, for the perfect functioning of a free market there should be no obstacles to the movement of factors of production, or to the entry of new firms into the production of a commodity. For example, if a license is required to enter a particular field of activity—a state requires beauty parlor operators to be licensed, or a city limits the number of permits to operate taxicabs—this reduces the supply of a service and forces its price higher than it would be if more providers of the service could enter the market freely. This is not to say that there are no good reasons for licensing; most of us would probably agree that not everybody should be able to start up as a surgeon, for example, without going through some licensing procedure. While reasons of public policy are invariably given to justify licensing schemes, the desire of practitioners already in the field to keep prices high is generally the motive force behind the establishing of licensing requirements, and it is not clear that licensing is necessary to safeguard public safety in many fields where it exists.

Fourth, the free-market model assumes that the players act rationally so as to maximize their income and material satisfactions. Perhaps on the whole, and in the long run, they do. But in any specific case that is being analyzed, factors of personal affection, tradition, or aesthetic and moral considerations may in fact serve to limit the rational maximization of income. An employer may hire a relative who will not be the most productive worker; he may refuse to stay open on a religious holiday, even though a high sales volume would be likely on that day. A worker may forego a job at higher pay if it requires her to move away from family and friends. That is, people may legitimately respond to motivations other than the maximization of income.

Fifth, the model assumes that there will always be an adequate supply of labor, materials, and capital, as these are needed to meet requirements of production. This assumption is not as far-fetched as it may seem. If a particular material is in fact not available, generally another one can be substituted, perhaps with some modification of the productive process. In other words, shortages are usually not absolute but only relative, in the sense that substitutes can be obtained, although perhaps at a higher price. Capital may be in short supply, but if the rate of return rises accordingly, people will save more out of their incomes, attracted by the higher rates of return. Nevertheless, entrepreneurship is always necessary, to see the opportunities, to raise the capital, and to organize the production process, and sometimes, especially in a developing country, it may not be available.

The free-market model, in other words, like other models of rational action, can serve both to describe and to predict reality, and to counsel desirable behavior, so long as one remembers that it is based on a series of assumptions that may or may not be actualized in the case at hand. Forgetting this principle is the curse of economists' policy recommendations. Awareness of the assumptions underlying the model also has the advantage that if predictions based on it fail, one is directed to a checklist of readily identifiable causes for the discrepancy: which of the assumptions failed to hold in practice?

GOVERNMENT REGULATION OF THE MARKET

An understanding that certain conditions need to hold if the market is to work in practice shows why it is fallacious to argue that government regulation of the economy is incompatible with the existence of a free market. In fact, government regulation of the economy—of a certain type—is absolutely necessary if the market is to function. Antitrust legislation, requirements for truth in packaging and advertising, and penalties for fraud and contract violation are clearly necessary conditions for the functioning of a viable market. We will refer to this first category of government actions as those which *support* the market system.

The second category of government actions would then be of those that *supplement* the market—that is, while they are not necessary for the market to function, neither do they impede its functioning. They simply make provision for areas of economic life that are not taken care of by the dynamics of the market. Thus social insurance programs, which provide protection against sickness, injury, or unemployment, may be desirable and may be constructed in such a way that they do not affect market behavior. For example, if unemployment benefits are set at such a rate and under such conditions that it is not in anyone's interest to quit work in order to receive unemployment benefits, then the functioning of the market should not be affected by having an unemployment insurance program.

A third category of government actions are those that *limit* the action of the market for noneconomic reasons, in the interest of protecting health, safety, or morals. That is, government may act to exempt certain areas from the action of the market—for example, by providing that addictive drugs may not be produced and sold; or that contracts to perform criminal acts are unenforceable. Most supporters of a free-market system would accept this kind of limitation on the operations of the market. However, one should acknowledge that the views of the public on the kinds of activities that can legitimately be exempted from control of the market on these grounds does change over time. At one time it was thought an illegitimate interference with the freedom of the market for a government to prohibit the employment of children in heavy factory labor. Today most people would accept that limitation as legitimate and desirable.

IDEOLOGIES OF THE MIXED ECONOMY

In what might be called the postsocialist era, it seems to be generally accepted that a modern economy cannot reasonably be socialist—that is, totally government-owned and -operated; but also that a purely capitalist economy needs to be limited in order to ameliorate the plight of the poor and underprivileged. Within that very broad consensus, at one extreme *neoliberalism* inclines to the view that pure capitalism has not been given a fair chance and the role of government needs to be minimized to the vanishing point; at the other, *social democracy* wants to put the satisfaction of human needs first and only allow capitalism to function on sufferance.

The German Federal Republic has had success with an economic model it calls the *social market economy*, in which welfare problems are taken care of by a strong social insurance program financed by employer and worker contributions rather than by taxes, while government interference with the free market is minimal.

Mexican President Carlos Salinas de Gortari (1988–94) seemed to have in mind in the doctrine he promoted as *social liberalism* a model in which neoliberal principles guide most of the economy but government retains a strong role in economic planning as well as in social programs, which can include subsidized consumption and investment.

Many parties have been founded with the *Christian Democratic* label, advocating a mixed economy in which the free market is moderated by principles of Christian compassion and solidarity, although once in power most Christian Democratic parties tend to the conservative side.

The fourth category of government action with respect to the market, *modifying market forces* for economic reasons, is more controversial. Although the general public interest is always claimed, often some powerful special interest is in fact involved. It is clear that a great deal of hypocrisy is involved in professions of loyalty to market principles, and support for the free market in general may evaporate when a special interest of one's own is at stake. The halls of legislatures are full of lobbyists for special subsidies, tariff protection against competing imports, special loopholes in the tax collection system, or government loans at below-market rates of interest. An ideological commitment, as we have seen, reflects an appreciation for what one's interests are in general, but not in every specific case.

Nevertheless, not all modifications of the incentives provided by an untrammeled free market respond to special-interest pressures. They may in fact be introduced in the general public interest by an economically sophisticated and public-spirited government. We shall delve into this subject at greater length when we discuss economic planning in Chapter 10. At this point it should be acknowledged that although at times the free action of the market may have drawbacks that one may wish to avoid, nevertheless on the whole it has very substantial advantages. This will become clear in Chapter 10 when we contemplate what happens in states that follow the fifth possible set of government actions with respect to the market, those that *replace* the market entirely with centralized state planning.

COMMON IDEOLOGICAL LABELS

Discussions of political ideology usually focus on the banners that have floated over the major European political movements. *Conservatism* has Edmund Burke as its most coherent theorist, with the thesis that institutions that exist have developed for good reasons, have been tested by time, and are adapted to the milieu in which they find themselves, and should not lightly be cast aside. Just as the content of conservatism may vary from place to place, according to which institutions ought to be conserved, the content of liberalism similarly varies.

Liberalism always stresses freedom; however, some old-fashioned Liberal parties in Europe, such as the one in Italy, still stress freedom of trade and are thus primarily business-oriented parties. Most Liberal parties stress freedom of speech and of the press; but some unsavory types show up in Liberal parties such as that of Austria, where the freedom most prized appears to be primarily the freedom from having one's pro-Nazi past investigated. Most Liberals anywhere, however, are supporters of civil liberties; most are also anti-clerical. However, in the United States, the term "liberal" is applied to those who favor not only civil liberties and equality of rights, but also redistributive economic policy measures designed to alleviate the lot of the more poor and miserable members of society.

Socialism comes in both Marxist and non-Marxist varieties. Based on opposition to the unemployment and class exploitation it believes to be inherent in capitalism, socialism opposes to the individual ownership of property the idea of collective social ownership of property. In practice, where socialist measures have been introduced, this has meant government ownership and control of segments of the economy, which has often had unfortunate results (see Chapter 10). Some present-day socialists have wanted to maintain the movement's tradition of opposition to the excesses of capitalism while abandoning government ownership of industry as the necessary prescription.

Although attempts have been made to give *Fascism* intellectual coherence, there is too much good sense among writers on political thought for Fascist ideology to be able to acquire any kind of respectability (despite the fact that Harold Laski once wrote that if Al Capone and Dutch Schultz shot their way into the White House, there would be some political scientist asking what their political philosophy was). Fascism is simply the use of violence by a self-selected minority for political purposes. Fascist movements frequently act against organized labor on behalf of employers, or against racial or ethnic minorities. Fascist ideologies are cobbled together out of elements such as extreme nationalism, racism, male chauvinism, glorification of war, and adulation of the leader.

EXTREMISM

A position on the political Left implies support for change in the existing situation, such as a reallocation of resources, in favor of those further down the social scale, while a position on the Right implies defense of a situation embodying inequality in the distribution of rewards.

The greater egalitarianism, or support of equality, to be found on the Left implies also a more benign attitude toward foreigners, as fellow human beings who also have rights. This means that a contrary right-wing position appears more patriotic, since the nation-state necessarily discriminates against foreigners: its government is concerned primarily with the welfare of citizens and not foreigners, and the doctrine of its military organization is based on the premise that it is legitimate in some situations to kill people of another nationality or citizenship.

This set of relationships implies in turn that left-wing extremism tends to be regarded as subversive and antinational, while even violent right-wing extremism may be regarded more leniently as patriotism that is perhaps a little too enthusiastic. Although many unhappy examples of the tolerance of state institutions for right-wing extremism are commonly cited from the Weimar Republic, there is no shortage of examples from other countries, including the United States.

NOTE

1. Donald Philip Green has summarized the evidence as indicating "the limited influence of narrow self-interest" on opinions with respect to policy questions, in "The Price Elasticity of Mass Preferences," *American Political Science Review*, March 1992.

KEY TERMS

ideology

empirical

normative

Left-Right continuum

French Revolution

free market

Adam Smith's *The Wealth of Nations*

neoliberalism

conservatism

liberalism

socialism

Fascism

CHAPTER 4

Legitimacy, Disobedience, and Revolution

POT-SHOTS NO. 784.

SHOULD I
ABIDE BY
THE RULES
UNTIL THEY'RE
CHANGED,

OR HELP SPEED THE CHANGE
BY BREAKING THEM?

Ashleigh Brilliant

LEGITIMACY

One of the most fundamental questions in politics is why people obey government. The obvious answer is that they do so in fear of negative consequences if they disobey—that is, from fear of punishment. Another part of the answer is that they do so out of habit; most laws are obeyed most of the time, automatically, without a conscious decision. A third part of the answer is that to some extent people obey government because they believe governments have a right to make laws that they should follow; in other words, they believe in the government's legitimacy.

Governments are very concerned to establish claims to legitimacy, since the more obedience can be founded on consent, the less coercion is necessary. If for no other reason, a government's having legitimacy means that it can economize on policing costs.

On what basis can a government claim legitimacy? The classic answer to this question generally cited is that of the great German sociologist Max Weber.[1] Weber classified legitimate authority as either traditional, rational-legal, or charismatic. By "traditional" authority, Weber meant principally forms of rulership such as monarchy, normally sanctioned by religion, found in premodern societies. "Rational-legal" authority to Weber meant essentially the authority of bureaucracies that ruled on the basis of clear and established procedures applying to all cases without favoritism, and based on sound technical criteria and a solid understanding of the factual situation involved. He seems to have had in mind particularly the Prussian and German bureaucracies as they had developed through the early twentieth century. "Charismatic" leadership claimed legitimacy on the basis of the personal characteristics of the individual ruler. Revolutionary leaders emerging outside of the established constitutional framework were certainly charismatic, but Weber also considered elected political figures in democratic societies to be charismatic leaders, since they are chosen on the basis of their personal characteristics.

This set of categories, or system of classification, is an *inductive* one—that is, it was established on the basis of familiarity with a number of cases, whose main features suggested what the different categories should be. An alternative method of establishing a system of classification is *deductive*, which establishes categories and a system of classification on the basis of abstract and *a priori* principles. Each method of proceeding has its strengths and weaknesses, and either one can be appropriate, depending on the circumstances of the particular case.

The advantage of a deductive over an inductive system is that it can be more comprehensive and orderly, and categories can be defined so as to include all possible variations, whereas an inductive system may overlook possible variations that happen not to be in the set of empirical cases from which its categories are derived. A deductive system, on the other hand, may be exhaustive in the sense that it includes all possible cases, but some of the categories it establishes may in fact be empty of empirical instances, while other categories may be too crowded to allow meaningful analysis.

This chapter will propose a deductive system of classification of types of legitimate authority which this writer believes to be more helpful for some purposes than Weber's schema, starting by posing the question of obedience in a rather different form: not "Why do people obey government?" but "When is it justified to disobey government?" Posing the question in this fashion makes it possible to draw upon a long tradition of political thought that focused on the questions of disobedience and of tyrannicide, or the justifiable assassination of a ruler. This raises an important methodological point: in analyzing a question it is generally preferable to build on an already established body of thought rather than to spend energy in starting completely from the beginning. As Isaac Newton put it, "I have seen so far because I have stood on the shoulders of giants."

A considerable body of doctrine was developed by the medieval Catholic Church with respect to these questions. This was so because the church, during various periods of its history, claimed the right to pass judgment on secular rulers, sometimes advising the faithful not to follow secular laws that conflicted with religious doctrine and principles, and even taking the position that there were instances when a Catholic could, or even should, participate in a revolt or an attempt to assassinate a tyrant. Clearly, it was thus of great importance for Catholic thinkers to develop criteria by which to define tyranny.

This attempt started with a distinction between origins and performance. A ruler might be a tyrant because of his origins. A ruler would be legitimate in his origins if he came to power in the prescribed manner according to the established laws and customs. For example, he could be the oldest son of a recently deceased king, universally acknowledged as the legitimate successor. Someone who seized power by force, removing a ruler universally accepted as legitimate, would be a tyrant in his origins, and he could thus in good conscience be resisted or even assassinated if no other remedy to remove him from power were available. But a ruler legitimate in his origins might become illegitimate on the basis of his performance. He might violate the laws, confiscate property without compensation, put people to death without trial, burn down churches, kill priests, and establish his own religion. He would thus become a tyrant by performance. Conversely, someone illegitimate in his origins might nevertheless prove to be a wise and benevolent ruler, concluding peace, causing the economy to prosper, and promoting the moral behavior of his subjects. Because of his performance in office he might then come to be regarded as legitimate.

A government may be legitimate, then, because of either its origins or its performance. These characteristics may be subdivided into *procedural* and *substantive* categories. That is to say, for example, a government may be legitimate *in its origins* for procedural reasons: it came to power according to established and accepted procedures—by election, inheritance, designation by the previous ruler, or whatever established law and custom provided (see Figure 4.1). Alternatively, a government may be regarded as legitimate in terms of its origins even if it comes to power outside traditional procedures, if it developed out of a transcendent and universally popular event—a war of independence, a popular revolution, and/or the availability of an individual with extraordinary personal charisma. George Washington was elected first president of the United States under the new Constitution partly so that the infant regime could acquire the legitimacy conferred by his personal prestige. The government of Fidel Castro in Cuba claims legitimacy not on the basis of elections or constitutional procedures but because it emanates from the revolution that overthrew the previous dictator and because of the great personal charisma of Fidel Castro himself.

Figure 4.1
Legitimacy: A Deductive Typology of Rulers

	By Origins	By Performance
Procedural	Chosen in constitutional or traditionally accepted manner	Governs in prescribed manner according to law
Substantive	Acknowledged hero of liberation or leader of independence movement, etc.	Governs wisely; policies successful

A government's claim to legitimacy *by performance* may also be divided into procedural and substantive categories. A government may lose legitimacy through its performance *procedurally* if, for example, it does not follow established rules—it tries to collect taxes not voted by the legislature, it imprisons people without due process of law, or it takes property without compensation. It may also lose legitimacy over time if the substance of its policies is extremely unpopular, even if the procedures by which they are arrived at are legitimate. Thus, for example, if over a long period a government fails to guarantee public security and/or if its policies cause severe and growing economic hardship among the population, they may come to reject not only the individuals holding public office, but even the system that put them there and keeps them there. This was the case, for example, with the long-established democratic regime in Uruguay: conditions deteriorated so severely, over so long a period, that finally in the late 1960s a military seizure of power occurred, an event without precedent in Uruguay in the twentieth century.

DISSIDENCE AND REVOLUTION

As can be seen from the preceding example, the question of a government's legitimacy is not a purely abstract and theoretical one. It is in fact an immediate practical question for military officers who are being importuned by opposition civilian politicians to overthrow an incumbent government. Of course in such cases the interests of the military themselves weigh very heavily, but the question of the government's legitimacy is also paramount.[2] It seems to be the case, from the Latin American evidence, that a government is more likely to be overthrown the weaker its claim to legitimate power: if it came to power illegally, if its margin of electoral victory was very narrow, or if it is headed not by a president who was himself elected, but by a vice-president who succeeded to the office on the death of the elected president. [Note: legitimacy is not an either/or matter, but a question of degree.]

The other significant factors in predicting the possibility of a government's being overthrown relate to its performance, where it can lose legitimacy on either procedural or substantive grounds—procedural if it habitually violates the constitution and the laws itself, substantive if its management of the economy is conspicuously unsuccessful.

Of course the overthrow of a government is the most extreme point on a scale of opposition activities that range from revolt at one extreme of the spectrum through tyrannicide, resistance, and civil disobedience, to simple verbal dissent (see Figure 4.2). [Note: previously we organized types of legitimacy on the basis of a fourfold table based on the distinctions between origins and performance, and between procedural and substantive; the other way of establishing categories, which we are now following, of ranging types along a spectrum or continuum, is possible where only a single dimension is involved—that is, where instances can be classified on the basis of whether they display more or less of one specific characteristic.]

REVOLUTION

As the term is generally used, a revolution consists of a major change in society, the economy, and political life, normally brought about by extraconstitutional and violent means. Revolution-like events that lack one of these features are described in modified terms, such as "a peaceful revolution" or "a palace revolt, not a real revolution."

A revolution involves the replacement of the existing ruling class. Although some historians still write of a revolution's occurring because the oppression of the masses reached such extremes that they could stand it no longer and rose in revolt, most analysts now believe that a revolution grows not out of oppression itself, but from an anomaly or incongruence in it: that is, from the frustration of a rising class that is improving its situation economically, but is blocked from achieving commensurate political power; or whose improvement in economic and political status is suddenly stopped and thrown into reverse.

However, it also appears to be true that a revolutionary situation can be created, not only by such broad historical movements as the long-term rise and fall of social classes, but out of the escalation of fighting that began over some minor point. The process of fighting itself may then mobilize large numbers of people, who expect the suffering they have endured, and sacrifices they have made, to result in worthwhile social change and not simply a restoration of the *status quo ante* (that is, the situation that existed before).

The strongest form of opposition, *revolt*, aims at changing the government. *Tyrannicide* does likewise, but if it is successful in removing the country's political leader, it may well be that the same group of people stays in charge and the subsequent leader is just as bad as or worse than the one who was assassinated. *Resistance* can take various forms, including

Figure 4.2
Degrees of Opposition to a Government

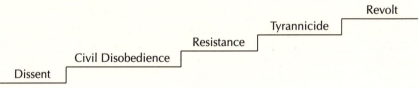

violent ones, but it aims at obstructing the actions of the incumbent government, not necessarily overthrowing it. One of the most famous examples of resistance, the French underground movement against the German occupation during World War II, had as its basic purpose to weaken the occupying forces and to assist the British government in its conduct of the war against Nazi Germany.

MOHANDAS GANDHI (1869–1948)

Gandhi, usually referred to by the honorific Mahatma, meaning "Great Soul," was trained as a lawyer in England and practiced in India and South Africa before becoming a community leader campaigning against the discrimination practiced against the Indian community in South Africa. Although his political activity focused on independence from Britain for India, finally achieved in 1947, he is best known outside India for the techniques of nonviolent political action he developed. Reflecting his understanding of the pacifism of Leo Tolstoy, the civil disobedience of Henry David Thoreau, and the message of Christianity, Gandhi cast the theory and practice of nonviolence into traditional Hindu categories. As well as for Indian independence, Gandhi conducted campaigns, which included mass demonstrations, fasts, and prayer, on behalf of the improvement of the status of untouchables; for peace between Hindus and Muslims; for abstinence from alcohol; and for women's rights, among other causes.

Revered around the world for his saintly way of life, the nobility of his ideals, and the inspirational quality of his leadership, Gandhi was not able to prevent the partition of India between India and Pakistan and the fighting among the religious communities that followed. He was assassinated by a Hindu extremist on January 30, 1948, but he has continued to serve as a source of inspiration for campaigners against war, inequality, and prejudice.

Civil disobedience has undergone an extraordinary flowering as a political technique during the twentieth century, being developed especially during the Indian anticolonial movement by Mohandas Gandhi and the Congress party, and then again in the American civil rights movement by Martin Luther King, Jr. The basic function of civil disobedience is to draw attention, to point out the absurdity or immorality of some government practice, to draw down condemnation on it, and to appeal to the conscience of the majority population. Civil disobedience thus operates in a moral dimension, so it is important that the actions of those involved be morally correct. This gives civil disobedience an ambiguous character. On the one hand, those involved are breaking a law they feel to be unjust; yet they act peacefully and are prepared to accept the punishment that the legal system metes out as a penalty for violating the law. Not only did followers of Gandhi and Dr. King permit themselves to be taken to jail without offering resistance, they also suffered extralegal attacks, which only served to draw attention to the peacefulness and good faith of their intentions and the moral weakness of those opposing them.

MARTIN LUTHER KING, JR. (1929–68)

As a young Baptist minister in Montgomery, Alabama, Dr. King was drawn into the civil rights movement of which he became by the middle 1960s the unquestioned leader. Of distinguished academic background, graduating from college at age nineteen with honors, finishing first in his class at seminary, and earning a doctorate in philosophy from Boston University, King drew from Hegel, the subject of his dissertation, an understanding of the power of ideas in forming the spirit of the time, which he combined with a Gandhian commitment to nonviolence and an understanding of the reasons for the effectiveness of nonviolence as a political tactic. Transposing this understanding into the idiom and spirit of traditional Southern black religion, he became the unquestioned leader of the civil rights movement by preempting the moral high ground, establishing a dialectic between the faith and hope of disadvantaged blacks and the guilty conscience of the white majority.

Under the impetus of the civil rights struggle, Congress passed the 1964 Civil Rights Act and later that year Dr. King was awarded the Nobel Peace Prize. His most-quoted works are his 1963 "Letter from Birmingham Jail" and his Washington speech "I Have a Dream." Harassed and hounded by the Federal Bureau of Investigation, for whose director, J. Edgar Hoover, King was a dangerous subversive, Dr. King knew his life was always in danger. On April 4, 1968, he was assassinated in Memphis; his killer, a professional criminal, seemed clearly a hired assassin, but went to jail without disclosing whether he had been hired and, if so, by whom. After Dr. King's death, his legend steadily grew as someone who had been able to channel protest against injustice into nonviolent but effective channels and had demonstrated that important moral ends could be secured by using only moral means.

Simple *dissent*, verbal disagreement with the policies of government, or even with the principles embodied in the reigning political or economic system, is of course perfectly legal in democracies. This does not mean that dissenters do not face unpleasant consequences. In fact, as Alexis de Tocqueville pointed out 150 years ago with respect to the United States—and as Plato pointed out long before—in democracies there may be a tyranny of majority opinion which imposes social penalties on deviance.

ANTI-COMMUNISM

During the 1950s in the United States, such a tyranny of majority opinion was known as *McCarthyism*. People suspected of even the mildest leftism were pilloried by congressional committees, placed on blacklists by self-appointed vigilantes, and smeared in the mass media. Independence of mind was discouraged; conformism was mandated. Many who refused to sign "loyalty oaths" or who had at some time been members of leftist organizations lost their jobs; some who refused to be browbeaten by congressional committees into accusing friends and associates, declining to answer leading questions, went to jail for contempt of Congress. Americans are still nervous about straying too far from mainstream certitudes, whether in politics, economics, or religion.

Yet anti-Communist hysteria was not generated solely by characteristics of Western societies. It was also provoked by certain characteristics of the Communist movement as this was established by Karl Marx, modified by V. I. Lenin, and developed further by Josef Stalin. Communism is, of course, a revolutionary doctrine that threatens the existence of the capitalist economy. Of course, the vegetarian movement threatens meat-eating and the prohibition movement the drinking of alcohol, yet they are opposed by people who disagree with them without evoking the particular passions associated with anti-Communism. This is partly because Lenin argued that Communist parties should become cadres of disciplined professional revolutionaries in order to succeed in the face of the repression and police terror of governments such as that of czarist Russia. Stalin compounded the problem by insisting that foreign Communist parties consider "proletarian internationalism" their primary obligation—that is, that they subordinate other considerations to the requirements of Soviet foreign policy. Like other governments, moreover, that of the Soviet Union engaged in espionage, especially to find out military information that might be of value to it.

All of these factors worked together and were confused in the minds of many, perhaps most, Americans so that no clear distinction was made between those who might share some of the ideas of Marx, people who criticized aspects of the capitalist system, those who didn't like features of current U.S. foreign policy, and spies for the Soviet Union. In fact, while some espionage agents acted on behalf of the Soviet Union out of ideological conviction, more of those who were caught appeared to be motivated by monetary rewards or personality flaws, and in any case had typically presented themselves as having conservative political opinions, which made better political cover.

Pressures for conformity in politics reduce a country's claim to be considered a democracy. A democracy requires the exercise of civil liberties if it is to function properly. Genuine choice among alternatives for the voters is not possible without freedom of speech, the press, and assembly. People must be free to propagate their views and to attempt to convince others, or the choice offered to a voter has little meaning. But what kind of free speech is it if one is free only to say what is popular? The real test of whether a country's claim to have free speech is genuine is if it protects speech that is unpopular and even offensive to a majority. Freedom of speech would not need constitutional protection if it extended only to government spokespersons and supporters, patriotic orators, or flatterers of those in power.

The problem is especially acute today in the United States and elsewhere where the mass media, and especially television, define the political issues and circumscribe what can be considered mainstream thinking; where views departing too much from the mainstream are regarded as "extremist," even vaguely disloyal. The framers of the U.S. Constitution knew what they were doing when they entrenched individual rights in the Constitution, making it impossible for it to be changed by a simple majority of the voters or their representatives. Sometimes, especially when a majority of the Supreme Court, the guardian of the Constitution, is not in sympathy with individual rights, even that is not enough.

Now that the Soviet Union, whose leaders claimed to be acting in line with the theories of Karl Marx, has passed into history, it would be tempting to regard Marxism as of no more relevance than the discarded scientific theories or religious heresies of the ancient world. But this would be a mistake. Understanding Marxism is important, not only to understand the period of history when the Soviet Union was a major factor in the world, but because Marxist thought still shapes the mentalities of many people in the world, and even more because not all of Marx's thought is obsolete. Much of it still raises interesting and important questions about capitalism, about human behavior, and about the nature of history.

MARXISM: THE BACKGROUND

To understand Marxism, one should appreciate that it grows out of a specific period of human intellectual history, which begins in the seventeenth and eighteenth centuries with the Enlightenment. Prior to the seventeenth century, human beings had not clearly improved on the ancient Greeks, technically or intellectually. Aristotle was still a good general source for what human beings knew. In the 1600s, this began to change.

Especially significant was the impact on the popular mind of Isaac Newton's great synthesis, in the law of gravity; of the breakthroughs in physics and astronomy of Johannes Kepler and others. The industrial inventions that followed in the nineteenth century, the improvements in the standard of living made possible by the growth of industry in Britain and France, and advances in the practice of constitutional government, especially in Britain, gave substance to the idea that history could in fact represent human progress. Progress was not necessarily inevitable, in the view of the best thinkers of the age, but it was possible and even probable. In fact, it became common to interpret the political history of Britain as a steady evolution in the direction of greater liberty though the steady accretion of powers to the parliament and the diminution of the powers of the monarchy.

KARL MARX (1818–83)

Born in Germany, Marx lived most of his life in exile because of the revolutionary character of his journalistic writings and his political activity. His writings on philosophy and economics, the most important of which is the massive three-volume *Das Kapital* (*Capital*), written in collaboration with Friedrich Engels, broke new ground in many respects and provided the foundation for the doctrine that became known as Marxism; Marx himself found his followers too inclined to convert his thought into a rigid ideological system and is supposed to have declared *Je ne suis pas Marxiste*.

Although it has become common to blame Marx retrospectively for the crimes committed by Josef Stalin, Mao Zedong, and other tyrants who called themselves Marxists, Marx himself can be quoted to effect on behalf of human freedom against oppression. It is certainly not necessary to identify as a Marxist or to subscribe to the whole system of thought derived from the works of Marx to appreciate some of Marx's fundamental contributions to social analysis, such as the importance of economic class identity in determining political attitudes, the dependence of social and political arrangements on economic realities, or some of his insights into the nature of the capitalist system. The best short summary of Marxist views is *The Communist Manifesto*, which Marx wrote in 1848 as the platform for a movement of German working class exiles in France and England.

Marxist thought grows out of this recently established view of history as representing human progress, and specifically out of the conception of history embodied in the work of the German philosopher G.W.F. Hegel. In Hegel's model, history was the story of the evolution of human liberty, and the dimension in which evolution took place was that of ideas. In the ancient world, slavery was practiced; in the Middle Ages peasant serfs were only semifree. In the modern world all people could be citizens and enjoy civil rights. Thus there had been a succession of types of society, each reflecting a different idea about the possible extent of human freedom. But change from one state of society to another, from one dominant idea to another, did not take place smoothly but "dialectically"—that is, by a clash of opposites. Opposition would grow to a dominant idea. Its limitations would become apparent, difficulties would develop in the society that embodied it, and it eventually would be superseded by a more advanced or superior idea.

Marx took this apparently unpromising model of Hegel's and made rather more sense of it by "turning it upside down"—by positing that the primary motivating principle in history is not ideas as such, but rather economic interests. Man's first priority is to make a living, to eat. To Marx, Hegel's insight that history moved by oppositions, or contradictions, by the movement of thesis and antithesis, was correct. It was correct to say that through these conflicts higher and higher forms of society evolved. But material conditions rather than ideas were the primary motivating force, and thus the conflicts that provided the creative motive power of history were not between ideas as such but between social classes and economic systems. One historical system succeeded another, then, because it was more productive.

Before we leave Hegel behind, however, we should not overlook the creative use made of Hegel's ideas by Martin Luther King, Jr. King wrote his doctoral dissertation on Hegel and it is possible to see in Dr. King's political thinking, along with the influence of Mohandas Gandhi, such Hegelian principles as that society progresses through struggle, that men are motivated by ideas, that superior ideas vanquish less adequate ones, and that ultimately human history is the story of the increasing actualization of the idea of human freedom.

PRINCIPLES OF MARXISM

The basic principles of Marxist thought are the following:

1. *Philosophical materialism*: Human beings must eat before they can think. Material conditions are prior to, and determine, other forms of human activity. In particular, in any society the economic base determines the superstructure of culture, religion, politics, and so on. Certain ideas and practices, such as those of religion, are appropriate to one type of society and not to another. Catholicism, for example, with its ideas of hierarchy, human weakness, and the expenditure of money on costly buildings and images, was appropriate for feudal times, but capitalism needs a religion of hard work, thrift, and success; thus the Protestant Reformation was born. Capitalism cannot tolerate internal barriers to trade; national unification movements thus arise. Rational calculation of profit and loss is impossible if the king can arbitrarily change the rules; thus capitalism supports constitutional government. Everything else, in other words—morality, religion, politics—flows from the specific character of the organization of production.

2. *The dialectic*: To Hegel, societies were organized around a dominant set of principles or ideas (the thesis), which over time would be found in-

adequate and opposed in various respects (by the antithesis) and would be replaced by a new set of ideas (the synthesis) reconciling the original principles and those attacking them; thus synthesis arose out of the clash between thesis and antithesis. To Marx also, everything contained its opposite—that is, each system created its own opposition. Capitalism, too, contained the seeds of its own destruction; it brought workers together in large numbers, taught them to read and write and organize, and then threw them out of work in its periodic depressions, provoking them to oppose and try to overthrow the capitalist system itself.

3. *Dialectical materialism*: History moves by these dialectical oppositions, and the basic motivations are economic. Thus the critical dynamic that motivates history is the conflict between economically defined entities, that is, economic classes. "The history of all hitherto existing societies has been the history of class struggles." A class is defined by its relation to the means of production—that is, one class of people is formed by the owners of property, another owns nothing but its labor.

4. *The labor theory of value*: What gives a product value? What accounts for the difference in value between a chair and the block of wood out of which it was made? The labor that went into making the chair. What accounts for the difference in value between the block of wood and the tree? The labor that was expended in cutting down the tree and splitting the logs. The value of a final product, therefore, is given to it by the sum total of the labor which made it, which mined or harvested the raw materials that went into it, which transported and prepared them, and also which managed operations, did the bookkeeping, and made the sales. However, under capitalism, there are returns to capital as well as to labor; capital earns profits, rents, interest, and dividends. These all come out of the end price of the product. In other words, although labor gave the product its value, the entire amount of that value is not paid to labor because much of it is siphoned off as payments to capital.

5. *Exploitation*: The difference between the value of the end product and the amount paid all of the forms of labor that went into making it constitutes the margin of exploitation. Labor is exploited to the extent that it does not receive the full value represented by the price of the final product.

6. *Crises, or depressions*: Under capitalism, a portion of the amount paid to capital as profits, dividends, interest, and rent is not spent but is saved. This means that not all of the money earned in the production of the total amount of goods manufactured in society is available to purchase them. Therefore, some goods remain unsold. As the warehouses fill up with surplus goods, the factory owners decide to close down production temporarily until the backlog is sold off. Of course, when the factories are closed the workers are not earning any money, so it becomes even more difficult to sell off the surplus produced. Thus a depression results, char-

acterized by widespread unemployment, a shortage of money in the economy, and quantities of unsold goods.

7. *The immiseration of the masses*: Unemployment thus grows out of crises of overproduction under capitalism. It also occurs continuously because it is the nature of capitalism to replace labor with capital. The amounts of capital that pile up through savings and profits must be invested, they must earn a return, and they are invested in machinery that is profitable because the factory need not employ so much labor to get the job done. In a continuous process, therefore, capitalism replaces labor with capital. Thus it continually creates unemployment. Because these great masses of unemployed people are desperate for a job, they compete for jobs and force down wages. The capitalists can lower wages because there are always desperate people eager to take a job at any pay. Thus workers become poorer and poorer.

8. *The revolution*: Finally, the great mass of the unemployed can stand it no more and rise in revolution. They overthrow the capitalist system that is responsible for exploiting them. After the revolution, a transition period takes place in which the proletariat—those who have nothing to sell but their labor—takes control. In Marx's thought, all governments are dictatorships. Because of its requirement for predictability and its need for freedom from government intervention, the bourgeoisie has constructed a constitutional and quasi-democratic state, but the bourgeoisie want freedom for themselves, not for their workers, so that the democratic character of the liberal bourgeois state is largely a façade, a disguised dictatorship. In any society the government is "the executive committee of the ruling class," since the political superstructure is determined by the economic base. Under capitalism, government is essentially a police force that has as its mission the protection of property. The bourgeois state exists to protect property, facilitate trade, and impede labor organization. The government that follows the revolution will be a dictatorship—as all governments are—but it will be a dictatorship of the majority, set up to liquidate the last remnants of capitalism.

9. *Socialism*: After capitalism is liquidated, the proletariat will construct an economic system without exploitation. Ownership of the means of production will be social (public) and not private as under capitalism. Under socialism, it will be "from each according to his ability; to each according to his work"—that is, the laborer will receive the full value of what he has produced without exploitation.

10. *Communism*: After socialism has created abundance for everyone, the system will change to one of communism, under which the principle of distribution will be "from each according to his ability; to each according to his need"—that is, distribution of wealth will be absolutely fair and just. Larger families will receive more; children and the aged will have their needs attended to even if they are not producers.

The economy will be abundant since there is no need to close down factories repeatedly until a surplus of unbought goods can be sold off. It will not be necessary for everyone to work every day, and there will be plenty of leisure time. Man will no longer be the greedy and selfish creature he was under capitalism—a new, generous, altruistic, public-spirited human being will emerge.

This is an overview of the main features of Marxism as a mode of understanding social reality, as a philosophy and an ideology. There are many more aspects to Marxism—it contains an epistemology, or theory of knowledge, for example, and an analysis in depth of the functioning of capitalism. However, those who followed Marx simplified and expanded on his ideas to the point that Marx himself is reported to have said "I am not a Marxist."

A CRITIQUE OF MARXISM

What are we to make of the Marxist approach to the world? Clearly, much of Marx's understanding of social reality has passed into the mainstream of human thinking. Any social scientist will try to interpret social structures and political dynamics in terms of social classes acting in their own interest. The conception of superstructure is insightful and provocative. However, no matter how valuable the analytic insights of Marxism, Marx's predictions were clearly off base. Under capitalism the condition of most workers has improved vastly since his time, despite the fact that depressions have continued to occur and short-term declines take place from time to time. Socialist revolutions have not occurred in the advanced industrialized countries, though some have taken place in backward agricultural nations.

The labor theory of value, moreover, is too limited and mechanical a way of understanding economic value, determined as it is by supply and demand. At the same time, the capitalist may make an important contribution as entrepreneur and risk-taker without "producing" anything directly.

A more fundamental criticism of the Marxist conception of the proletarian revolution that will overthrow capitalism is that it is really itself quite un-Marxist. Why should the proletariat be expected to overthrow capitalism? Previous societies embodying distinctive forms of economic organization were not brought to an end by revolutions of the exploited classes. Revolts of slaves were not the reason for the passing of slave society, nor did revolts of serfs determine the end of feudalism. Feudalism was not replaced by a dictatorship of the serfs that prepared the way for the construction of capitalist society.

In his concept of proletarian revolution, Marx seems to have confounded two different kinds of historical struggle. *Within* each society a struggle goes on between the property-owning class and the "exploited" class over distribution of the burdens and the benefits of the production system. In this struggle, the interests of the proletariat are opposed to those of the bourgeoisie. A quite different struggle, however, goes on between the dominant class in a society and the emergent dominant class of the society that is to replace it, which is in no way the same as the exploited class in the existing society. Feudalism was brought to an end not by the serfs but by the bourgeoisie, the emerging representatives of a new form of social and economic organization who wanted an end to monarchical absolutism, feudal privilege and obstructions to trade, and the economic burden to society of expenditures on royalty and established religion.

Thus capitalism as Marx knew it will no doubt be replaced in the fullness of time; perhaps the changes going on in the world today—the development of new forms of financial manipulation, the growing importance of the computerized retrieval of information, and new forms of direction and control—are part of that process, but it is the people who will benefit from the new forms of organization that will take the lead in bringing about the changes, not the working class of the present system.

It was in fact the failure of Marx's predictions, and especially the failure of his predictions as to how the revolution would come about, that led Lenin to make his own contributions to Marxist thought, modifying it drastically and in many ways contradicting its basic spirit.

LENINISM

Lenin tried to extend and adapt Marxism to take account of the fact that the situation of workers in the industrialized West European countries seemed in many respects to be getting better rather than worse, and that therefore there seemed to be no prospect of the development of a revolutionary workers' movement that would seize power and bring capitalism to an end. In explaining what had happened, he drew on the work of British economist J. A. Hobson, who had explained imperialism—the seizing by the West European powers, especially Britain and France, of territories overseas—as a way of resolving the crisis of overproduction. Marx had predicted that because wages were relatively low there would not be enough money in the economy to buy all the goods produced and that therefore the factories would have to close periodically until the surplus was consumed.

Lenin, following Hobson, wrote in *Imperialism: The Highest Stage of Capitalism* that the colonies were conquered to become captive markets for the sale of surplus production and for the investment of excess capital, as well as to secure raw materials. With captive markets for their surplus, factories could keep producing; in this way capitalism was able to extend its life without a series of crippling crises of overproduction. The imperialist stage of capitalism, wrote Lenin, incorporating developments occurring especially in Germany at the time, was also the stage in which banks would increasingly take control of the economic system. With the super-profits made possible by the exploitation of the colonies, the capitalists would then be able to bribe leadership elements in the working class to ensure that the class did not take a revolutionary line.

V. I. LENIN (1870–1924)

Vladimir Ilyich Ulyanov took the *nom de guerre* Lenin as a revolutionary working against the czarist regime in Russia. Lenin's tactical sense led his faction within the Russian exile Social Democratic party to dominance within the movement and, during the chaos of the Russian Revolution, brought the Bolsheviks to power in November 1917 (October, according to the calendar then in use in Russia). It was also Lenin's sense of tactical realities that led to his modifications in Marxist theory, so that the official ideology in the Soviet Union was always called Marxism-Leninism.

Leninism explained the failure of the Socialist Revolution to come in the developed countries by means of the theory of imperialism, and stipulated that the revolution would be brought about by a secretive disciplined revolutionary party. After the drastic policies of the first years of Bolshevik power, Lenin reversed course with the "New Economic Policy (NEP)," beginning in 1921, which allowed for the functioning of a free market.

On the basis of the NEP, liberal Communists such as Mikhail Gorbachev have argued that Lenin's legacy was that of a more open kind of socialism, not the totalitarian system that Stalin gradually imposed after he succeeded Lenin in 1924; and Lenin had warned his colleagues about the crudeness and ambition of Stalin. Although Stalin carried dictatorship to paranoid and totalitarian extremes, however, there seems no doubt that the basis for the dictatorship was laid by Lenin, who not only set up the Communist Party of the Soviet Union on a disciplined and conspiratorial model, but also established the secret police.

This was a neat and plausible way of accounting for the rising standards of living and the lack of a revolutionary consciousness among the working class in a way that seemed superficially to correspond with the Marxist approach. In a sense, it was truer to Marx's basic insights than Marx's own conclusions were; the proletariat attempted in fact to secure a better deal for itself within the capitalist system, not to bring the system to an end. Marx's conception that the proletariat would try to overthrow capitalism, as we have said above, involved a confusion of two different kinds of economic struggle.

Left to itself, then, the proletariat would not achieve anything beyond "trade union consciousness," the attempt to improve its conditions within capitalism by securing higher wages and shorter hours of work. Many socialists drew from this fact the conclusion that the aims of socialism could be attained by means of peaceful political action within the framework of democratic capitalist societies. These "revisionist" social democrats were by far the larger component of working-class political movements in Western Europe. Lenin was, however, a Russian, citizen of a country ruled by absolute czars, where there were no possibilities of peaceful democratic action. Accordingly, Lenin made his second contribution to Marxist thought: the doctrine that the revolution could be brought about only by the organization of a dedicated cadre of professional revolutionaries, which would be disciplined and secretive—since the czar's spies were everywhere—and ready to resort to extreme measures—since absolutism was too deeply entrenched to be removed otherwise.

Although Lenin's faction was a minority of the Socialist party of Russia, as it was a minority of other parties too, Lenin took advantage of one particular occasion when lack of attendance of more moderate delegates gave his faction a temporary majority to name it the majority, or "Bolshevik," faction. Subsequently, after the Bolsheviks had attained power in Russia, Socialist parties all over the world split, with those willing to follow Lenin's line of policy calling themselves "Communist." Communist parties thereafter were saddled, rightly or wrongly, with the image given them by Lenin, of being secretive, conspiratorial, extremist, and violent.

Marx had thought that the revolution would come after capitalism had run its course; that is, the revolution would come first in the most advanced capitalist societies, such as Britain or Germany. Yet the proletarian revolution was first proclaimed in Russia, where the Bolsheviks took over in the chaos of the country's defeat by Germany in World War I. In Russia the beginnings of industrialism were just becoming visible. Lenin's rival before the seizure of power and close collaborator thereafter, Leon Trotsky, explained this by what he called the "law of combined development"—capitalism was a single world system and the revolution would begin when capitalism as a whole had attained the appropriate stage of development; however, the chain that bound the workers would then snap at its weakest link, which was Russia. But revolution did not in fact extend from Russia to other capitalist countries and the new Bolshevik government felt itself surrounded by hostile capitalist powers. Especially under Lenin's successor, Josef Stalin, the Soviet leadership developed an obsession with security which led to a tight and brutal dictatorship and the transformation, at least as long as Stalin lived, of foreign Communist parties into tools of Russian foreign policy. In Stalin's Russia, it was hard to recognize the anguish over human suffering and the concern for human freedom that had characterized the young Hegelian Karl Marx.

NOTES

1. Weber's work on legitimacy was published as part of his massive tome *Wirtschaft und Gesellschaft* (*Economy and Society*). Most of those who cite Weber on legitimacy have seen only an extract from the book and do not fully understand his work on legitimacy because they have only seen it out of context.

2. This is made clear by John S. Fitch in his *The Coup d'Etat as a Political Process in Latin America: Ecuador, 1948–1968* (Baltimore: Johns Hopkins University Press, 1977).

KEY TERMS

legitimacy	resistance
inductive	civil disobedience
deductive	dissent
procedural	McCarthyism
substantive	Marxism
revolution	dialectical materialism
revolt	Leninism
tyrannicide	Bolsheviks

CHAPTER 5

Political Development

POT-SHOTS No. 1374.

I'M GROWING OUT OF
SOME OF MY PROBLEMS,

BUT
THERE ARE OTHERS
I'M GROWING INTO.

Ashleigh
Brilliant

THE BASIC MODEL

The lexicon of development has become a permanent part of the political vocabulary. Countries are referred to as "developed," "developing," or "less developed." What does this terminology mean? It means that a model is generally accepted that groups countries into three categories. Some are conceived of as underdeveloped—completely traditional, not exposed to the modern world or adopting its ways. (Today, in fact, hardly any societies completely of this type still exist.) At the other end of the spectrum lies the developed modern state, in which people are urban, educated, and participant, with industrialized economies, constitutional governments, and rational bureaucratic practices. In general, this is the kind of state to which most peoples of the world aspire. Much of the world is then conceptualized as "developing"—lying in a transition zone between stagnant traditional society and dynamic modern society. (The term "Third World," often used to characterize undeveloped and developing countries, grows out of a different model, in which countries were divided into Western democracies, Communist regimes, and those neither Communist nor Western.)

What are the political characteristics of the three stages of development in this model? Generalizing and no doubt oversimplifying, one could say that politics in traditional societies is primarily court politics; that is, politics consists of jockeying for the ruler's favor within his or her immediate entourage (see Figure 5.1). Under Jean-Claude Duvalier of Haiti, for example, gossip would have it at one time that his mother had the most decisive influence; at another time, his brother-in-law. The masses of the people did not know what was going on in that closed arena, and certainly did not participate in decision-making.

Figure 5.1
Arenas of Politics

Type of Society	Characteristic Political Arena
Underdeveloped traditional societies	The private arena: the ruler's "court"
Developing societies	The streets
Developed societies	Constitutional institutions: the press, elections, parliament, the courts

Contrast this with politics in a fully developed state, a constitutional democracy like Sweden, which probably approximates closer than any other the "ideal type" of the developed country. There politics is participant—everyone votes, joins political parties and unions, keeps informed by reading newspapers, listening to radio, and watching television. The press is free and takes its reporting and commenting responsibilities seriously. Elections take place at regularly scheduled times; the votes are scrupulously counted, and the government that issues from those elections takes office and serves out its appointed term. Legislation is debated openly in the parliament and laws are passed according to the prescribed constitutional procedures. The judiciary and the bureaucracy discharge their duties in compliance with the law.

In a developed constitutional state, therefore, the arena in which politics takes place is the open one of constitutional institutions. Debates are held in the parliament, which passes the laws. Different contending parties meet in the elections, which decide the issues between them. Vigorous opposition and a free press help to insure that constitutional procedures will be faithfully followed and power not abused.

The "developing countries," which are intermediate between those having traditional political structures and those of the modern world, feature a mix of practices from both traditional and modern societies, together with some characteristics deriving from the fact of transition itself. Participation in politics is not total, although it grows as people learn to read and write, and move to the cities. Elections usually take place, but they are not necessarily held honestly, nor is their result automatically respected. The institutions of a constitutional democracy—press, bureaucracy, judiciary, and legislature—function but not always as they are supposed to, and bribery and corruption are common.

Under these circumstances, political conflict goes on in all arenas—in the private circle of the ruler, as in traditional societies; to some extent in the press and the legislature, as in the developed world; but characteristically, more than in traditional or modern societies, political activity takes place in the streets. That is, it consists of violence and the threat of violence: demonstrations, marches, and strikes. The masses cannot yet trust the political system to be fair, but neither are they indifferent and intimidated, as in traditional society. Political parties have been organized, but they cannot simply rely on the outcome of elections, which may be rigged. Interest groups have started to organize, but are not assured their views will be heard unless they threaten violence. Politics is a matter of sublimated conflict in what Charles W. Anderson has called a system of "the demonstration of power capabilities." And frequently things get out of control and actual violence occurs, in the form of police repression, riots, the military seizure of power, and authoritarian rule.

THE MILITARY SEIZURE OF POWER

Most frequently, the armed forces seize control of the state when there is a vacuum of power or of legitimacy. For this reason, the military seizure of power occurs frequently in newly independent and developing countries. After the old colonial symbols of legitimacy are gone, power may pass to the leaders of the independence movement, who are regarded as national heroes. But if they quarrel among themselves, or prove unable to govern effectively, loyalty to the new regime is too short-lived for its institutions to command the unquestioning respect and obedience that only develops over time. In such a situation, force may be the only arbiter of the occupancy of power, and when that game is played, as Thomas Hobbes observed, "clubs are trumps." But even an old-established political system may eventually begin to lose its legitimacy after a prolonged period of government ineffectiveness—for example, in dealing with economic crisis.

Within the armed forces, some ambitious officers may be eager to seize power, but most officers are as a rule reluctant, and will discuss among themselves whether the government has in fact lost legitimacy and whether the seizure of power would be widely supported by civilians. Professional-minded officers are not eager to abandon the tasks for which they are trained and to assume unfamiliar obligations, especially if they risk courting public hostility.

Typically, the seizure of power occurs when the group favoring the coup either outmaneuvers the moderates or else wins them over. The latter occurs when it becomes clear that the great majority of the people favor a coup, or when the moderates become convinced that the incumbent government threatens the interests of the military institution itself. Such a threat can consist, for example, of political interference in what the military see as purely professional/technical matters; heavy cuts in the military's budget allocation; or an attempt to establish a rival, politically controlled, military force, such as a party militia.

A military seizure of power is sometimes sponsored or incited by the hegemonic regional power. During much of the Cold War the United States worked through the armed forces of the Latin American countries to assert its control of the region, much as the Soviet Union maintained its control of Eastern Europe by working through the local Communist parties.

Figure 5.2
Levels of Overt Political Violence

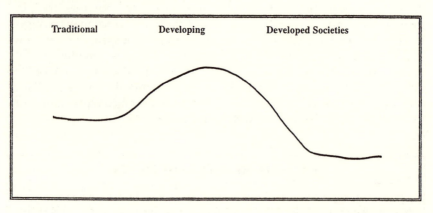

Political development thus consists of a transition in a country's political practices toward those confined to the constitutional arena. This is a possible, but not a necessary, course of development, however, and there is no *a priori* reason why movement cannot take place in the opposite direction—that is, toward a less developed state of affairs. Moreover, even where development does take place, the transition may not be smooth, but may occur in fits and starts, with abrupt reverses. In fact, however, for many countries political development does indeed take place, more or less keeping pace with the country's development in social and economic respects—that is, with its growing literacy and urbanization, and its higher income levels.

During the transition period, the level of violence in the society typically increases before it declines. This paradoxical situation has confused the issue for many people, who have taken it to mean that political development does not accompany economic development. It does; but during the transition phase from stable authoritarian rule to a more open society, violent behavior is likely to occur as the old system breaks down and the circle of those who participate widens (see Figure 5.2). Violence and the threat of violence may initially become more common until new rules of political behavior become generally accepted.

THE SOCIAL DIMENSIONS OF CHANGE

How and why does political development normally accompany social and economic development? The key link is the increase of *mass participation* in politics. In the developed polity, almost the whole of the national population participates in the system through voting, through informing itself on the issues, through joining political parties and other social formations that are active in politics, such as labor unions. In a politically transitional country, participation begins to express itself in these ways, but it also takes the form of direct action, of marches, strikes, and demonstrations.

Why does popular participation increase? Because of several social and psychological causes. Greater awareness of what is happening on the political scene and the desire to participate grow out of the extension of education, the growing literacy of the population, its movement to urban areas, and its exposure to the national communications network. A city resident has more opportunity and more motivation to get involved in political life than a peasant or villager—although the spread of the transistor radio has made it possible for dwellers in rural areas to become much more aware of national and international developments than they used to be, even if they are illiterate.

STUDENTS IN POLITICS

In the countries that are politically transitional, where democratic institutions are not yet firmly established, university students usually play a major role in politics. Intelligent, idealistic, and aware, they may be the only sizable group of people that can be quickly organized for a demonstration or march. Not yet having the jobs to lose and the families to care for that inhibit the participation in opposition politics of older people, students usually take the lead in denouncing corruption and abuse of power. Elections for officers in student government may be fought along party lines and student politicians who are successful may move directly into leadership roles in national party politics. In many developing countries, student organizations provide the most effective counterpoise to the armed forces in national politics.

Improved communications, in the sense both of the communication of information through the electronic media and the improved means of transportation, have facilitated the great increase in political participation. But psychological factors have also been involved in what has been called the *revolution of rising expectations*. That is, in a traditional village culture, the expectation was always that the child would follow the occupation of the parent, whether housewife, peasant, or craftsman; would remain in the same village or local area; and would live at about the same economic level.

With the changes in communications and greater exposure to the outside world, people can now envision a new world of possibilities, and can hope for a higher standard of living, a less arduous occupation, and freedom from the concerns about illness and premature death that beset the life of the peasant. If the prospect of substantial change seems unrealistic for oneself, one can expect it for one's children. Typically, migrants to Third World cities tell interviewers that the primary motive for the change was to secure an education for their children, so that they could enjoy a better life than their parents.

Thus technical changes have both motivated the great movement of urbanization that has occurred and, by improving transportation, made it possible. Technology has also contributed to another cause of urbanization, the population explosion.

DEMOGRAPHIC CHANGE

In traditional societies, under conditions of traditional technology, birth rates are typically high and families containing eight or twelve children are not uncommon. For most of us, this was true in our own families, in our own parents' or grandparents' generation. At the same time, it was highly unlikely that all of those children would reach maturity or die of old age. In the least developed countries, even today, the normal expectation is that half of all infants will die before their fifth birthdays. The chief cause of infant mortality is gastrointestinal complaints, particularly those deriving from polluted water. In tropical zones, insect-borne diseases are also a major factor. Thus birth rates are high; but so are death rates—that is to say, average life expectancy is short, as low as the late twenties in the very poorest countries, but around forty years in most less developed countries even today. This contrasts with average life expectancies at birth in the seventies for today's most developed countries.

In those developed countries where the population is predominantly urban, the normal family has one, two, or perhaps three children. The children are all expected to survive and most can look forward to living out their natural span. Artificial birth control is widely practiced.

THE DEATH RATE

The death rate—what proportion of the population dies in a given year, usually stated as so many per thousand—is another way of indicating the average length of a life span, or life expectancy at birth. Of course, the meaning of the term is not necessarily immediately apparent, as in the story of the demographer who asked "What's the death rate in this village?" and was told "One per person."

The normal transition in a country's demography, therefore, as it undergoes development, is from a predominantly rural society of high birth rates and high death rates to a predominantly urban society of low birth rates and low death rates.

Characteristically, however, the transition does not take place evenly in all respects. Typically, what drops first is the death rate. Death rates can be brought down by a few simple and relatively inexpensive public health measures. The provision of clean drinking water is critical here; it helps if mothers still breast-feed and have not been induced by advertising to buy powdered baby formula. The spraying of DDT to eliminate mosquitoes can also be significant. Thus death rates are brought down right away, but birth rates decline only after an interval, perhaps of a generation or two.

Birth rates decline as efficient birth control methods become generally available; as mothers grow to expect that all of their children will survive; and as people move to cities where living space is much more restricted than it was in rural areas, and where children are expected to attend school rather than participate in the family's economic activities. Thus for a period of a generation or more, during which death rates have already dropped but birth rates remain high, an extremely rapid increase in population takes place, which has been called the *population explosion*.

The population explosion is in popular commentary often linked to the fact that in many areas of the world, especially in areas of Africa contiguous to the Sahara Desert, there have been recurrent outbreaks of famine in recent years. Closer examination, however, indicates that although population increase has led to an increase in herds and some consequent overgrazing, shifts in rainfall patterns are particularly responsible. On a global level, in fact, food production has increased along with population growth, and there are many areas in the United States, and elsewhere, that could be brought into, or back into, food production if there were enough effective demand. If people could pay for it, they would have enough food; the problem is not so much an absolute shortage of supply, but a lack of purchasing power. At least so far, the problem is fundamentally that of unequal distribution of resources rather than of overpopulation as such. In fact, the development of techniques making possible substantial increases in agricultural production—improved seed varieties, pesticides, and artificial fertilizers, together sometimes called the *Green Revolution*—has led to a substantial increase in world food production figures.

The problem of unequal distribution of resources takes various forms. One of these is the shortage of land for those who wish to farm, and in many countries along with population growth has come increased pressure for agrarian reform—that is, the division of larger estates and the allocation of small parcels of land to landless workers.

One of the effects of the population explosion is to intensify the movement to the cities, which have grown extremely rapidly. The largest, Mexico City, now exceeds 20 million inhabitants. This rapid increase in population lets loose an avalanche of problems in the city: shortages of housing, of employment, of schools, and of the provision of services such as sewage disposal, water supply, and electricity. Some cities adjust better than others, and adjust better at some times than at other times. For at least part of the period during which populations are increasing rapidly, many cities present symptoms of breakdown: polluted water supplies, inadequate housing, and filthy streets crowded with beggars.

In this the cities of today's Third World reproduce the experience of the cities of Western Europe during that region's industrial revolution: the dreadful slums of Manchester and other cities of the industrial north of England, which helped to form Karl Marx's ideas of the evils of capitalism, and created the milieu for Charles Dickens's stories, were as miserable and degrading as the worst areas of the cities of Asia and Latin America today.

THE "INFORMAL" ECONOMY

A difference is that in some of today's developing countries, especially in Africa and Latin America, the industrial revolution is providing proportionally fewer jobs than it did in Europe. As a result, most people must create their own jobs. This gives rise to the phenomenon of *underemployment*, with people working at semi-jobs or pseudo-jobs doing things that don't need to be done, provide no addition to the sum total of the country's wealth, and produce very little revenue: shining shoes, guarding parked cars, or peddling odds and ends on the streets. Housing, too, is often self-built. At its worst, it may consist of shacks built out of flattened oil drums, odd pieces of wood, and even cardboard, by the city dump, by the railway tracks, or stuck on a hillside and likely to be washed away with the first heavy rain.

Outside observers are often horrified by the conditions they encounter in settlements of this type. Nevertheless, it never does to underestimate the resilience of the human spirit. If not harassed, intimidated, or extorted by local police and authorities, the poorest urbanites will gradually improve their position, rebuilding their unsatisfactory housing into more substantial living quarters, finding jobs that more adequately provide for their needs, and becoming self-supporting members of society.

One difficulty is provided by city administrations that try simply to eliminate shantytowns by bulldozing them without providing their residents alternate housing—or else by moving them to soulless high-rise projects outside the city, too far to commute to where there is employment—instead of helping to improve their existing housing by supplying cheap building materials, technical assistance, and legal title to the land. In addition, sometimes the poor have to surmount archaic and pointless licensing regulations that make it difficult for people to develop occupations or ply trades that could provide a decent living. Since it is not possible, given the society's resources, to provide everyone with a regular job in the industrial sector or a home in a professionally built house, there is no point in making more difficult people's efforts to help themselves. If governments assist instead of obstructing them, lower-class urbanites will improve their position gradually.

In returning to Third World cities he has previously visited, this writer has often been impressed by the improvement that has taken place, demonstrating that people are not inevitably condemned to misery, not by the growth of population nor by the difficulty in providing for their wants—provided that economic theorists, political leaders, and bureaucrats are helpful and not hostile.

An increase in population need not lead to a reduction in standards of living; as Mao Zedong put it, every stomach comes attached to a pair of hands, and it is possible in principle for people to work and produce more than is necessary to feed themselves, so that with increased population the average standard of living can still improve. The experience of Hong Kong has shown that it is possible for millions on millions of people to achieve a high standard of living in a restricted space.

THE POLITICAL ECONOMY OF THIRD WORLD INDEPENDENCE

In fact, however, for most developing countries, economic problems have grown more acute. Sometimes, as was mentioned earlier, increased population may lead to an increase in herds and overgrazing of available lands. More important, specialization in one or two export crops may produce an excessive dependence on fluctuations in world market prices and thus great vulnerability of the economy to sudden shifts over which it has no control.

Typically, land on which people once grew their own food becomes converted to producing cash crops that bring high revenue in good years, but leave people hungry when export prices crash—and sometimes even when they don't, if the new farming techniques mean that most small farmers are forced off the land, which becomes concentrated in the hands of those with access to the bank credit necessary to buy machines, insecticides, and fertilizers. Especially in African countries, the fact that city populations are politically more important than rural ones, whether it is a question of votes in an election, demonstrations, or street fighting, means that governments will try to keep food prices low. This provides disincentives for farmers to produce food crops and leads to shortages. To continue to keep food prices low, governments then frequently get into importing foodstuffs and selling them at subsidized prices, creating a tremendous drain on government resources and on foreign exchange, which in turn may begin a process of financing expenditures through contracting debt, until more of national earnings go to pay interest on debt than to funding economic development.

Often, especially in newly independent countries in Asia and Africa, government personnel lack training and are guided more by ideological considerations than by economic logic. Caution and moderation may seem like abandonment of the struggle for national liberation, while the laws of economics may seem part of the old colonial restrictions that must now be thrown aside.

The process of political development entails placing rising demands on government. The population is growing, and at the same time is growing more assertive. Not simply content with living in the same way and at the same level as their parents, people's expectations are rising and they place demands on government for schools, jobs, housing, and the provision of urban services. If the economy is growing, if international prices for the country's products remain strong, if production is expanding, then the government is able to gratify these demands, and social peace can be maintained. If times are hard, jobs are not available, and government does not have the resources to satisfy demands being placed on it, people strike, demonstrate, and riot. Where there are free elections, voters will listen to more radical candidates. If demands cannot be satisfied by distributing new wealth that is being created, perhaps they can be satisfied by redistributing existing wealth. Even when the economy is not growing, it is possible to build schools and create jobs by taxing the wealthy; it is possible to provide land to the landless by expropriating it from the owners of large estates.

When the possibility of economic redistribution is raised, when a newly mobilized mass population demands benefits and services that a stagnant or deteriorating economy cannot provide, when radical or populist politicians propose to meet popular needs by taxing the well-to-do, then the wealthier members of society become alarmed, and cast about for a way to bring to an end the political mobilization of the masses and the programs of populist politicians, which they regard as Communist demagoguery. At this point the most common outcome in the Third World is for the political representatives of the wealthier classes to solicit a military seizure of power that will bring the democratic political process to a halt.

The general principle underlying this situation, which was pointed out long ago by Aristotle, is that the distribution of power tends to follow the distribution of property. If people have money, they also have political influence, which they use to maintain their possession of money. At the same time, the converse is true: the distribution of property tends to follow the distribution of power. That is, if the masses are allowed to acquire power through the political process, their representatives are likely to attempt to redistribute wealth and income in their favor. For this reason, when political competition becomes serious, the wealthy in poor countries oppose democracy. Superficially, they may seem to accept its procedures, which are generally in style throughout the world. But democracy's underlying logic implies economic redistribution and this they necessarily oppose.

The process of development may thus seem self-contradictory or para-doxical. Popular participation is growing. In the long run, this means more democracy. In the short run, however, it is just as likely to lead to a military coup, and dictatorship, and the repression of popular demands. This sequence of events is likely to occur especially when the economy is not growing. For if the economy is growing, it may be possible for the demands arising out of increased popular participation to be met without redistributing existing wealth, and a democratic political system can be maintained and strengthened. Economic development can thus contribute to political development. If economic growth is not taking place, on the other hand, the beginnings of social mobilization may raise the specter of redistribution of income; and that will likely lead to military rule and an end, for a shorter or longer period of time, to the process of democratization.

THE LOGIC OF MILITARY INTERVENTION

When this occurs, the military will, in effect, be serving the interests of the country's economic elite. This is commonly, but not invariably, the case. The military force's primary identity is as the servant of the state and of national security, and in this capacity it has two formal purposes: to defend national borders and national integrity against external enemies; and to supplement domestic police forces in defense of law and order. These are the interests it is established to defend. Nevertheless, as a corporate body, it also develops its own interests, which go beyond the formal purposes for which it is established. For most of the time, the military treats its own institutional interests as simply an extension of the national interests it is supposed to defend. For example, it resists any cut in the military budget, which is in its own interest to do, by arguing and to some extent believing that such a cut would threaten its ability to defend the nation's borders.

Examples of other institutional interests that can be defended as necessary to its discharge of its official functions are: retaining a monopoly of the use of force against any attempt to establish a militia, or to arm labor unions or peasants' syndicates; resistance to any interference with its systems of promotion and of hierarchy and discipline; and opposition to any measure that might make the military forces unpopular with the citizens at large.

There are various "fringe benefits" of military service, such as special clubs, subsidized prices in military commissaries, and posts—sometimes with a second salary or the possibility of illicit additional income—in the economic enterprises controlled by the state, which will also be defended by the military, although it is hard to maintain that such privileges are necessary to the military's performance of its primary national security function. Conservative politicians representing the interests of the economic elite can usually persuade military officers that important military interests are threatened by the same political forces that threaten the elite's interests. A leftist or populist political party, for example, if it is allowed to come to power, may be expected to reduce the military budget so that social benefits can be increased, and might arm workers' or peasants' organizations to prevent attacks on them by security forces working for the *oligarchy*. So these conservative politicians can usually convince military officers that a threat exists, and are readily able to enlist military aid in preventing leftists or populists from coming to power, or in removing them once in power.

Occasionally, however, military interests are clearly not the same as the oligarchy's; the military may even see its interests as opposed to those of the oligarchy. For example, the military may come to believe that an unjust social order perpetuated by the economic elite is the cause of insurgency and breakdowns in law and order that could be prevented by the timely adoption of reforms. This logic motivated a sector of the Peruvian armed forces to operate a reformist government from 1968 to 1975. Similar reasoning was behind the attempt of the Carter administration (1977–81) to enlist the support of the military for a land reform program in El Salvador. Important sectors of the military accepted this policy, which required them to oppose the interests of the country's oligarchy, although the policy was watered down and finally brought to an end by the Reagan administration.

As this example illustrates, in much of Latin America the military forces have come to respond primarily not to their own oligarchies but instead to the hegemonic power, the United States. Put in another way, it is primarily through the military connection that the hegemonic power of the United States in the region is made manifest. The connection is maintained partly by overt methods, by military economic assistance, the supply of weapons on concessional terms, training missions, expense-paid visits, courses in U.S. military schools, and the like; and to some extent by covert relations with specific individuals in Latin American armed forces, who are put on the payrolls of clandestine U.S. agencies.

The military is not always responding to oligarchic or hegemonic pressure when it plays a political role, however. It has its own interests, and it also responds to social pressures. As we have seen in discussing African politics, the military, as an organized force in being that possesses weapons, is necessarily the residual holder of power when it passes from the grasp of others. When the imperial power passes from the scene, the national independence movement, its leader, and its party usually dominate national politics; but if they do not, if for some reason the new authorities lack legitimacy in the eyes of the people, or if the new regime loses legitimacy by a sustained period of economic decline, corruption, or incompetence, then the military rushes in to fill the vacuum of legitimacy and authority.

KEY TERMS

political development

Third World

demonstration of power capabilities

mass participation

revolution of rising expectations

death rates

population explosion

Green Revolution

"informal" economy

underemployment

oligarchy

GOVERNING

CHAPTER 6

Elections, Parties, and Interest Groups

© ASHLEIGH BRILLIANT 1981.

POT-SHOTS NO. 2076.

WILL ALL THOSE
WHO FEEL POWERLESS
TO INFLUENCE EVENTS

PLEASE SIGNIFY
BY
MAINTAINING
THEIR USUAL
SILENCE.

Ashleigh Brilliant

THE POLITICAL PARTY

In political systems where competitive elections are held, the principal function of a political party is to elect candidates to office. It is this characteristic that distinguishes the party from other organized political groups, generally known as pressure groups or interest groups, which seek to promote the interests of their members in the political arena by lobbying and by public education or propaganda campaigns, but do not themselves nominate candidates for office.

The strategies of political parties—how they define themselves, what policies they espouse, and the kinds of candidates they nominate—are strongly affected by the nature of the competitive system in which they operate. The rules of the game, and the number of other players, largely determine party strategy and tactics. As was suggested in Chapter 2, a strong causal relation exists between the nature of the electoral law and the number of major political parties in the system. It is almost universally accepted, for example, that the single-member-district plurality, or *first past the post*, system tends to limit the major parties competing in politics to two, since it is extremely difficult for third parties to secure any representation.

PROPORTIONAL REPRESENTATION

The major contrasting system in use today is that of proportional representation (PR), which attempts to have each party's representation in the legislature reflect its proportion of the vote. This it achieves by organizing multimember districts, so that seats may be assigned proportionately. Thus, for example, if ten members are to represent the district, they can be assigned so that each party receiving more than 10 percent of the vote has at least one representative. Thus the faithfulness of representation of the partisan vote increases the larger the number of members for that district. If the district has only five members, a party must secure at least 20 percent in order to win representation; if the district has fifty members, a party can elect a member with only 2 percent of the vote. The highest degree of proportionality is achieved in Israel and the Netherlands, which do not divide the country into districts at all; the whole country constitutes a single electoral district. Thus, for example, in Israel, to elect the 120 members in the Knesset, the national parliament, the voter chooses not individual candidates but a party's entire candidates' list. The candidates on a party list are numbered in sequence. If a party is entitled to eighteen seats on the basis of its share of the vote, then candidates one through eighteen are declared elected. It should be noted that this system confers great influence on the party leadership, which determines each candidate's place on the ballot. If you are assigned the number 1, you are as good as elected already; if you get number 70, don't count on it.

What are the other effects of a proportional representation system? Quite clearly, it encourages rather than discourages small parties. In Israel, any party securing at least 1 percent of the vote elects at least one member. Clearly, if 1 percent of the vote nationally is all it takes to become a member of parliament, then everyone and their brother-in-law form their own political parties. In one extraordinary case, a fugitive financier from France acquired Israeli citizenship and ran for the Knesset so that as a member of parliament he could acquire immunity from extradition to France to stand trial for illegal financial manipulation. Having lots of money for electoral propaganda, he was successful; ironically, when he ran for reelection he was too successful, attracting enough votes to entitle him to two seats in the Knesset when he was the only candidate on his party list.

THE MULTIPARTY SYSTEM

Small parties are encouraged not only by the ease of electing members, but also by the prospect of exercising significant influence in the legislature. In a parliamentary system the government needs to maintain a legislative majority in order to remain in power. Where a multiplicity of parties secure parliamentary representation, as they do in a PR system, then the votes of minor parties may become a significant factor in putting together the minimum majority necessary to support a government. A minor party with a handful of seats may thus be in the position of deciding which coalition shall take office, and of course can use this power to exact important concessions when a cabinet is being put together. During the French Fourth Republic (1946–58) the extremely small party to which François Mitterrand then belonged, the Democratic and Social Union of the Resistance (UDSR), found itself in this position,[1] and despite its minuscule size, its leader, René Pléven, was twice prime minister.

This feature of a PR system, the significance it gives to small and even tiny parties, has a great many drawbacks. A small party can hold up a big one for ransom, and acquire influence out of all proportion to the size of the electoral bloc that supports it. Thus what is obviously a more fair system in representing voters' opinions becomes quite unfair at the level of the formation of cabinets. Moreover, in a parliamentary system that has PR, normally no party can hope for a clear majority on its own, so that coalition cabinets are necessary. This means that a great many compromises need to be made among parties' programs and principles before a mutually satisfactory coalition program can be adopted.

While under PR voters are able to pick parties closely representing their views and do not have to settle, as they do in a two-party system, for a party representing simply the lesser of two evils, this may make no difference at all to the extent to which voters can expect their views to be enacted into legislation. The voters do not have to compromise their views and settle for the lesser of the evils when they go into the voting booth, but the parties that represent them have to do exactly the same thing when it is a question of putting together a cabinet; so the result ends up the same.

Where many parties are represented and coalition cabinets are necessary, one of either of two situations tends to result: either coalitions are unstable as minor parties withdraw because they cannot agree with the position the majority of the cabinet wants to take; or, to maintain the coalition parties together, the cabinet avoids making decisions and postpones facing issues, with resultant negative consequences for the country. In either case, the normal outcome is that the country is in effect run by the bureaucracy rather than the people's elected representatives. The French Third Republic (1870–1940) is generally regarded as having been unable to prepare itself to meet the threat posed by Hitler's Germany because weak coalition cabinets were unable to take the decisions required to raise the money needed to arm and equip the military in adequate fashion.

In fact the Third Republic did not operate with a proportional representation system, but with another electoral system that also encourages a multiplicity of political parties. This is the single-member district with a runoff election if no candidate receives an absolute majority of the vote. In this system, a candidate must receive 50 percent of the vote to be elected on the first ballot; if no candidate does so, then a second election is held (in France, two weeks later) at which the candidate who gets the most votes is declared elected.

This *single-member* district *majority* (rather than *plurality*, as in the United States, where it is necessary only to get more votes than any other candidate) system also encourages minor parties to some extent, because a bargaining process goes on between the first and second ballots during which a minor party may be able to exact concessions in terms of program or patronage in return for throwing its support to one of the larger parties on the second ballot. Moreover, the peculiar effect is created that, since the eventually winning candidates in each district have made different bargains and agreements in return for getting the votes of minor parties, members of the same party in the national assembly may represent different local coalitions; some members of a center party, for example, will have committed themselves to vote with the left on some item of legislation, while other members of the same party are committed to vote with the right. Under these circumstances the single-member majority system with runoff may come to have similar effects, resulting in unstable or immobile governments, to those of the proportional representation system. In the French Fifth Republic, however, which has mostly used the runoff system, government instability has not occurred because a strong presidency has been introduced that drastically modifies the rules of cabinet formation and accountability normal to a parliamentary system.

PROPORTIONAL REPRESENTATION OR SINGLE-MEMBER DISTRICT? THE GERMAN SOLUTION

Proportional representation is favored because it produces results that mirror more faithfully the electorate's preferences. The single-member district, on the other hand, attracts supporters because it reduces the number of parties represented in the legislature, and gives voters a specific representative to whom they can take their complaints. The constitutional draftsmen at Bonn produced an ingenious compromise that has begun to be emulated, in Eastern Europe and also in Latin America. It has been referred to as "personalized proportional representation" or "the two-vote system," since the elector votes once for a representative in his or her district, and once for the political party he or she favors.

The German Federal Assembly has twice as many seats as there are districts. The first vote cast by the voter, for the first set of seats, elects one representative in each district, just as in Britain or the United States. The second set of seats is then distributed so that when added to the seats already filled, the total allocation for each party in the legislature will bring it into line with what it should receive based on the voters' second-vote choices.

Let us suppose a state has a total of twenty representatives and is divided into ten districts. On the second, proportional, vote the Christian Democrats receive 50 percent, the Socialists 30 percent, and the Liberals 20 percent. That means that, of the total of twenty seats, the Christian Democrats are entitled to ten, the Socialists six, and the Liberals four. On the basis of the first vote, let us say that the Christian Democrats have won eight district seats and the Socialists two. Thus the electoral authorities then declare elected an additional two representatives for the Christian Democrats, four for the Socialists, and four for the Liberals, to bring the total elected up to the allocation to which each party is entitled. (In addition, German electoral law provides that a party must receive a minimum percentage of the vote to receive any seats in the proportional distribution, and outlaws antidemocratic parties.)

Nevertheless, it may not always be true that a multiparty system, of the kind created by proportional representation elections, is necessarily unstable. It may happen, as was for many years the case in Italy, that one center party is larger than the others and dominates all possible coalitions. Where a distribution of votes is of this type, government in a multiparty system may in fact be very stable, since the representation of the different parties in the legislature usually changes very little at elections, not being subject to the exaggerations caused by the single-member-district plurality system, where a shift of a couple of percent in the vote may mean a landslide for one party or the other. Under proportional representation, for example, a shift of a couple of percent in the vote means only a shift of a couple of percent in the legislature, rather than a landslide.

Where a presidential system exists, the negative effects produced by a multiparty system under a parliamentary regime are not so important, since the president remains in office even if he loses his majority in the legislature. Of course, such a situation can create a deadlock between president and legislature. This is not only bad in itself, in preventing action on national problems, but also bad in that it tempts presidents to try to circumvent the legislature and rule in dictatorial fashion.

The basic premise of the parliamentary system is thus that the prime minister and cabinet represent a majority of the legislature. Normally this implies the enforcement of *party discipline*—that is, the requirement that all legislators from the party vote the same way, so that the government retains its majority. If the government doesn't always command a majority in the legislature, the possibility arises that someone else would command a majority and that someone else should be prime minister and not the present incumbent. Party discipline is thus necessary to see that the majority remains intact.

Because party discipline normally holds, in a two-party system an incumbent government has no excuse for not passing into law the program on which it competed in the elections. In a separation-of-powers system like that of the United States, different parties may be in control of the presidency and the Congress. But in any case there is no necessity to enforce party discipline in the legislature, since the president has a fixed term and will continue in office even if a majority of Congress votes against his legislative proposals. Without party discipline, each legislator goes his or her own way and the process of legislating involves extensive compromises and the trading of favors. Under these circumstances, the legislation that emerges from the Congress is hardly ever exactly what the president, or indeed anyone else, wanted. In a parliamentary system, on the other hand, the government has a legislative majority by definition, so there are no obstacles to its enacting the program it espoused during the election. The party platform, accordingly, is a carefully drawn series of specific pledges as to what the government will do if elected, unlike the vague attempt to appeal to all possible interests usually represented by the platforms of U.S. political parties.

A country's electoral system helps determine how many parties will flourish and which will be dominant. For this reason a particular dominant party or group of parties will maintain an electoral system or, sometimes, change to another one that favors it. In the French Fourth Republic, as elections approached, the ruling coalition would often pass modifications in the electoral law shamelessly designed to secure its advantage. The causal relation between electoral system and party system thus runs in both directions: a particular electoral system tends to promote a certain type of party system; because it does so, a particular configuration of parties will impose a specific kind of electoral system to help them stay in power.

The single-member district—with majority or plurality, that is, with or without a runoff—and proportional representation, as it has been described here, are not the only possible types of electoral systems. Various other types can be found in effect in local jurisdictions or private organizations, and many variations on the PR model are possible. The main questions in establishing a PR system are how large and how equal districts should be—that is, how many members should represent each; and what formula should be used for allocating members in proportion to the winning parties' vote, since members cannot be divided into fractions.

PARTY SYSTEMS AND PARTY STRATEGIES

Under different conditions of party competition, it is rational for parties to adopt different strategies. Where there are two large parties, one with a reputation for being more to the left than the other, it is rational for the party leadership, trying to win the maximum number of votes, to develop a moderate, centrist, program. This is because the more left-wing party can take for granted the voter to the left; it must try to capture those in the middle of the spectrum who are undecided as to which party to vote for. The logic is similar on the right, so that normally in a two-party system both parties' programs and leadership will tend to be centrist on policy questions, both trying to appeal to the centrist voter. When this happens, voters grumble about choosing between Tweedledum and Tweedledee, and threaten to vote for third parties or to stay home on Election Day. In the end, however reluctantly, they usually vote for "the lesser of the two evils."

Now this is what happens "normally." But if the United States could elect Ronald Reagan in two landslides and if Margaret Thatcher could be the longest-serving British prime minister in over a hundred years, clearly things are not always normal. Why is a major party leadership not always centrist? There are several reasons:

1. Because the leader is picked by noncentrists. Although the key general election voters may be in the center, the candidate may be nominated

by party militants of more extreme views. This is because centrists who don't feel strongly in favor of one party or another are unlikely to be the active party members who participate in the party's internal selection processes.

It should be noted, however, that often even when candidates of more extreme views get picked, they abandon their previous political positions and move to the center in the drive to attract votes. This is a very common occurrence in two-party politics, particularly in the British Labour party and the U.S. Democratic party. Neil Kinnock, leader of the Labour party during the 1980s, exemplified this pattern; Bill Clinton is generally said to have made his move to the center when he was defeated for reelection after his first term as governor of Arkansas.

MARGARET THATCHER

Margaret Thatcher, née Roberts (1925–) served as prime minister of Britain from 1975 to 1992, the longest-serving prime minister in the twentieth century and the first to win three consecutive general elections. The first woman to serve as prime minister, she won the leadership of the Conservative party, despite the fact that her extreme views on economic questions were not representative of a party majority, by being the only person bold, or foolhardy, enough to challenge an incumbent party leader, Edward Heath, in a leadership election in 1975.

As a dominating personality and forceful speaker, Mrs. Thatcher's pro-free-market views were more uncompromising than those hitherto prevailing in British politics, to the extent of being willing to see unemployment rise to a record 3 million, allowing many businesses to fail and whole industries to go out of business.

Her electoral successes were due in large part to the fact that the opposition Labour party split over the question of participating in the European Community, and on military and other issues, so that the Conservatives were able to elect overwhelming majorities of the House of Commons with around 40 percent of the popular vote. Mrs. Thatcher also derived some electoral advantage out of the victory of British forces over the Argentines who had invaded the British colony of the Falkland Islands in the South Atlantic, and because she started a program of selling housing owned by local government authorities to renters on favorable terms. However, Mrs. Thatcher was unable to survive a strong popular reaction against her attempt to divorce local taxation from wealth or ability to pay, and have everyone pay an equal amount (the so-called poll tax).

After she resigned from the leadership of the Conservative party, the party started a drift back to the center, where traditionally most votes are to be had. However, Mrs. Thatcher left a permanent mark on British politics, and also had an influence on the promotion of "neoliberal" economic ideas elsewhere in the world, including in the United States of Ronald Reagan.

2. Because the leader needs to court not only voters but also contributors to party funds, who, in conservative parties, may have extreme rather than centrist views. In progressive parties, the influence of private contributors is usually to pull leaders away from the left and toward the center, but organizational contributors such as unions may sometimes exert a leftward pull.

3. Because the leader believes he or she need not just appeal to people's present views, but can change those views. Margaret Thatcher said "I am a conviction politician, not a consensus politician." Normally, "conviction politicians" of this type are not successful in a two-party system. Mrs. Thatcher was lucky in taking over the leadership of the Conservatives when the opposing Labour party was about to split, making it possible for her to win a great victory with only 40 percent of the popular vote.

4. Because—and this may be the most important factor—issues may be important to voters other than those of economic policy that define what constitutes left, right, and center. Questions of personality and perceived competence may be important, and sometimes questions of social morality become election issues; but the dimension that most frequently supersedes economic policy is that of foreign and defense policy. Despite his extreme economic views, Ronald Reagan defeated Jimmy Carter for president primarily because Carter had been unable to secure the release of Americans held hostage in Iran, an issue magnified and made central by the media and, in a short-sighted and self-defeating way, by Carter himself.

5. Because the voter have become confused by party propaganda and the laziness of the media into not understanding economic policy issues.

Despite these reasons for deviations from the norm, it remains most often true that in a two-party system the parties seek the center of the spectrum of political opinion, which usually is defined in terms of economic policy and usually reflects economic interest.

The dynamics of a multiparty system are quite different from those of a two-party system. Where many parties flourish, the rational strategy for a party leadership is not—as it is in a two-party system—to attempt to appeal to voters in the middle, taking for granted voters to one extreme or another. In a multiparty system no voters can be taken for granted, since if they are dissatisfied with a party's program another party will arise that can find electoral success by representing the views of that group of voters. The indicated behavior for a political party, therefore, is to identify a specific group of voters who are not being represented or whose representatives are not faithfully expressing their maximum demands and seek to be the most perfect representatives possible of precisely that point of view or interest. Thus in a multiparty system everyone can have their own party—religious extremists, farmers, pacifists, schoolteachers.

The advantages of such a system are clear. Voters do not have to settle for the lesser of two evils when they vote, nor is the party system even telling them that the socioeconomic dimension is more important than any other. If to the voters women's rights or the protection of the environment are more important than economic issues, then they can search out parties that are primarily concerned with those issues. The strength of a multiparty system, therefore, is its greater representativeness of voters' opinions. Its greatest weakness, as we have seen, is that very often it makes for governments that are ideologically incoherent, less stable, and less effective. If frustration grows in a two-party system because the parties are so similar and present little choice, in multiparty systems it grows because parties cannot deliver on their promises.

THE SINGLE-PARTY SYSTEM

In the world today many political systems are still dominated by a single political party. Sometimes this is because only a single party is permitted and the rest are outlawed, but not always. In India, which won independence in 1949, one party, the Congress party, has long dominated at the national level, even though a vigorous multiparty political life exists and indeed opposition parties come to power at the state level. Some of these, however, are purely local parties, appealing only to a specific language group in a particular state. Once in power at the state level, many of these parties find no problem in cooperating with the Congress party, which is usually (though not always) in power at the national level. In Mexico, at the time of writing, the same party has ruled for over sixty years, although opposition parties have started to take over state governments.

In most cases where a single party dominates the political system, the opposition suffers from legal disabilities of one kind or another. However, there are factors that tend to single-partyism even where the opposition parties are not repressed. One of these, as in India, is that the dominant party has developed from the liberation movement that led the victorious struggle against the colonial power and retains the patriotic prestige it earned at that time. The United States, too, had such a single-party system, its candidate George Washington, the hero of independence, for the first presidential election under the current Constitution.

In many countries, moreover, characteristically in Africa but also in Asian countries such as Malaysia, societies are split by ethnic conflicts; parties, seeking to represent the groups into which people's most salient identity divides them, may each represent a different language or racial group. In such a case, competitive elections might not be fought over issues of policy so much as being simply a sort of ethnic census. Most important, the emotions of political campaigning among parties constituted in this way could easily degenerate into racial violence and civil war. Leaders of the single-party system thus argue that it avoids the ethnic conflict that would result from a multiparty system. However, it is often true that instead of avoiding ethnic conflict a single-party system embodies it; that a single ethnic group dominates the ruling party and discriminates against other ethnic minorities.

The long-established single-party system in Mexico resembles in some respects both those in Africa and those that used to rule in Eastern Europe. As in Communist-era Eastern Europe, in Mexico the party claims to represent a revolution that meant a progressive departure in the country's history; but it also has consistently won national elections and so can also claim democratic legitimacy. This claim has become thinner in recent years as opposition parties have grown and as the minor electoral fraud that was always practiced has come to seem an obstacle to a possible opposition victory.

Where expectations are that a ruling party will remain in power, its rule is reinforced by the adherence of opportunists who are interested in government jobs and contracts. Filipino parties and traditional parties in Brazil are notoriously based primarily on expectations of patronage. Nevertheless, there are countervailing forces working against the dominance of the single party, such as the expansion of education. Such systems are most stable when they rule over an uneducated population that accepts government propaganda claims at face value and where the average educational level does not exceed that of grade school—in other words, where people have been exposed in the schools only to the civic indoctrination that strengthens incumbent governments but not to the analytic thinking that promotes opposition to them.

Long-established single-party states, those in Africa and Eastern Europe as well as in Mexico, tend also to be characterized by the growth of a "new class," as government party politicians and bureaucrats develop privileges that set them apart from the masses of the population. In Eastern Europe the paradoxical situation was that political parties claiming to assert the values of equality, liberty, and popular welfare finally ruled over a system that restricted political freedoms and protected special privileges.

INTEREST GROUPS

One of the most difficult questions for normative democratic theory is that of the proper place of interest groups in a constitutional democracy. Interest groups in this sense are organizations of people with a similar set of beliefs or set of interests that act to influence public policy. This they may do through campaigns of public education, or by direct influence on the policymaking process through contact with legislators, elected officials, or civil servants. These latter activities are generally referred to as "lobbying." Lobbying may take the form of testifying before legislative committees to make the organization's views known and to present arguments in favor of its position. Many legislators are predisposed to favor positions taken by a group they identify with, and need only to be told how to vote on an issue, or to be given a draft bill to introduce. Or a pressure group may want to impress legislators with the strength of its support among the voters—for example, by organizing a letter-writing campaign.

The organization may also seek to influence a legislator's position by giving him or her money or other things of value. Direct payment in return for a vote constitutes a bribe and is of course illegal everywhere—though it has nevertheless been known to occur in most countries, including the United States. But more subtle forms of transferring funds exist that are quite legal. Laws vary from country to country as to which practices are legal and which are not. In the United States, interest groups may donate funds to a candidate's campaign, although there are regulations governing the amount that can be given and requiring that they be reported. Sometimes controls on how such donations may be used are quite lax. In the United States, a variety of other methods are used for transferring funds: large fees, as well as money for expenses, may be given to legislators for delivering speeches to an organization's meeting; the legislator's law firm may be retained by the organization and given little work to do; large quantities of the candidate's campaign biography may be bought for free distribution to organization members. Some countries regulate such practices strictly, while most others are even more lax than the United States, but the United States is lax enough.

Does the existence of such organizations deform the democratic process? Is their existence compatible with the pursuit of the general interest? How is it possible to characterize the role of such groups in general as it affects the democratic process? Different students of the problem have suggested different answers to these questions, which are both descriptive and normative. We can summarize these answers in the form of alternative models of the relation of interest groups to the state in a constitutional democracy:

1. *The Rousseauian model*: The great French-Swiss philosopher Jean-Jacques Rousseau believed that the existence of organizations of this type was incompatible with republican government. His position has strongly influenced French political theory and French constitutions. When voting, he thought, citizens should "ask themselves the right question"—What is in the general interest?—not what is in their own individual interests. In Rousseau's terminology, a popular assembly should express the general will, not simply the sum total of particular wills. The doctrines animating the French Revolution followed these ideas, and were hostile to "intermediaries," organizations standing between the individual and the state. These would just aggregate particular wills, and get in the way of the expression of the general will.

In the practice of modern democracies, however, it seems impossible to take such an extreme position. How can interest groups be outlawed if freedom of speech and association are guaranteed, if people are assured of the right to petition their representatives for redress of grievances, indeed if legislators and administrators solicit people's opinions to help guide them in their work? The Rousseauian view, for all its merit and the clarity with which it states the issue, seems too extreme to be relevant to modern democracies.

2. *The pluralist model*: This model of the relation of interest groups to the political process is analogous to that of the economic free market. In the pluralist model, there is no restriction to the organization of interest groups, which proliferate and represent every conceivable type of interest. Because there exists such a wide variety of such groups, however, they compete with and counterbalance each other. Just as the action of many individuals, each freely pursuing his or her individual economic interest, manages to result in the most productive economic system, maximizing consumer satisfaction, so, in the pluralist model, the free competition of interest groups produces a result that approximates the general public interest.

While this logic has a certain plausibility in many circumstances, it remains flawed as a general account of the matter. This is so because some sets of people are in fact underrepresented or not represented at all in the free market of interest groups. Some sets of people are particularly weak or difficult to organize—homeless people, migrant farm laborers, and in general the most poor, powerless, and needy members of society. Conversely, groups representing the more affluent members of society are likely to be better organized and better financed, and thus more effective. Accordingly, the result of free pressure group activity is likely to be a policy outcome biased in favor of upper-income groups.

3. *The class rule model*: Of course this is what a Marxist would expect. Carrying the preceding criticism of the pluralist model a step further, in the Marxist analysis it is a coalition of interest groups representing the lords of the economy, those who control the factories and the banks, that in effect gives orders to legislators and public officials. In this view the apparatus of constitutional democracy merely conceals the ultimate reality that in a capitalist system the capitalist class is in control. In general, after all "the state is the executive committee of the ruling class."

There is certainly a great deal of truth in this insight. Any government operating within the context of a capitalist economy must take care not to undermine the premises of the system—that is, it must maintain investor confidence, not allow a chain reaction of bank failures to begin, try to avoid a total crash of the stock market, and so on. In other words, it must be nice to the wealthy. It is certainly true, moreover, at least of the United States, that the role of money in politics has become very great. Election campaigns are extremely costly and officeholders are inhibited about offending large contributors to their campaign funds.

FOR EXAMPLE: OIL

Through continuous public relations campaigns, powerful and well-funded special interests try to convince the public at large that the general public interest is the same as that of the pressure groups. An example of this is how the domestic oil industry seems to have convinced the public that there is danger to national security in "dependence on foreign oil," and that imports of oil should be discriminated against in various ways. It is hard to avoid the conclusion that this is the exact reverse of the truth; that in fact, since oil is a nonrenewable resource, it would be in the national security interest of the United States to conserve domestic oil—that is, not to use it but to keep it in reserve against the day when shortages from abroad might be interrupted by suppliers for political reasons. It would thus make more sense, accordingly, to consume only foreign oil while it was available; this would conserve the more secure domestic supply. "Reducing dependence on foreign oil," as this concept has been sold to the American public and taken up by contribution-dependent politicians, means, in fact, using domestic sources more rapidly and hastening the day when they will be exhausted and the United States will indeed be dependent on foreign oil.

How has the U.S. Department of Energy—which, since the days of its first secretary, during the Carter administration, James Schlesinger, reflected the views and interests of energy producers—responded to this criticism? It has set up a "strategic petroleum reserve," consisting of vast stores of oil, bought by the U.S. government and pumped into underground storage, which may be used in the event of an interruption of foreign supply. The principal difference between the maintenance of a strategic petroleum reserve of this kind and just leaving underground oil that has not been extracted in the first place seems to be that the oil industry receives money for oil placed in the strategic reserve but would not receive money for oil left unexploited underground.

---

4. *The state autonomy model*: In the pluralist conception, all interests compete against each other and the result is a sort of automatic balancing-out of special interests. The state autonomy model goes further, taking the view that since interests exist that balance each other out, this leaves the state authorities, political officeholders and bureaucrats, free to act in their own conception of the public interest. Better put: the various interests do not balance each other out automatically, but can be made to do so by strong-minded political leaders. As against the point, for example, that legislators may need campaign contributions and so become beholden to special interests, the state autonomy model argues that so many interest groups exist with diverse points of view that legislators may freely make up their own minds how they should vote. They can then go out and finance their campaigns adequately with contributions from whichever groups support that position, on the premise that no matter what position

they take there will always be some group with funds to contribute that will support them. Bureaucrats, similarly, are free to make independent decisions within their areas of discretion, since some group will object to whatever decision is made, in any case.

While there is a great deal of insight in this point of view, one must bear in mind that bureaucrats in fact have their own interests and that an autonomous bureaucracy decides issues not solely in the interest of the general public. Bureaucrats have their own corporate interest as a particular type of pressure group wishing to defend its privileges. In addition, individual bureaucrats act on behalf of their individual careers and the maintenance, defense, and expansion of the interests of their particular offices and departments.

Interestingly enough, the possibility of state autonomy is taken account of in the Marxist schema. In trying to account for the phenomenon of Napoleon and his nephew, Napoleon III, Marx wrote that while of course the state is the executive committee of the ruling class, there are times of historical change, when one ruling class is on the decline and another, representing a new economic system, is in the ascendant, during which no one class is dominant. Thus, for example, the rule of the feudal lords in France was brought to an end in 1789 by the French Revolution, but the bourgeoisie who were lords of the capitalist system did not establish their rule firmly until the late nineteenth century. This created an era during which there was no single dominant class, making possible the temporary autonomy of the state. During this era it was accordingly possible for the two Napoleons to rule in an arbitrary manner without reference to a ruling class.

Similar arguments have been advanced in other contexts. The difficulty for Marxists has been that so many cases have needed to be explained on the basis of state autonomy that the instances of class rule diminish, and it becomes unclear whether in the whole course of history class dominance is the rule and state autonomy the exception, or state autonomy the rule and class dominance the exception.

5. *Neocorporatism*: A model of the relation of interest groups to the state that has acquired wide currency in recent years is that of neocorporatism. The older corporatism, a common way of treating the state in medieval Catholic thought, was that the state was like a body, with the monarch at its head, so that it was unreasonable to expect everyone to have equal rights and duties, just as the different parts of the body perform different functions but work together for the good of the whole. The neo- (or "new") corporatist approach is that interest groups are not like firms in the free market competing freely with each other. Instead, interest groups are built into the machinery of government itself. This is an important insight, throwing into relief aspects of the functioning of the modern state that might otherwise have been ignored. In the neocorporatist model, interest groups are guaranteed regular institutionalized

access to the decision-making process, in effect becoming part of it. In the United States, before Congress acts, the relevant congressional committee will solicit testimony from affected interests in order to learn their points of view. By law, the Food and Drug Administration has to circulate to the pharmaceutical companies drafts of proposed regulations and take into account their comments before it can make the regulations final. In Europe, it is very common to require by statute that the minister solicit and take into account the opinion of advisory bodies and commissions before making his or her own recommendations or before drafting legislation.

There has developed something of a controversy among specialists in West European politics in recent years over whether the neocorporatist or the pluralist model more accurately describes the actual situation. The upshot of that controversy seems to be that the different models describe the situation under different governments. For example, in its early years the Thatcher government in Britain made clear its dislike of the neocorporatist arrangements that had evolved under previous governments—the advisory commissions, the regular luncheons with representatives of the trade unions, and so on—and as a result relations between government and interest groups moved decisively in a more pluralist direction. The various advisory boards and commissions had been known in Britain by the quaint acronym "quangos," for quasi-autonomous nongovernmental organizations. Mrs. Thatcher's abolition of large quantities of these advisory groups became referred to as her "quangocide." Later in her government she drifted back in a neocorporatist direction, however.

Thus it seems to be that different models of the role of interest groups describe reality more accurately at some times and in some places, and others at other times and in other places. This is true, in fact, of competing theories of how the world works; they may each be true enough of a limited range of the data, while a general formulation that would include them all might be too general to be helpful.

NOTE

1. Actually, the Fourth Republic changed its electoral system several times. It is a good example of multipartyism, though not necessarily of proportional representation.

KEY TERMS

first past the post

multiparty system

proportional representation

single-member majority system

prime minister   pluralist model
party discipline   state autonomy model
interest groups   neocorporatism
lobbying

CHAPTER 7

Constitutions and Constitutional Principles

POT-SHOTS NO. 1094.

MY GREAT AMBITION
IS
TO BUILD
SOMETHING
THAT WILL LAST,
AT LEAST UNTIL
I'VE FINISHED
BUILDING IT.

Ashleigh
Brilliant

© BRILLIANT ENTERPRISES 1977.

THE LIVING CONSTITUTION

A country's constitution is the set of rules governing how its institutions function. Americans typically conceive of a country's constitution as being contained in a single document. This is never altogether true, however. In practice, each country has a "living constitution," the actual way institutions work, which is both more and less than the constitutional document. The reality is more than the mere document, because a great many practices—what the British would call "conventions"—are incorporated into constitutional practice though they find no place in the document itself. Thus, for example, for almost a century and a half after George Washington had left office, presidents followed his example of not seeking a third consecutive term. It was, in effect, part of the U.S. Constitution that a president would serve no more than two terms, although that was nowhere provided by law. Congress decided it needed to be written into law and took the steps necessary to do so after Franklin D. Roosevelt successfully defied the customary prohibition, and was reelected to third and fourth terms. Now that the 22nd Amendment has been passed it is no longer legal for a president to serve a third successive term.

On the other hand, some portions of the written document fall into disuse. Henry Clay was elected to the Senate before he had reached the age of 30, which the Constitution prescribes as a minimum, for example. Legislators are not supposed to be appointed to "offices of honor or profit" by the president, to maintain the separation of powers, but senators have in fact accepted appointment to the U.S. delegation to the United Nations.

Again, many of the most important constitutional practices are not clearly specified in the document although they are compatible with it; for example, the power of judicial review—that is, the authority assumed by the Supreme Court to declare that certain acts of Congress are incompatible with the Constitution, and thus null and void, nowhere appears in the written Constitution. Other practices, while not in contradiction of the provisions of the written Constitution, define a process quite different from that envisaged by the constitutional framers. The electoral college system for electing a U.S. president, for example, assumes a meeting of popular delegates in each of the state capitals to discuss the merits of the various candidates and decide who will get the votes of the state. In current practice, of course, what determines the election is the popular vote, although the allocation of electoral votes to the different states may conceivably distort the final result. An actual operating constitution, then, a living constitution, has something of the same relation to the written document that the body has to the skeleton: it follows its outline, but on the basis of the skeleton alone it would not be possible to predict the shape and mass of the whole organism with complete accuracy.

THE ELECTORAL COLLEGE

Probably most Americans are not aware that the president of the United States is not elected directly by popular vote. In fact, Article II of the Constitution provides that the voters of each state choose electors, who then choose the president. The electoral college was a compromise adopted at the Constitutional Convention to break the deadlock between those who wanted direct election of the president and those who wanted indirect election, either by Congress or by the state legislatures.

Each state has a number of electors equal to the number of its representatives in both houses of Congress; since representation in the House of Representatives is based on population, but each state no matter what its size has two senators, this means that small states are overrepresented in the electoral college. Moreover, each state's votes are cast as a bloc under the so-called unit rule, so that a candidate receiving a majority of the popular vote in a state receives all of that state's electoral votes. However, because the unit rule makes the electoral vote of the largest states especially valuable, candidates adopt positions that will appeal to those states, generally ignoring the smallest ones. A further peculiarity of the electoral college system is that if no candidate receives a majority in the electoral college—because there are more than two candidates—then the president is chosen by the House of Representatives from among the top two contenders, in an election in which each state has one vote.

Normally, these distortions average out so that the winner of the popular vote is also the winner of the electoral vote, but there have been occasions in American history when that did not in fact occur and the loser in the popular vote was the winner in the electoral college.

THE FUNCTIONS OF THE CONSTITUTION

A constitution has several major functions. First, it allocates powers among the organs of government and indicates how those who staff them are to be chosen. In the second place, it specifies the limits of government power—that is, it defines what rights citizens will have as against government bodies. In the third place, most of the world's constitutions specify in general what the policy objectives of government should be. The Constitution of the United States does this in a very limited way in the preamble; twentieth-century constitutions typically go into great detail as to the objectives of policy—full employment, old-age pensions, guaranteed medical insurance, and the like often figuring prominently. In most cases these provisions are simply hortatory and not self-executing.

Constitutional government is then government whose powers with respect to those subject to it are limited, which has a defined allocation of powers among different organs of government, the occupants of which are chosen for specified terms in a prescribed manner. Although we are accustomed to the existence of constitutional democracies, a constitutional government is not necessarily the same as a democracy. On the one hand, a democratic government is possible in which the power of the majority of the people or their representatives is not restrained, but extends to any matter without limit. To some extent, the democracies of ancient Greece were like this, and the assembly could make judicial decisions, confiscate property, and condemn individuals to death, without restraint. On the other hand, constitutional systems have existed that are not democracies. A constitutional monarchy may clearly define the relative roles of the monarch, the nobility, and the commoners, without providing for majority rule. The developed countries of North America and Western Europe today are, of course, constitutional democracies.

As noted above, one function of a written constitution is to allocate powers and another is to specify the rights of citizens against government action. In fact, these two objectives complement each other, in the sense that one of the purposes of dividing powers among different organs of government is that none of them become strong enough to tyrannize over individuals. It was made clear in the brilliantly argued Federalist papers that this was a leading purpose of the U.S. Constitution. The bulk of the legislative power was given to the Congress and the bulk of the executive power was given to the president, but each organ checks the other in the discharge of its functions, so that the president's assent to legislation is needed, as is Senate confirmation of the president's appointment of judges and ambassadors.

THE FEDERALIST PAPERS

In the effort to persuade public opinion of the desirability of the ratification of the U.S. Constitution, three of the Founding Fathers of the U.S. government—Alexander Hamilton, James Madison, and John Jay—wrote a series of articles in *The Independent Journal* of New York City, which were published during late 1787 and early 1788 over the signature "Publius." The collected papers have become a classic of political thought, transcending the circumstances that called them forth.

The majority of the papers were written by Alexander Hamilton, but the most profound were the work of James Madison, whose mastery of a vast range of data and whose penetrating insights qualify him to be considered America's first political scientist.

The article with the most lasting value is probably Federalist No. 10, written by Madison. The ultimate reason for different political groups, wrote Madison, is the unequal distribution of property, which gives rise to different economic interests and to the various social classes based on those interests, which are then reflected in political attitudes and programs. It is utopian to think that in a civilized society, these interests could ever be suppressed or ignored; the only remedy is to organize a political order that is broad enough to include the representation of a wide variety of interests, whose competitive interplay will allow something approximating a general interest to emerge. This point of view, so much more sophisticated than the Rousseauian attempt to suppress factional interests and insist on public-spirited virtue, which was shortly to animate the thinking of the French Revolution and to lead to its downfall, has always provided the most hopeful basis for a reasonable politics in the United States.

Moreover, the different organs of government were given different constituencies so that they were unlikely to be all dominated by the same set of interests, and the rivalries and divergences of interest of their separate constituencies would induce them to watch jealously each other's exercise of power, thus ensuring that no organ became too powerful. In fact, in the United States the division and restraining of power, the checking and balancing, often becomes excessive, so that it is generally easier to block action than to take action, with the result that a great many abuses of various kinds continue to exist without the policymaking machinery being able to come to grips with them. Today, the main check on the arbitrary action of governments is less the constitutional checks and balances than the existence of a competitive party system whose existence is guaranteed by the norms of free speech, regular free elections, and independent courts.

Today virtually all countries have written constitutions—among the Western countries, only Britain and Israel lack them. In the case of Britain this is because the system has evolved over a very long period so that there are various documents and pieces of legislation with constitutional status, but much constitutional practice is based on tradition and custom, and no single document contains all of the constitutional rules. Israel has no written constitution as such, since so many basic questions that a constitution would have to resolve would be divisive, especially those that would provoke battles between devout and secular Jews, that the country operates with constitutional provisions established by ordinary law.

In cases where the basic procedures of the state are established only by ordinary law, they can of course be changed by ordinary law. Where a written constitution exists, its provisions have a special status and they can be changed only by extraordinary procedures. These procedures for constitutional amendment vary from one country to another. Sometimes they require passage by the legislature, but by an extraordinary majority—for example, a two-thirds vote, or a two-thirds vote of all members, not just those present at the time. Some constitutions require a popular vote on amendments, sometimes also qualified by an extraordinary majority. In federal systems the separate assent of state populations or state legislatures may also be required. Thus it is not possible to change basic constitutional procedures or principles easily or lightly. They have a special fundamental status that is protected by their being entrenched in this way. Let us now review in summary form some major questions that are taken up and dealt with by constitutional provision.

CONSTITUTIONAL PRINCIPLES

The principle of *separation of powers*, derived from the *Esprit des Lois* (Spirit of the Laws) of Henri Secondat, Baron Montesquieu, is embodied in the U.S. Constitution and those modeled on it. Its premise is that liberty is best protected if the powers of making rules, enforcing them, and interpreting them are lodged in separate bodies that are separately chosen. These are generally known, respectively, as the legislative, executive, and judicial branches of government. An earlier version of the doctrine can be found in James Harrington's *Oceana* (first published 1656). In Harrington's version, the way to assure justice was by the same principle on which two boys would divide a cake into equal portions: one boy would cut the cake, and the other would pick which piece he wanted. This would guarantee the cake was cut equally, since otherwise the boy who did the cutting would end up with less than half.

Montesquieu's principle was based on his understanding of how the government of Great Britain, the government of his time that best assured the liberty of the individual, functioned. As seems to be the case with all such interpretations of the British system, it was not completely accurate. Moreover, the British system, which has evolved continuously, has changed since Montesquieu's eighteenth century and is now a totally different kind of system, although it nevertheless continues to assure individual liberty as well as it did, more or less, back then. The separation of powers principle, however, was a very good way of limiting the power of a hereditary monarch.

The history of the evolution of British constitutional practice can be understood, albeit with some oversimplification, as the story of the steady reduction of the powers of a hereditary monarch from the days when he or she was all-powerful, until today, when the monarch herself is only a figurehead virtually without independent powers. During the eighteenth century, this process had evolved to the point that the division of power between the monarch and the Parliament could be described in the terms Montesquieu used. Of course, this was also the period in which the U.S. Constitution was being drafted and adopted, so it is not surprising that it is based approximately on the British practice of the time and justified by reference to the interpretations of Montesquieu.

Another principle embodied in the U.S. Constitution is that of *checks and balances*, which is sometimes confused with the principle of separation of powers. The checks and balances of the U.S. Constitution are partly based on the separation of powers but in part contradict it. That is, the premise of the separation of powers doctrine is that each power will be assigned to a different agency; the doctrine of checks and balances implies that each agency cannot exercise its power in complete freedom but is checked by another organ of government; this in turn implies that part of the power in that category is shared in another organ.

Specifically, for example, while Congress has the power to legislate, the U.S. Constitution has in practice given the power of veto to the president. Thus, in effect, the president constitutes a third house of the legislature, and Congress does not have all of the legislative power. Similarly, the authority to make appointments to implement the laws is presumably part of the executive power, and indeed the president appoints cabinet officers and ambassadors. They must nevertheless be confirmed by the Senate, which appears to give a legislative body some executive power.

The judiciary is of course a separate branch of government, and it is clear that a free political system could not survive if either the executive or the legislature had the power to tell a court how it had to decide a case. Nevertheless, in the U.S. system the president appoints federal judges and he may take into account their views, including their political views, in making such an appointment. Moreover, it is not out of the question that judges might have their career interests in securing promotion to a higher judicial office in mind when they make judicial decisions that have political implications. There is clearly a case to be made here that with respect to the judiciary the U.S. Constitution does not go far enough in assuring a separation of powers. Some other countries make a greater effort to insulate the judiciary from political influence—for example, providing a separate, hopefully nonpolitical, body to control the appointment and selection of judges. In Colombia, for example, the Supreme Court, and not the president, makes appointments of judges to inferior courts.

The decisions made by judges may, on occasion, have political implications. This is particularly so in the United States since Chief Justice John Marshall asserted the authority of the Supreme Court to strike down laws that conflicted with the Constitution, which proclaims itself to be the supreme law of the land and therefore takes priority over ordinary legislation with which it is in conflict. This power of *judicial review* of legislation exists quite generally in countries with written constitutions, and indeed many modern constitutions establish a separate court in addition to their supreme court, specifically to hear constitutional questions. However, most courts are circumspect about striking down legislation and will generally make every effort not to do so, limiting the validity of their decisions solely to the specific case at hand, or deciding the case on narrow grounds that do not call into question the legislation itself.

The independence of the judiciary is a necessary feature of any political system that pretends to the status of a constitutional democracy, or indeed simply to that of a civilized society. The separation of powers between executive and legislature, however, is clearly not a necessity for a successful constitutional democracy. The evolution of the British political system has in fact brought it to where it is characterized by a fusion of powers rather than a separation. Britain today has what is known as a *parliamentary system*, under which the head of government is a prime minister who is the leader of the party or coalition of parties that has a majority in the legislature, and is himself or herself a member of that body. Members of the cabinet, who are selected by the prime minister, are also members of the parliament. This is in contrast to the separation of powers in the presidential system, under which normally cabinet members cannot be at the same time members of the legislative body.

A feature of a parliamentary system is that there is a separation of the roles of *head of state* and *head of government*. The head of state is the ceremonial representative of the state—in Britain, the king or queen—who presides on great state occasions, makes formal speeches, and confers awards and titles. The head of government is the active initiator and coordinator of policy, the elected political leader who represents a particular party and political viewpoint. The head of state, on the other hand, must remain nonpartisan and politically uncommitted. In a presidential system the two roles are combined in the same person.

CENTRAL/LOCAL RELATIONS

States whose population varies a great deal in language, religion, or culture from one area to another often find it advisable to recognize such differences by allowing different regions a certain degree of autonomy. When provisions for autonomy are constitutionally guaranteed, the system may be a federal one. In a *federal system*, the regional or provincial authorities are directly elected by the local populations, and not appointed by the central government. These state governments (provinces in Canada, cantons in Switzerland) have powers of their own and a distinct sphere of authority guaranteed them by the constitution.

The alternative to a federal system is a *unitary system*, in which local governments may have powers of their own, but these can be taken away, and the local governments themselves can be abolished, or regional jurisdictions divided or consolidated, at the wish of the central government. In Great Britain, which has a unitary system in which counties are the next level of government below the national level, during the prime ministerships of the Conservative leaders Edward Heath and Margaret Thatcher, county lines were redrawn, with some counties and special metropolitan jurisdictions being created or abolished. In the United States, on the other hand, specific areas of jurisdiction are reserved to the states, as are allocations of powers that can't be changed by ordinary law but only by constitutional amendment or new judicial interpretations of the Constitution.

In practice, although legally a unitary central government can redraw local boundary lines and abolish provincial authorities, normally the existence of traditional local governments is respected. At the same time, in a federal system the central government may exceed its traditional powers at the expense of the state governments despite the constitutional provisions. This was certainly what happened in the United States during the Depression, when the government of Franklin D. Roosevelt decided that in order to meet the country's economic needs effectively, it had to act in areas traditionally reserved to the states. At first, the U.S. Supreme Court struck down such acts of Congress passed at the urging of the Roosevelt administration. But after President Roosevelt developed a scheme that would have expanded the size of the Supreme Court and given him authority to appoint new justices (the so-called court packing scheme), a key justice, Owen Roberts, changed his views and the new Supreme Court majority voted in a series of cases to allow a shift in the balance of power between the federal government and the states to occur, even though the court packing plan was unpopular and was dropped by the president.

Different federal systems draw the lines between federal and state authority in different ways. The German Federal Republic has a particularly interesting type of federalism, in which most laws, both state and federal, are administered by the state governments. They also collect both state and federal taxes, while state courts hear cases arising under both state and federal law. State administration of federal law is supervised by federal authorities, while federal courts hear appeals from state courts.

GERMAN FEDERALISM

The particular characteristics of German federalism, like other features of the German constitution, show the effects of compromise between different factions and among different approaches to government, and also the influence of historical circumstances peculiar to Germany. The upper house of the federal legislature, the Federal Council (Bundesrat) is neither equal in power to the Federal Assembly (Bundestag) nor totally without power; its decisions can be overridden by the Federal Assembly, but only by a larger majority than the vote against the legislation in the Federal Council. That is, legislation defeated by a 51 percent vote in the Council needs to have a two-thirds vote in its favor in the Assembly for the Council veto to be overridden. A state's representatives in the upper house are not elected, but are appointed by the state governor. That means they actually represent the views of the state government, unlike representatives in the U.S. Senate, each of whom interprets his or her mandate to represent the state however he or she wishes. In a compromise between equality and proportionality, a state has no more than five representatives in the Bundesrat no matter how large, and no fewer than three representatives, no matter how small.

In both administrative and judicial areas, there is integration between the state and federal governments. The state governments administer both state and federal law, although they are supervised by the federal ministries; while state courts can hear cases arising under both state and federal law, but appeals can be made from them to federal courts. This is unlike the situation in the United States, which has separate structures to administer and adjudicate state and federal matters.

THE RULE OF LAW

In constitutional states, the *rule of law* prevails. This means principally that everyone, no matter what his or her rank, is subject to the law; that courts will be independent of political control; and that established procedures, known beforehand, will be followed. This last provision is referred to in the U.S. Constitution as "due process of law." It includes, in the United States, such rules as that persons cannot be prosecuted for an act that was made criminal by laws passed after they committed the act; that everyone accused of a crime is entitled to trial by a jury; that accused persons shall normally be allowed to be free until the date of their trials subject to their depositing a reasonable sum of money ("bail") that they forfeit if they do not appear for trial; that evidence can only be gathered in certain fair ways, including that an individual cannot be forced to confess to a crime. While the specific procedural rules differ in different jurisdictions, the basic ideas of fairness and due process remain constant.

In fact, the ideal of the rule of law is never fully complied with, anywhere, but in many countries the degree of compliance is quite high, and in any case the situation is vastly preferable to that in countries in which no pretense of having a rule of law is made—despite the fact that everywhere people of high status are normally treated more leniently than people of low status in terms of race and income.

A difficulty is that the purpose of the protections of individual rights represented by the rule of law is often not generally understood by the population, so that there is often public support for violations of rights or for politicians who promise to curb "abusers" of such rights. For example, majorities frequently feel that someone arrested for a crime is bound to be guilty and any evidence gathered against him or her, no matter by what methods, perhaps even evidence faked or concocted, should be used to convict. Under the rule of law, of course, the person must be presumed innocent unless and until his or her guilt is proved by established methods. Testimony against oneself cannot be compelled, since this would legalize confessions forced by torture or beating. Not only would the truth of such confessions be naturally suspect, but who would want to live in a system in which the police were allowed to use forcible measures of this kind? Similarly, evidence obtained, let us say, by police burglary of a private residence may indeed prove that someone is guilty of a crime; but methods such as these are outlawed because civilized societies do not want to encourage police to commit burglaries.

Countries differ with respect to whether specific practices are forbidden or not; for example, most but not all countries have abolished the death penalty, believing that it is in itself a savage practice; and that if an error is made and an innocent person convicted, which sometimes happens, it is not possible to bring the executed person back to life when new evidence emerges, or someone other than the person found guilty confesses.

CIVIL LIBERTIES AND EMERGENCY POWERS

The civil liberties that are guaranteed in constitutional systems—rights such as freedom of speech, of the press, and of assembly—are not only desirable in themselves, but represent necessary practices if a democratic constitutional system is to function. If free elections are to be held it is necessary for the press to be free to criticize officeholders, for parties to organize and hold meetings, for public discussion to take place in which government figures are criticized. Again, often the public does not understand the necessity for these provisions and supports attempts made to limit unpopular speech. Of course, it is precisely unpopular and outrageous speech that needs to be protected; conformist truisms, patriotic oratory, and government propaganda hardly need legal protection.

Nevertheless, extraordinary circumstances arise, such as in cases of rebellion or invasion, in which it is temporarily not feasible to follow normal procedures, but it may instead appear necessary to jail people without immediate indictment or release on bail, situations in other words that call for the suspension of constitutional protections for a short time. Now obviously provisions for emergency procedures are subject to abuse, and it is critical that constitutions that include provisions for emergency powers, *state of siege*, and martial law also include careful safeguards against a permanent dictatorship being erected under cover of the emergency provisions. For example, in Paraguay the president may declare an emergency, but it can last only for ninety days. With only brief exceptions, for the thirty-five years that General Alfredo Stroessner remained in power, he simply declared a new state of siege every ninety days, on the expiration of the old one, thus making a permanent dictatorship ostensibly legal. The provision contained no effective safeguard against its abuse.

Article 16 of the constitution of the French Fifth Republic, which essentially reproduces article 48 of the constitution of the Weimar Republic of Germany (1919–33), provides that the president may declare an emergency and then take any measures, including issuing decrees with the force of law, that he thinks necessary. Clearly, this provides a loophole for a legal presidential dictatorship. Although as the leader of the largest single party in the Reichstag he might well have come to power without it, this provision in the Weimar Constitution played its part in the process that brought Hitler to power. [Note: Hitler came to power as chancellor, or prime minister, not as president.]

Various limitations can be placed on emergency powers so as to bring them under constitutional control. The ancient Romans placed an automatic limit of six months on an emergency dictatorship. The dictator had to render accounts to justify his actions, subsequent to his term of office, and he could be prosecuted if his actions were thought not justifiable; and if he retained dictatorial power past the end of the six-month period he became an outlaw and could legally be killed by anyone. Less drastic safeguards in present-day constitutions seem effective. In Costa Rica, a presidential declaration of a state of siege is automatically a call for the Legislative Assembly to meet within forty-eight hours and vote either to confirm the state of siege or to end it. In Germany today, the president, who is primarily a figurehead head of state, can declare an emergency, but only on the request of the chancellor; after an emergency has been declared the chancellor does not need to secure the approval of the Federal Assembly for emergency measures, but must still get the approval of the Federal Council, the upper house in the two-chamber legislature.

THE GERMAN FEDERAL PRESIDENT

The Federal Republic has a parliamentary system, so the key governmental leader is the chancellor, who is elected by the Federal Assembly. The formal head of state (the equivalent of the British monarch), whose picture appears on coins and postage stamps, the president is not totally a figurehead, but has one or two residual powers that can be used in unusual situations. If no candidate for chancellor receives an absolute majority of the Federal Assembly vote, the president has the option of appointing the candidate who received a plurality of the votes, or dissolving the assembly and holding new elections. If the chancellor cannot get a majority of the assembly for a piece of legislation he regards as urgent, he can ask the president to declare a state of legislative emergency. If the president agrees to do so, then the bill can become law without the approval of the assembly if it is passed by a majority of the upper house, the Federal Council, which represents the state governments. Both of these provisions were designed to deal with the kinds of crises that occurred in the late 1920s and early 1930s, under the first German Republic, and were associated with the rise of Adolf Hitler, without opening the way for the kind of abuse of power by the president that occurred at that time under a much more permissive constitution.

The Federal president is elected by a special electoral college consisting of the members of the Federal Assembly plus an equal number of representatives elected by the state legislatures. This is designed to see that the president is neither a puppet of the chancellor, as he might be if elected only by the assembly, nor a powerful figure likely to threaten the authority of the chancellor, as he might be if elected by direct popular vote. So far, the system has worked more or less as it was intended to work.

KEY TERMS

living constitution	head of government
constitutional government	federal system
separation of powers	unitary system
checks and balances	rule of law
judicial review	state of siege
presidential system	Bundestag (Federal Assembly)
parliamentary system	Bundesrat (Federal Council)
head of state	chancellor

CHAPTER 8

Parliamentary and Presidential Systems

POT-SHOTS NO. 1019.

THE TIME FOR ACTION
IS PAST!

NOW
IS THE TIME
FOR SENSELESS
BICKERING!

Ashleigh
Brilliant

$\mathbf{A}$lmost all constitutional democracies in the world today have either parliamentary or presidential systems, with the exceptions of the Swiss *collegial executive*, in which there is no single president but the cabinet of ministers exercises the functions of the presidency; and of some hybrid forms that attempt to combine parliamentary and presidential features. While each political system has its own specific characteristics, there is nevertheless a logic to how parliamentary and presidential systems work. Although the two logical structures are quite different from each other, ironically both systems originated in the British political system. The presidential system is based on the model of British government as it existed in the sixteenth century, before the king had lost all of his power; the parliamentary system is based on the model of nineteenth-century Britain, after the monarch had become mostly a figurehead. (Table 8.1 lists the U.S. presidents in the twentieth century.)

THE LOGIC OF THE PARLIAMENTARY SYSTEM

In its most simple form, the parliamentary system works as follows. The voters choose representatives to the national legislature. Any method of election is compatible with a parliamentary system, although the system operates somewhat differently under two-party and multiparty circumstances. Use of the single-member-district plurality system in Britain leads to a predominantly two-party configuration, in which a single party normally enjoys an absolute majority of seats in the House of Commons.

The leader of the majority party (or coalition) then becomes head of government. In Britain the term used for this office is prime minister, in West Germany chancellor, in France and Spain president of the Council of Min-

Table 8.1
Twentieth-Century Presidents of the United States

1901–1909	Theodore Roosevelt
1909–1913	William Howard Taft
1913–1921	Woodrow Wilson
1921–1923	Warren G. Harding
1923–1929	Calvin Coolidge
1929–1933	Herbert Hoover
1933–1945	Franklin D. Roosevelt
1945–1953	Harry S. Truman
1953–1961	Dwight D. Eisenhower
1961–1963	John F. Kennedy
1963–1969	Lyndon B. Johnson
1969–1974	Richard M. Nixon
1974–1977	Gerald R. Ford
1977–1981	Jimmy Carter
1981–1989	Ronald Reagan
1989–1993	George Bush
1993–	William Clinton

isters. In West Germany the head of government is actually elected by the Federal Assembly, in France he or she is designated by the president and then approved by the National Assembly; in Great Britain the monarch simply appoints whoever is the recognized leader of the majority. These variations don't affect the nature of the office, which is leader of a cabinet representing the majority party or coalition.

Collectively, a prime minister and his or her cabinet set policy and guide the work of the legislature. Individually (except in Sweden, where the civil service is autonomous), they administer the various departments of government, exerting political control over the civil service and overseeing the implementation of the government's program.

This model has a great many strengths. The system is democratic in that everything flows ultimately from the choice made by the voter. It is simple, easy to understand, and easy to follow; there are no separate elections of executive and two houses of the legislature, no division of powers so that no one is quite sure who was responsible for a given policy, no possibility of arguing at the next election "We wanted to implement that policy, but we couldn't get a legislative majority." Problems can be dealt with in a straightforward, efficient, and timely way.

HEAD OF STATE AND HEAD OF GOVERNMENT

The logic of the parliamentary system implies other features and practices. There is a separation between the roles of head of government and head of state, which in a presidential system are filled by the same person. Following the British model, parliamentary systems have a head of state, either a monarch or a figurehead president, who represents the state for ceremonial purposes but who also has the function of designating or ratifying the choice of prime minister. In Britain, as in other predominantly two-party systems, this is not normally a significant role since it is known in advance who the leader of each party is and therefore who will become prime minister if the party wins a majority in the general election. In a multiparty system where a coalition government must be formed, however, it may be that several possible alternative coalitions might command a majority. Under such circumstances, typically the head of state asks a leader of one of the major parties to serve as the prime minister-designate—that is, to sound out the leaders of the various parties to see if it would be possible to put together a coalition under his or her leadership. Since several people might be able to command a majority under these circumstances, there may be an advantage in becoming the first one to make the necessary inquiries, which gives some significance to the president's power to designate a prime minister.

If the head of state is a monarch, obviously he or she inherits the position. Where the head of state is president of a republic, however, constitution-makers need to devote a considerable amount of thought to how that person will be chosen. The difficulty is that if a figurehead president is to be elected by popular vote, different parties, in seeking to win the election, may feel it necessary to put forward their strongest candidate. If a candidate of this type is elected with a large popular majority, it will be hard for him or her to be contented with merely a figurehead role, and conversely easy to argue that as a strong popular choice he or she should be the dominant figure in the government and not simply a figurehead. For a long time, in fact, the French were afraid to have a constitution providing for a popularly elected head of state, since on the only occasion before 1958 on which that was tried, at the formation of the Second Republic in 1850, the first president elected turned out to be Louis Napoleon Bonaparte, the nephew of Napoleon, who had no qualification for office except his name, and who soon staged a coup and proclaimed himself Emperor Napoleon III. After Napoleon III was overthrown as a result of the French defeat in war with Prussia in 1870, the leaders of the Third Republic were careful, after some initial difficulties, to try to pick presidents who would serve only as figureheads. The president was elected not by the people but by the politicians of the National Assembly, who were careful to pick somebody who would not try to encroach on their prerogatives, very often a distinguished but aging and feeble individual. Georges Clemenceau, the great Radical leader and prime minister during World War I, said "I always vote for the stupidest."

CABINET AND PARLIAMENT

Although ministers are individually responsible for the administration of the department of government they head, and are expected to resign if that department is guilty of serious errors, the cabinet as a whole is collectively responsible for the overall character of government policy. In Britain a minister may have opposed the adoption of a particular government policy in cabinet meetings, but once it has been adopted he or she is expected to stand by it and defend it in public if necessary. This is felt to be a necessary aspect of party discipline. The government cannot be expected to be backed by a solid majority of the assembly if it is itself split over policy questions.

The *civil service* is supposed to play a nonpolitical and impartial role, in that it must carry out the policies of whichever political party has a majority. Just as the government is united, in a two-party system the majority opposition party is similarly united in that it also fought the election as a disciplined party behind a coherent platform that it was pledged to implement if victorious. In Britain, the opposition forms a "shadow cabinet," each member of which "shadows" one of the government ministers—that is, has the responsibility of leading the opposition's criticism of government conduct in that particular policy area. The Leader of the Opposition stands ready to assume the prime minister's role if members of the government majority sufficient to swing the balance of power should come over to the opposition. This has not occurred in Britain in recent times, but did occur in the German Federal Republic in 1982, when the liberal Free Democratic Party abandoned its alliance with the Social Democrats and brought the Christian Democrats to power, with Helmut Kohl as chancellor.

If there are two chambers to the legislature, normally the government will be responsible only to one. Being responsible to two different chambers, possibly with different political complexions, makes cabinet government extremely difficult, as the experiences of the French Third Republic, which tried to operate in that fashion, demonstrated.

If the cabinet loses its majority in Parliament, as demonstrated for example by the passage of a vote of no confidence, the prime minister and cabinet should resign and the head of state may then appoint a new prime minister and cabinet to represent the new majority; alternatively, the prime minister may take the view that his or her government and policy are still supported by a majority of the electorate and, instead of resigning, may request the head of state to call new elections that will either confirm the incumbent in office or give the majority to someone else. That is, the prime minister may appeal the vote of a majority of the present Parliament to the decision of the majority of the next Parliament. The basic norm still holds that the government cannot function without the support of a parliamentary majority.

These are the essentials of the parliamentary system, the components of the logical mechanism. There are other features of the British system that are extraneous to the model, which happen to be present in Britain but do not need to be copied by other countries trying to implement a parliamentary system. For example, there are survivals of an older political system that have not been abolished—the hereditary monarchy, the partially hereditary House of Lords. The single-member-district plurality system of electing members of the British parliament is not a necessary part of a parliamentary system, and other parliamentary systems function on the basis of proportional representation. However, the parliamentary model does work more smoothly, providing a clearer choice of alternatives and a clearer resolution of issues, if the electoral system helps to promote two-partyism.

THE DISADVANTAGES OF THE PARLIAMENTARY SYSTEM

A discussion of the disadvantages of the parliamentary system, then, must begin with the observation that if many parties are represented in the legislature, a parliamentary system will depend on coalition-building. Coalitions are likely to be unstable, depending for their success as they do on the agreement of many centers of decision-making; moreover, they give excessive weight to small parties.

A disadvantage of the parliamentary system even where a single party enjoys a stable majority in the legislature is that it overloads members of the cabinet with responsibilities. They are typically members of Parliament, and must run for election in districts and represent their constituents, for example, in complaints against the bureaucracy; they must keep in touch with local district opinion, and hold office hours in the district. As leaders of their party in the subject matter field of their responsibilities, they must also take a major role in parliamentary debates, in public speeches, and in interviews with the press. As members of the cabinet they must participate in the formation of overall policy and also serve on cabinet committees that deal with policy subfields. At the same time, as ministers for individual departments they supervise the operations of the permanent civil servants in that department, who have their own concerns and objectives that are not necessarily those of the party in power.

In view of the variety and sheer weight of these responsibilities, it is not surprising to find cabinet ministers who neglect important parts of their duties. Staff members may take care of many of the functions related to the constituency, and some of those dealing with parliamentary debate. More important, many cabinet members do not participate fully in the setting of overall policy, confining themselves to matters affecting their own departments; and yet it has been estimated that half of the members of the British cabinet exercise only marginal influence in their departments, which are essentially run by the senior civil servants. Very commonly, the minister simply adopts the "departmental point of view," becoming an advocate in the cabinet and to the outside world of the permanent policies of his or her department, as formulated by the upper civil servants.

It might be thought that one of the disadvantages of the parliamentary system, in its British form, is that it concentrates power excessively. Given in effect an automatic majority in the legislature, an ineffective second chamber, and a head of state who approves all parliamentary acts, there would clearly seem to exist the danger of a dictatorship by the ruling party or by a strong prime minister. Events in some of the former British colonies in Africa that have adopted a parliamentary system seem to illustrate this danger. In point of fact, however, most ex-British colonies that have taken the road of dictatorship have instead found it more convenient to switch to a presidential system. Apparently the separation of powers and other constitutional protections of a presidential system provide little effective obstacle to a dictatorship where a strong single party holds the reins of government, while a president does not face the necessity of justifying policies to a parliament to the same extent as a prime minister. The chief reason for the changeover, however, is most likely the higher status ranking at formal international conferences and state visits of a president, who is head of state as well as head of government, as compared to a prime minister.

In fact the most plausible complaints of abuse of power in Great Britain refer not so much to the concentration of power in the hands of the majority party or of the cabinet as to the autonomy left to the civil service by the lack of effective ministerial and party control. Although the monarch has no power today, there are many survivals of monarchic power exercised by the cabinet and the civil service. The gravest threats to a regime of ordered liberty in Britain seem not to come from the power of the cabinet and ruling party with relation to the Parliament as much as from infringement on a free press by rules keeping official information secret, from the ability of the civil service and the police to operate independent of political control, and occasionally from the illicit exercise of political influence on the courts. It seems generally to be true that in modern political systems of any type, the most effective guarantees of democracy and individual liberty are not the form of government as such but the requirement of regular elections, with their necessary implication of the tolerance of a free opposition and a free press, together with guarantees for the independence of the judiciary.

One of the curious features of parliamentary systems is that, given the existence of party discipline, there is commonly a feeling of ineffectiveness and alienation among members of a parliament. They feel that they are being marched to the division lobbies[1] to vote like so much "voting cattle," in the German phrase, and they pine for the independent power of legislatures in a separation-of-powers systems. Some of this feeling of powerlessness is an illusion; legislatures may in fact be more important than they feel themselves to be. Part of their importance lies in what they don't do but could: by maintaining a majority for the incumbent government, they force it to keep within certain boundaries, to overstep which would provoke a revolt and its removal by majority vote of the parliament. They thus form a sort of silent electoral college in continuous session.

They perform other valuable functions for the health of the political system, however. Debate in the chamber, even when a majority for the government is a foregone conclusion, serves to clarify issues for the public and promote general political education. In fact, one of the striking features of a parliamentary system, as opposed to a presidential one, is the way that the entire political life of the country is focused on the legislature. The lead stories on the front pages of the newspapers have to do with the previous day's debates. New policy initiatives are usually announced in the chamber and not to news conferences or television audiences. Questionable policies are not put through without public awareness or discussion because the opposition party is intimidated by the high popularity ratings of a president, as sometimes occurs in the United States. In a parliamentary system an opposition exists whose job it is to marshall the best arguments that can be made against the government's policies, day after day.

A parliament is also a place where new recruits to political activity are socialized into the system, are trained, are able to show off their talents and have their strengths and weaknesses spotted, and in general are scouted by the leadership for future positions of leadership themselves.

Finally, of course, the members perform services for their constituents whose importance should not be underestimated in these days of omnipresent bureaucracy and overwhelming red tape. This is a function complained of by parliamentarians but jealously guarded by them, so that when a special official empowered to investigate alleged abuses of the bureaucracy has been appointed (usually known by the Swedish term "ombudsman") parliamentarians have typically insisted he or she be able to act only at the request of a member of parliament.

OMBUDSMAN

The original ombudsman, or chancellor of justice, was a Swedish official given a roving commission to investigate complaints of government abuse of the rights of citizens, and to institute proceedings to remedy the situation if he found the complaint well-grounded. The ombudsman is placed outside the regular administrative chain of command so that he or she can be free to pursue the investigation no matter where it leads.

Although the institution of ombudsman had existed for 200 years in Sweden, it was not until the twentieth century that it began to be copied elsewhere. Sometimes officials of this type, whose powers differ somewhat from country to country, are called ombudsman, as in New Zealand; in Britain and Germany, the term "parliamentary commissioner" is used. Somewhat similar powers are wielded in Chile and Costa Rica by the controller-general.

The point is that modern governments have become so complex and administrative officials so enmeshed in bureaucratic procedures that is it sometimes necessary to have someone whose authority can cut across established administrative lines in order to act effectively on behalf of an individual citizen. Because this role is also played by elected representatives who do not wish to abandon it and the political support it can generate, in Britain and elsewhere the parliamentary commissioner acts only if asked to do so by a lawmaker.

THE PRESIDENTIAL SYSTEM

The presidential system is the principal alternative to the parliamentary system among democratic countries in the world today. It owes its origins to the attempt by the founding fathers of the American Constitution to adapt the British political tradition as it existed in the eighteenth century to the realities of life in the new republic they were trying to form. Their objective was to create a government more effective than what had existed under the Articles of Confederation (1781–89)—which had loosely tied together the former British colonies after the success of the Revolution—but in which power would not be subject to the kind of abuse they had experienced when the colonies were ruled by George III. Like many political products, the U.S. Constitution was a compromise—in this case between those more concerned to make the new federal government a strong promoter of economic progress and those concerned that it would create a concentration of power dangerous to local and individual liberties. As was pointed out in Chapter 7, the principles on the basis of which the compromise was worked out are known as the separation of powers and checks and balances.

The development of the principle of the separation of powers, like other doctrines believed in by human beings, can be explained either logically—

that is, as a rational solution to an intellectual problem—or genetically—as an outgrowth of the events that preceded it at a particular time in history. The logical basis for the separation of powers was the theory developed by Baron Montesquieu that was discussed in Chapter 7. The genetic, or historical, mode of understanding the separation of powers is that it was a way of describing what was assumed to be the satisfactory division of responsibilities in British constitutional practice between the monarch, Parliament, and the courts that had been arrived at in the course of the evolution of the British political system to the second half of the eighteenth century.

As was mentioned previously, England had been evolving away from a situation in which the monarch had all power toward, ultimately, a situation in which the monarch had no power to speak of and all power was wielded, in principle, by the representatives of the people in Parliament. During the second half of the eighteenth century a middle point in this evolution had been reached, in which the monarch still retained some important powers, although a substantial portion of them had passed to the legislature.

In order to maintain the separation of executive and legislature, to see that one is not dependent on the will of the other, it is necessary that they be separately elected. Clearly, if the executive were to be chosen by the legislature, as is more or less the case in a parliamentary system, it could be controlled by the legislature and the separation of powers would be ineffective. (In fact, the relationship is reversed: if the cabinet is chosen by the legislature, then it tries to control the legislature.) Thus in a presidential system, the president and the legislature are elected by different constituencies for terms of different lengths, which ensures that even if they respond to the wishes of the same electorate, it is an electorate animated by different moods at different times, and their political complexion will be different.

The system is organized so that presidents do not need a majority in the legislature in order to discharge their functions (although it is certainly helpful to have such a majority); a president need not resign if he or she lacks a legislative majority, but continues to serve till the end of the four-year term. This means also that there is no difficulty in having two houses of a legislature each with significant powers. In a parliamentary system this would create an extremely difficult situation, as the cabinet would have to be responsible to two different masters. In the United States, in fact, both Senate and House of Representatives can be potent bodies, in contrast to the normal situation in parliamentary systems, where, following the British model, the upper house, the one less directly responsive to the popular vote, plays only a marginal role.

In the presidential system there is no separation of the roles of head of state and head of government. The president is the effective head of government, setting policy and dominating the cabinet; but he or she is also the ceremonial head of state, receiving foreign ambassadors, issuing proclamations, and being attended by ceremonial guards. This always seems to the party out of power an unnecessary and counterproductive arrangement. Presidents are, after all, merely politicians who got lucky. When they are attended by all the ceremonial trappings of head of state and become the symbolic representative of the nation's sovereignty, this surrounds them with an aura, a dignity, and a patriotic significance that make it harder to attack them, criticize their performance and policies, and scoff at their mistakes. However, there is also an advantage in this arrangement so far as foreign policy is concerned. The greater prestige and stature of a head of government who is also head of state strengthens the hand of the president somewhat in his personal relations with the heads of other governments.

Since a presidential government does not stand or fall by its maintenance of a majority in the legislature, it is not necessary to enforce party discipline there as it is in the parliamentary system. Each legislator elected in a single-member district is responsible for his or her own election and owes relatively less to the party campaign than does a representative in a parliamentary system. Thus party discipline is not only less necessary in a presidential system, it is more difficult to achieve. This means that in a democratic presidential system, such as that of the United States, the assembly functions as a genuine legislature, making decisions as it goes along, defying the president's wishes from time to time, with the outcome of its debates often quite unpredictable. This contrasts with the functioning of a legislature in a parliamentary system, where the government's projects almost always have a majority.

The presidential-system legislature does not control the cabinet, as in parliamentary systems. Instead, it has its own subject matter specialists in the form of specialized committees, whose chairpersons may acquire an expertise and authority that can challenge that of the cabinet minister of the relevant department.

The strengths of this system are also its weaknesses. The complexity of the system, the independent roles of the president and the two houses of legislature, the specialized committees—and then the conference committees, which must reconcile different versions of a bill passed by the two houses—creates a series of "choke points," where it is easy to block legislation, or hold it hostage, passing it on only in return for some favor. This means that in a system of the American type it is very difficult to get legislation passed, and almost impossible to get it passed in exactly the form the government wants; which means in turn that it is difficult to meet problems fairly and squarely, and they tend to persist and get worse before anything effective is done. It is sometimes said that the United States is forty years behind Britain in legislating to meet specific problems.

In addition, the fact that the system is so complicated and it is relatively simple to obstruct legislation promotes corruption of all kinds, such as the introduction of legislative provisions that benefit only small special interest groups, sometimes even specific individuals, with the benefit involved being disguised in complex and even impenetrable language. Bills passed by the U.S. Congress are full of special loopholes and "hidden ball plays," with provisions inserted by powerful committee chairmen or subcommittee chairmen, or members of the conference committee, to benefit special interests to which they are beholden.

The complexity of the American legislative process also contributes to the fact that the public is ill-informed and confused about the nature of issues and the positions on them of politicians and political parties. It has to be said that this confusion is often deliberately created by political figures who, in keeping with the dictates of rational action in a two-party system, seek always for the middle ground and try to be all things to all men. The ideal situation of congressmen, for example, is to be recorded on both sides of every issue, so that they can always point to something in their records in enlisting the support of whatever group they are appealing to. This can be done in various ways; for example, a congressman or congresswoman may vote for a bill, but also for an amendment that would cripple it. He may vote to authorize some program, but vote against appropriating the funds necessary to implement it. She may speak in favor of some measure in general terms, but work behind the scenes against it. The system acts to diffuse responsibility, blur issues, and encourage dishonesty. Under these circumstances, where so many possibilities exist of blocking needed changes and it is so difficult to pass reform legislation, the power of those already established and wealthy is enhanced. The general atmosphere of duplicity that surrounds the U.S. legislative process renders ironic the usual congressional criticisms of the president for concealing executive policies of dubious morality, legality, and even intelligence under the veil of national security.

It remains true, nevertheless, that the very complexity of the system, the number of positions of power that it contains, mean that any interest can find an advocate somewhere in the system. Although the preponderance of power seems, perhaps as always, to lie with the established and wealthy, the underprivileged also have their advocates, and there is enough flexibility in the system, and things appear to come out right enough of the time, that it always seems premature to abandon hope completely.

NOTE

1. This is a British term reflecting the fact that Members of Parliament vote by walking past tellers into either the "aye" or "nay" lobbies situated to either side of the legislative chamber.

KEY TERMS

collegial executive

cabinet

monarch

figurehead president

civil service

"shadow cabinet"

House of Lords

departmental point of view

ombudsman

CHAPTER 9

Bureaucracy

POT-SHOTS NO. 2074.

HOW
COULD THERE
EVER POSSIBLY
BE ANY
CONFLICT
BETWEEN
MY
PRIVATE INTERESTS
AND
THE PUBLIC GOOD?

Ashleigh Brilliant

The study of bureaucracy—that is, of workers in the civil service—has had something of a distinctive character within political science. The difficulty here lies in distinguishing professional or vocational training for future public servants from scholarly analysis of what actually occurs. Clearly, if one is engaged in vocational training, one teaches the student the way things should be done. Engineers are not trained to build bridges badly, nor surgeons to botch operations. Programs in public administration are concerned with teaching future bureaucrats how to perform competently; political scientists, on the other hand, are interested in what actually occurs in bureaucracies, not what is supposed to occur.

THE WEBERIAN MODEL

The great German sociologist Max Weber, more than anyone else, described the way a modern bureaucracy should ideally function. Weber's model of a perfectly functioning modern rational bureaucracy (what we have previously termed a model, he called "an ideal type") consisted of several elements. A rational bureaucracy is organized on a hierarchical basis. There are clear lines of responsibility. Every person knows to whom he or she reports and who reports to him or her. Jurisdictions are clearly defined, and responsibilities are unambiguous. The personnel of a rational model bureaucratic system are recruited and promoted solely on the basis of merit. They are admitted to the service on the basis of their performance on examinations—personal and family connections have no relevance. They are then promoted on the basis of their performance in office, as periodically evaluated by their supervisors or by consulting panels. After a period of probation, civil servants can be removed only for a specific cause, and only after procedures are followed that fully safeguard their interests; if they appeal against their dismissal, they are entitled to review by a board, which must consider the evidence they present on their own behalf. On their retirement, civil servants receive a pension and perhaps other benefits. The obstacles to their arbitrary removal, and the guarantee of their pensions, serve the purpose of protecting civil servants from political interference, and enable them to perform their jobs impartially without fear of consequences if someone should be offended.

In its norms of operation, the civil service is governed by preestablished rules; civil servants do not act simply as they wish, but are bound to follow the laws and the regulations established for the implementation of those laws. In applying these regulations, civil servants are impersonal, taking no account of the wealth or social prestige of the individuals with whom they deal; they are honest, fair, and nonpartisan in the discharge of their functions.

Clearly this model represents an ideal that can never be perfectly realized. As we shall see, there are certain characteristic ways in which bureaucracies tend to depart from this normative model. However, even if it were possible to implement the model as it stands, problems would inevitably arise because of tensions within the model itself. One of these is the conflict between the requirement that bureaucrats adhere strictly to preestablished regulations, and the fact that each case presents its own peculiarities, which make a certain amount of flexibility in the application of the rules desirable. We have surely all had the experience of coming up against an official, private or public, who was unwilling to agree that the rules needed to be varied slightly in a particular case in order for justice, or some other patently desirable objective, to be realized. Thus one intrinsic tension within the bureaucratic model is that between general rules and specific circumstances.

Another intrinsic source of tension is that confidentiality is necessary to protect personal information about some citizen that a bureaucrat needs to have, for example, for purposes of tax assessment or for determining whether a law has been broken, but that, if it became generally known, would needlessly violate the individual's privacy. Some information would give an unfair advantage to one business competitor over another; other information might be of use to the country's potential adversaries in war. Yet, at the same time, this requirement for confidentiality, or for secrecy, conflicts with the freedom of speech and of the press that must exist in a democracy, especially if the democratic electorate is to hold elected officials responsible and form a correct evaluation of the performance of one political party rather than another. To what extent should officials be allowed to withhold information from the public?

BUREAUCRACY IN DEVELOPING COUNTRIES

The problems cited are presented by the implementation of the model even in its purest form. Yet another series of problems arises when the model, designed for a developed country with high standards of education and competence and with advanced political institutions, is adopted by a developing country still in transition to the norms of the modern world. The protection of bureaucrats from political interference, represented by the system of hearings and quasi-judicial procedures necessary before someone can be fired, for example, may prove quite counterproductive. In a transitional situation in which the country needs substantial reforms, and needs a civil service dedicated to implementing changes, provisions for tenure designed to protect bureaucrats against political interference, and complicated rules of procedure, tend to entrench a conservative bureaucracy linked to an established elite class that has an interest in preventing reforms, while the complex procedures designed to assure fairness give them tools with which to delay and circumvent reform efforts. A conservative high bureaucrat, an Ecuadorian friend of this writer, when asked how the new reformist government of his country was doing, replied with a wink, "The revolution above, the counterrevolution below."

The opportunities for obstruction are endless. The new reformist government, let us say, wishes to implement a land reform. Of course, says the conservative bureaucrat; but before we can implement the land reform we must first take a survey of actual landholdings to see which landowners hold extensions of land in excess of the amounts permitted under the new reform. Unfortunately, we are short of surveyors to do that job, so we must establish a school for surveyors. That is, we must contract with a foreign technical corporation to train the surveyors. In order to do that we must draw up specifications for bids from foreign technical concerns that wish to set up a training course for surveyors. The first question is therefore the composition of the committee that will draw up the specifications on the basis of which to choose the foreign company to train the surveyors to do the surveys to find out which landholdings are too large. The procedures can proliferate endlessly and the reformist government will be long gone before any land is actually scheduled for distribution under the reform measures.

Merit bureaucratic *systems* were introduced to end the evils of the "spoils system," under which bureaucratic jobs were regarded as the spoils of victory by the political party winning an election, with the civil servants of the previous administration fired wholesale. The spoils system may have resulted in public servants of less-than-optimum quality and impartiality, and a lack of continuity in government programs. But such a method of appointing bureaucrats might be more serviceable for a reformist or revolutionary government coming to power in a Third World country and trying to end long-standing practices of exploitation and oppression.

LAND REFORM

In temperate regions of Africa, in Latin America, and in some countries of the Far East, representatives of the colonial power or members of the ruling class occupied the best land. The resulting uneven distribution of the land, with large tracts in the possession of a few while many laborers were landless, can be regarded not only as unjust in itself but also alien to the requirements of a democratic society, since economic power translates into political power, so that those without land may not be genuinely autonomous as citizens. Perhaps more to the point for most governments is that an increasing number of dissatisfied people may lend support to a revolutionary movement; while conversely people are likely to feel well-disposed to the government or political party that made it possible for them to own their own plots of land

For these reasons, the governments of newly independent states, at least those representing the more progressive political forces in the country, frequently institute land reform programs, by which is meant the division of large estates into small plots of land that can be farmed by the hitherto landless. Land reform of this type is generally a feature of the political programs of progressive political parties in the developing world.

Economists sometimes argue that land can be more productive in the hands of those with capital to develop it and farm it with machinery, so that reforms that break up large landholdings make them less productive. However, this need not be true if landless laborers who would otherwise be a drag on the national economy are given small plots to farm. Under circumstances of mass unemployment, labor is in effect free of social cost, so there may be no point in trying to introduce machinery to save labor, especially expensive machinery that must be bought abroad.

Although the introduction of a land reform program or the election of a government pledged to institute one may panic the wealthy and become the catalyst for a military seizure of power, there are also many political and bureaucratic ways in which a land reform can be sabotaged or perverted from its original purpose, and that is probably the fate of most land reform programs. However, the recent history of countries such as Japan and Taiwan suggests that a land reform is desirable not only for social justice, but also for economic development.

ADMINISTRATION AND POLITICS

The model of a nonpartisan, impersonal, and fair bureaucracy sets standards that are difficult to reach. One of its premises is that it is possible to separate politics from administration, and confine the bureaucracy to nonpolitical administrative matters. Needless to say, the line separating politics from administration is difficult to draw.

Curiously enough, that line is drawn at quite different points in different political systems. Thus, for example, when a new party comes to power in Britain, perhaps 200 positions in the cabinet and subcabinet change hands. In the United States the figure is something between 3,000 and 4,000 positions, regularly including jobs several levels further down the bureaucratic structure than the cabinet. Some U.S. administrations go further than others in staffing positions with political appointees. This writer was told in Nepal that at the beginning of the Reagan administration the Peace Corps representative there was replaced because he was not an active Republican. It is rather unusual, even for the United States, to have partisan considerations enter into positions that low on the bureaucratic ladder.

In some other countries, the problem is posed in rather different form. In France and Germany, for example, rather than political appointments being made to bureaucratic positions, the deviation from Weberian norms tends to be in the other direction: that career civil servants get involved in politics. In the United States, for many years, the Hatch Act prohibited federal bureaucrats from involving themselves in partisan politics. In France or Germany, however, many politicians are high bureaucrats on temporary leave from their civil service positions.

The Federal Republic of Germany has continued the long-standing German tradition of emphasizing technical expertise in politics, and defining political issues as far as possible in bureaucratic terms. Each party feels that it must be represented on legislative committees by experts in the particular subject matter in question and will attempt to recruit the bureaucrats who have been professionally concerned with that subject matter to be legislative candidates who, when successful, would then become the party's specialists in that field. The upper house in the German legislature, the Bundesrat, moreover, consists of delegations from the governments of the states of the federation, and the political heads of the delegation generally leave most of the work to their staff members, who are state-level bureaucrats. Since many of the legislators in the lower house, the Bundestag, are themselves officials on leave, the legislative process in Germany has a bureaucratic tone to it, and one can have the feeling of being present at an interdepartmental meeting rather than at a session of a legislative body.

In France the situation is somewhat similar. The admissions standards for the higher civil service are so rigorous, and the training so demanding, that training at the National School of Administration produces an intellectual elite of high competence, who frequently leave administration for politics permanently after having attained a high level in the bureaucracy. A majority of the Fifth Republic's prime ministers, and all five of the presidents elected in the Fifth Republic since it began in 1958, started their careers as officials, either civil or military.

This predominance of bureaucratic figures in a country's political life reaches its high point in Mexico, which has long been ruled by a dominant single party. The last five presidents of Mexico at the time of writing were career administrators, none of whom had ever run for a political office before being nominated for president. This tends to be a characteristic of single-party systems: since there is no alternation of parties in power, there need not be so clear a distinction between permanent civil service jobs and political appointments.

THE LOGIC OF BUREAUCRATIC BEHAVIOR

A realistic analysis of bureaucracy must go beyond the classic normative model of a nonpartisan merit service impartially executing the political will of the democratically chosen government. Bureaucrats are charged with pursuing the public interest, which they do; but at the same time they pursue other interests, based not only on their identities as public servants, but also on their identities as individuals pursuing a career and as members not only of the public service as a whole but of particular bureaus, agencies, and branches of government. Public servants do not conceive of their devotion to the interest of their own departments as something opposed to their loyalty to the general public interest; on the contrary, socialized into their departments' norms, they tend to believe that the missions of their own departments or bureaus are a critical part of the general public interest. If they serve in the Department of Defense, then of course the country's national security necessarily takes priority over all other objectives; if in the Treasury ministry or budget bureau, then of course the country lives or dies by its financial health. The future of the human race depends on the safety of the environment, if its protection is one of their department's responsibilities; or its future depends on the education of the young, if they work for the education ministry. This commitment to the bureau mission has given rise to the saying "Where you stand depends on where you sit," meaning that your views are determined by the position you occupy. Certainly in a cabinet meeting it is not hard to predict in advance what the position of each member of the cabinet will be, depending on which ministry or department each one represents.

In most cases, even though the heads of departments, cabinet ministers, are political appointees, they tend to take on the *departmental point of view*, as propounded by their chief permanent officials. As a minister is briefed on department activities, he or she tends to absorb the rationale of the department's existence, its pride in the dedication of its personnel, its particular conception of how its mission is central to the public interest. The traditional departmental point of view can be elaborated in great detail: there may be a doctrine as to why some subject matter should lie within the territory of the department rather than that of some other department, or why some particular terminology should be used rather than an alternative. It has been estimated that in Britain about two-thirds of cabinet members simply take on the departmental point of view instead of dominating their departments and imposing on them the government's own political orientation. Of course, in a parliamentary system cabinet ministers are overloaded with their nondepartmental responsibilities, in the constituency, in parliament, and in the cabinet itself, and it is a rare cabinet minister who performs all of his or her other tasks well and also succeeds in dominating and reorienting his or her department.

There are many techniques by which senior civil servants can manipulate their minister, even when he or she is a strong, "take charge," type. For example, when a minister asks the staff to prepare a description of the alternative courses of action possible with respect to a specific problem, it is always possible to describe each of the alternative policies in such a way as to make them undesirable, except for the alternative favored by the staff.

Winning over the minister or cabinet secretary is but one of the games bureaucrats play that grow out of the self-identification of individual bureaucrats with the departments or offices in which they work. Another game is defending the turf—that is, maintaining the scope of the department's mission against the attempt of other departments to encroach on it. The budget game is aimed at increasing the department's budget over what it was the previous year. The question to be asked is not what functions need to be performed and how much they will cost; it is rather, first, how much can one reasonably expect the budget to be increased, and only then what new activities can be proposed to justify that increase.

This writer learned to operate in this manner as a university administrator for fourteen years during a period of generally expanding budgets. The procedure I followed was to estimate how much of an increase in the previous year's budget I could reasonably hope to get from the dean, given the university's financial circumstances, and then draw up a budget asking for an increase of twice that amount. The amount of the increase requested would be justified partly on the basis of increased costs, partly on the basis of expanded programs; but these would be listed in such a way that the more obviously desirable ones could be funded with the maximum budget increase that I could reasonably hope for, so that the dean could feel frugal by approving only half of the requested increase, denying the request to fund the less essential activities.

Identification with the bureau mission can lead, with some personality types, to a policy of bureaucratic imperialism, the aggrandizement of the bureau by its taking on new functions and expanding its sphere of control. The wise bureaucratic imperialist, someone like J. Edgar Hoover, who headed the *Federal Bureau of Investigation* (FBI) for over thirty years, will be careful not to take on tasks that are impossible to perform, or are unpleasant, or may lead to poor public relations. Hoover's management of the FBI was in many respects a masterpiece of bureaucratic politics: he resisted having the bureau's responsibilities extend to enforcement of drug laws or combatting of organized crime,[1] reasoning that both tasks were inherently hopeless, while exposure to the drug trade would corrupt some bureau agents. Hoover developed a formidable public relations operation, which glamorized his bureau in the public eye and made it virtually impossible for Congress to refuse him any request; he made doubly sure of this by building up dossiers on the activities of congressmen themselves, which made many of them especially reluctant to provoke his wrath.

Having the fighting of crime as his mission also made it possible for him to point to spectacular successes he had had, while at the same time bemoaning the fact that the problem was getting greater each year, thus necessitating large annual budget increases; and the fact that basic law enforcement was the responsibility of local police forces, and not of the FBI, made it possible for Hoover to limit the bureau's involvement to easy-to-crack, high-visibility cases. Sometimes a fugitive was placed on the sensational "The Most Wanted Men" list, for example, after his whereabouts were already known and his apprehension was being planned.

The example of the FBI indicates how much bureaucrats' hands are strengthened by their being able to cover those operations they wish with a veil of secrecy. Of course, the official version is that secrecy is necessary to protect ongoing investigations or confidential information about individuals; or to prevent criminals or hostile foreign powers from acquiring valuable information. In fact, however, their ability to classify information as secret enables bureaucrats to cover up their errors or keep the public ignorant as to the true extent of unpopular practices. Fortunately, the United States now has a Freedom of Information Act, which makes it possible, at least in principle, for the public to request and receive information the secrecy of which is not absolutely necessary. (In practice, difficulties can be created and released material censored.) In this respect the United States has started to follow the example of Switzerland, where official files are normally available for inspection by the public.

A notorious counterexample is that of Great Britain, where the Official Secrets Act makes it a crime for public servants to disclose any information whatsoever acquired as a result of their government position, except where such disclosure is authorized by a superior official. The coming to light of various cases in which scandalous behavior has been hushed up, and others in which the government has made itself ridiculous by attempting to prosecute former government officials for publishing information quite without national security value, has created pressures in Britain, which have so far been resisted, for changes in the law.

FREEDOM OF INFORMATION

In 1966 the U.S. Congress passed the Freedom of Information Act, which provided that federal agencies must make their records available to individuals on request. Exceptions could be made for confidential personnel and financial files, or for material bearing on national security and law enforcement. Individuals may sue government agencies in federal court if they fail to comply with the terms of the Act.

Although the limits that can be placed on the material made available are often enough to enable government wrongdoing to be covered up, nevertheless the Act has made possible much greater openness in the conduct of public business, and is widely envied abroad.

Bureaucratic behavior and the protection of departmental interests is not necessarily aggressive and imperialist. It may be purely defensive, aimed at avoidance of trouble. While the public interest may not be served by a bureaucrat's attempt to expand his role and promote his career in an aggressive fashion, it may also not be served by his declining to do his job in implementing the laws because of his fear that he will offend somebody and thus jeopardize his career. Excessive timidity is just as much a problem in bureaucrats as aggressive self-promotion.

BUREAUCRATS IN UNIFORM

Tendencies to serve the institutional interest rather than the public interest can be found in bureaucracies all over the world, in military bureaucracies as well as civilian. Like their civilian counterparts, army officers try to defend their turf from encroachment, to maintain good public relations, to expand their budgetary allotment. The difference is that in many countries of the world the military forces are prepared to use the monopoly of armed force entrusted to them for national defense in order to promote their collective interests. Víctor Villanueva once observed that every government of Peru that tried to cut the military budget had been overthrown.

In some countries, attempts to limit the role of the military or reduce its prerogatives run the risk of provoking a military seizure of power, although for public consumption reasons of national interest are always asserted. To be sure, when a military force intervenes in politics, it may be doing so at the behest of an oligarchy that feels itself to be threatened, or of a hegemonic power. But even in such cases it is necessary to engage the interest of the military by pointing out to them the specifically military interests that would be threatened by a continuation in power of the incumbent government. For example, if a political party that represents the oligarchy—that is, the ruling moneyed elite—feels threatened by an incumbent populist government's plans to legislate a land reform, party leaders may point out to the military that such a land reform would occasion a great deal of disturbance and probably violence in the countryside, requiring the military to be called out and used in a policing role. This kind of role is despised by the military, as unfitting for those whose mission it is to defend the nation against foreign enemies, and also as tending to lead to bad military relations with the civilian populace.

CIVILIAN CONTROL OF THE MILITARY

In a democracy, a military force is established to serve as an instrument of the elected political leadership. Samuel P. Huntington pointed out in *The Soldier and the State* (1956) that there were two ways in which a military force could be democratic: one was for it to be absolutely disciplined from top to bottom with the officers at the top taking orders from the civilian political leadership; this he called "objective" civilian control. In "subjective" civilian control, the military is democratic because its members are indoctrinated with democratic values, but its discipline is more relaxed, and soldiers are encouraged to think for themselves. Huntington thought "subjective" civilian control dangerous because unelected military leaders might be free to deviate from what the political leadership desired. Paradoxically, therefore, he argued that a democracy was better served by having a totally authoritarian institution in its service rather than one that tried to be internally democratic.

This analysis is true in general—rank, hierarchy, and discipline should characterize an effective military force, since on occasion men and women will be sent to fight and if necessary to die, and this is more reliably achieved if they are trained to follow orders without questioning them or thinking them over. It seems clear, on the other hand, and has been established as an internationally valid principle, incorporated into the codes of military justice of developed countries, that soldiers have no obligation to obey a criminal or illegal order. They may refuse, for example, to obey orders to perform personal services for an officer outside the line of duty; they should refuse to participate in a massacre of noncombatant civilians; they should be able to refuse an order to arrest their country's political leaders in order that some general can take power. That is, while discipline should normally prevail, it may sometimes be necessary for an order to be disobeyed. This means that soldiers must be able to recognize illegal orders, and must have the confidence to back up their refusal to obey them.

This need not disturb us overmuch, however. The unthinking automaton assumed in Huntington's model of objective civilian control does not exist, after all. Even in the best-disciplined military services, soldiers do not automatically and unthinkingly obey all commands and standing orders. In fact, like people of other walks of life, soldiers usually try to manipulate the rules to their own advantage.

Alternatively, an oligarchic party trying to provoke a military intervention may point out that a populist government attempting to improve conditions for the masses is likely to divert funds from military to social welfare spending; that it is likely to create a popular militia based on the trade unions and on peasants' syndicates, which would threaten the military's monopoly of the legitimate use of force; and that such a tendency might result in the complete replacement of the traditional military by a people's militia, or even, as in the case of Fidel Castro's revolution in Cuba, in the execution as war criminals of military officers who had served under the old regime. Most cases of the military seizure of power can thus be viewed as simply another instance of a bureaucratic organization, established to serve the public interest, serving only the public interest as it conceives of it, and moreover deviating from the public interest in order to protect its own private corporate interests.

IS A MILITARY SEIZURE OF POWER EVER JUSTIFIED?

Not only must soldiers be free to decline to obey orders that they believe to be illegal; on rare occasions the military may even be justified in acting to remove from office a leader who has committed major violations of the laws and constitution and may be driving the country to ruin, where no other remedy exists. The tyrant may have closed the legislature and the courts, so that no constitutional recourse exists, for example. Clearly such a military intervention should occur only in extreme and generally agreed circumstances. It is not quite adequate, however, to say that if a president was elected by popular vote he or she should invariably be obeyed. Tyranny, after all, may be tyranny by performance even if the ruler was legitimate in his or her origins. In the regrettable case that such an act becomes necessary, however—for example, where a tyrant has prevented parliament and the courts from functioning—the military intervention should end with the removal of the tyrannical incumbent. A democratic military should then yield power as soon as possible to those constitutionally next in line of succession.

CONCLUSION

Bureaucrats are not always narrow-minded and self-serving. A great many are dedicated and selfless public servants, who perform prodigies of work in the public interest. Nevertheless, since much of the study of civil-service behavior is based on Max Weber's model of what ideal bureaucratic behavior should be, it is necessary to provide a corrective in the form of this discussion, which reemphasizes the basic principle of political analysis presented in this book: most behavior can be explained as rational pursuit of self-interest, so long as it is remembered that an individual's "self" is complex and multidimensional.

NOTE

1. Evidence has subsequently come to light suggesting that Hoover's refusal to move against organized crime was also based on his fear that if he did so, crime figures would release material they possessed exposing his secret homosexuality.

KEY TERMS

bureaucracy	departmental point of view
ideal type	Federal Bureau of Investigation
merit system	Freedom of Information Act
spoils system	Official Secrets Act

CHAPTER 10

Economic Policy

© ASHLEIGH BRILLIANT 1982.

POT-SHOTS NO. 2627

IN A DEMOCRACY,

EVERY LITTLE WRONG IDEA
MAY GROW UP
TO BECOME
NATIONAL POLICY.

Ashleigh Brilliant

Since so much of politics is concerned with economic policy, a book on politics must discuss the principal economic issues and the different positions people take with respect to those issues. We will select for discussion six major areas of economic policy: taxation, spending on social benefits, labor relations, the public/private mix (i.e., the question of how much of the economy should actually be owned and operated by public authorities rather than left in private hands), demand management, and planning.

TAX POLICY

Tax policy can have several objectives. Its primary purpose is to raise revenue to finance the operations of government. At first glance, it may seem strange that a government cannot simply print the money it needs to finance its own operations and not bother raising taxes; but this would produce, or increase, inflation. If taxation takes the same amount of money out of the economy, out of the hands of consumers who would spend it, as is spent by government—and thus put back into the economy—then it is not inflationary; that is, it does not make the level of prices rise.

Taxes can also have purposes besides raising revenue: to increase production and productivity by changing the rewards and punishments attached to different courses of action; to redistribute income by taxing the rich to pay for services provided to the poor; or—not acknowledged overtly—to appeal to some group in the population the governing party wants votes from in the next election, or to repay some group for its votes in previous elections, or for its campaign contributions.

CAMPAIGN CONTRIBUTIONS

One of the principal modes in which economic interests influence legislation is that of the campaign contribution to a member of Congress. A campaign contribution is not the same as a bribe, in return for which a congressman or senator agrees to vote a certain way. Nevertheless, if the contribution is substantial, it is likely that a member will think twice before voting to damage the interests of the generous donor. Campaign contributions are necessary because of the huge costs of running an election campaign under the present American system. It has been said that senators spend two-thirds of their time raising funds and only one-third attending to the nation's business.

There is general agreement that the system needs to be changed. Since the main campaign expense is for television advertising, a simple way of drastically reducing the money needed to run a campaign would be to provide that television stations give free time for election programs of the candidates, as they do in Great Britain. Of course that would mean a considerable loss of revenue for the television networks, which presumably have enough influence so that Congress would not enact a reform of that type.

In general politicians favor, in their tax policies, those groups they particularly represent. In the U.S. Congress provisions are sometimes introduced into tax legislation that benefit only small groups of favored individuals. This actual purpose may deliberately be hidden by obscure and confusing language or some public purpose may be alleged for the favoritism. Thus, for example, companies producing oil in the United States have been given special tax breaks ostensibly so that the country will "reduce dependence on foreign oil," but in fact because they are owned by influential individuals who may make large campaign contributions or who employ a lot of workers. The central role placed in the U.S. Congress by representatives from Texas and Oklahoma has been important in getting such legislation passed.

Tax policy is normally discussed on the basis of principle rather than favoritism, however. From a disinterested and impartial position, what principles should guide tax policy? One principle that might be suggested is that those who particularly benefit from a specific government service should pay taxes to finance it. This is comparable to buying a particular product in the private sector. In the United States, for example, one pays a fee to enter many national parks; sometimes those who drive on a particular road must pay a toll. This principle cannot be extended too far, however. Apart from the fact that the public regards such "user fees" as a nuisance, most feel that they are already paying enough to government through general tax collections that they are entitled to re-

U.S. OIL POLICY

The policy of the United States with respect to petroleum supply, as we saw in Chapter 6, has been heavily influenced by the interest of the oil-producing companies to drive prices up by fostering the impression of limited and unreliable supply. In the *long term*, supply is limited in the sense that petroleum resources are finite and at some date in the long distant future may actually run out. This presents no cause for alarm, since there are very many other energy sources that can substitute for petroleum. Fuels that are somewhat more expensive than oil, but could readily be substituted, would gradually be used more as increasing scarcity drove up the price of oil.

But in fact the earth's supplies of petroleum are enormous and very far from being exhausted. Many well-meaning people in the general public have been misled, however, by the commonly made statement that proven oil reserves in such and such a country or such and such an area will be exhausted in thirty years, or some similar period of time. The reason why any particular petroleum field is likely to be exhausted in about thirty years is that recovery is optimal when the oil is maintained at a certain level of pressure, and pressures would be too low if a recovery rate were set to last over a period of time much greater than thirty years. Moreover, a "proven" reserve is normally one that is under production. There are vast quantities of "probable" reserves that are not "proven" in this sense.

Panic and feelings of scarcity are generated not only by the prospect of eventual exhaustion of petroleum supplies but by *short-term* interruptions of supply due to economic, political, and technical factors. Because of the possibility of such short-term interruptions of supply, the dogma has become established that the United States should seek not to be dependent on foreign sources of oil. This is in fact an unrealistic objective, since U.S. demand far exceeds domestic supply and there is still no way—even after switching to alternative fuels that could be substituted for oil in the near term—that purchases of foreign oil could be discontinued or even greatly reduced; nor should they be, given the advantages in price and ease of use that oil has over competing fuels.

Moreover, the fact that the oil is of "foreign" provenance does not necessarily mean its supply is less reliable than that produced domestically. "Foreign" Mexican oil, which can easily reach the United States by pipeline, is more reliable than "domestic" Alaskan oil, which needs to be loaded on tankers and then offloaded into pipelines on the California coast, and is thus subject to the hazards of the maritime journey—apart from being considerably more expensive to produce and ship.

ceive the services government provides without facing additional charges. Moreover, many of the services government provides, such as national defense, cannot be charged to individual users, but are used by everyone.

In all developed countries today, tax policy is instead based at least in part on another principle, which is ability to pay. Of course, ability to pay is inevitably part of any tax policy: you can't get blood from a stone, as the saying goes. There is no point in demanding $100,000 in taxes from someone whose income is $10,000. But the more sophisticated forms of tax policy attempt to use ability to pay in order to equalize the hardship faced by taxpayers of different income levels as they pay their tax bills. This means going to a tax system that is *graduated,* or *progressive*, in the sense that higher tax rates are progressively imposed on increments of income so that the wealthier person not only pays more money in tax than the poor person but also pays a higher proportion of his or her income.

The logic behind the progressive tax system is that each increment in income has a decreasing value to the recipient (there is a declining marginal utility of income). Thus the first thousand dollars of income you earn is vitally important; it enables you to buy food. The last thousand dollars of income to a multimillionaire is of trivial importance. Accordingly, the argument goes, the first thousand dollars of income should not be taxed at all—that would impose too great a hardship, meaning that the recipient would have to do without food in order to be able to pay the tax. Successive increments of income would be taxed, at first very lightly, then gradually more heavily, since each additional increment of income would be less vital to the recipient, so that yielding an increasing proportion of it to the government would impose less hardship. In some countries the principle of progressivity was so generally accepted that until recently the marginal rate of income tax, for extremely high incomes, reached 90 percent. A reaction against these extremely high rates took hold in the 1970s and 1980s and the pendulum swung drastically in the other direction, so that before the Clinton administration took office the highest marginal income tax rate in the United States—the rate on the last thousand dollars of the multimillionaire—was only 31 percent.

Of course, income tax is not the only tax modern governments impose on their citizens. This is largely a matter of convenience, tradition, and—quite frankly—of trying to disguise taxes so that taxpayers will not notice they are paying them and therefore will not be inclined to revolt against paying. Logically, it should not matter what taxes are paid "on"—whether on property, or sales, or other activities—because the money used to pay them always comes *out of* income. You may pay a property tax on your house, but you don't sell a bit of your house in order to pay the tax; you pay it out of your income. Taxes can also be disguised by calling them "user fees" or "contributions." The Social Security system, for example, is financed not by a tax but by a contribution. Making a contribution presumably hurts less than paying a tax.

Because of the presence of so many other taxes, an individual's total tax burden may be assessed in an unprogressive, or *regressive*, way even if the income tax itself is progressive. The sales tax, for example, has a regressive incidence; poorer people must spend all of their income, so they must pay a sales tax on most of it. Wealthier people save and invest a lot of their income, on which they therefore don't pay sales tax.

The Social Security system presents an example of a tax that does not merely happen by accident to be regressive, like the sales tax, but is in fact designed to be regressive—that is, to fall more heavily on the poor than on the rich. At the time of writing, the Social Security "contribution" in the United States is 6.2 percent of the first $55,500 of earned income. Additional income above the level of $55,500 pays no social security tax at all. The maximum amount of social security tax paid thus represents a smaller and smaller percentage of income over $55,500 as that income gets larger—the exact definition of regressiveness in taxation. Of course, there are many standard rationalizations for this state of affairs: we have here a contribution, not a tax; Social Security is not a benefits scheme but a quasi-insurance system; the system must be kept "solvent." In fact, this seems to be politically the easiest way of raising the large sum of money required. One could blame public prejudices and misconceptions for a system in which tax collection policy departs from elementary principles of fairness; but one might have hoped that political leaders would not play to these prejudices and misconceptions but would instead try to correct them.

It should be noted that tax policy may not aim only at raising revenue and distributing burdens fairly, but may also be designed to bring about certain behavior by rewarding specific courses of action and penalizing others. A tax deduction or credit, or a reduced rate of tax, may be allowed in order to encourage a particular kind of activity. Of course over time these incentives originally designed to produce behavior that promotes economic growth become "loopholes" in the tax law and may be taken advantage of in ways that do not in fact promote the original purpose.

SPENDING POLICY

The counterpart of tax policy, which determines how money is raised, is policy on government spending. A government politically committed to favor the poorer classes in society tries to derive tax revenue from a graduated tax system whose burden falls more heavily on the wealthy. In its policy on spending, it emphasizes social benefits—spending for schools, medical care, welfare benefits targeted at children, and so on. These kinds of spending are "progressive" in their incidence in that they provide services that the wealthy either do not need, or would be able to buy for themselves. In fact, even where public services are provided for all, people who can afford to do so may prefer to buy those services on the free market, trusting that privately provided services will be superior in quality, less crowded, or patronized by more congenial types of people. If one can afford it, one expects to send children to private schools, for example.

Traditionally, political parties representing the more affluent members of society, such as the Republicans in the United States or the Conservatives in Great Britain, tended to oppose government taxing and spending as such, on the premise that taxation would necessarily be more onerous on the wealthy and spending would be primarily for the benefit of the poor. The reality may depart from the rhetoric, however. The Reagan administration in the United States (1981–89), for example, which was paralleled to some extent by the administration of Margaret Thatcher in Great Britain (1977–91), while maintaining antitaxation and antispending rhetoric, and cutting taxation of the wealthy and spending on the poor, nevertheless increased spending on projects that aided business, particularly industries involved in military production; the increase in relative poverty also led to higher expenditures for social control (e.g., prison construction and the war on drugs).

The fact that, in the United States, government spending for military purposes was substantially raised while taxes on the well-to-do were being cut opened a sizable budget gap, requiring deficit financing. This proved to be something of a benefit program for the investor, as the federal budget deficit was covered by borrowing money through the mechanism of floating Treasury bond issues. This meant that a substantial portion of the budget then became dedicated to paying interest to those who had bought Treasury bonds. Given the increased regressiveness in both taxing and spending, the poor were being denied services in order to transfer money to the wealthy. It could be said that the money to fund government was still being taken from the wealthy as before, but now they were being paid high interest rates for it.

LABOR RELATIONS POLICY

Another area of economic policy on which "left" and "right" disagree is policy on labor relations. Modern democratic states guarantee the right to form unions, and the right to strike. These rights were not won easily by labor; throughout the nineteenth century and even into the twentieth century, people died in defense of the right to unionize as against the conservative view that a labor union was a subversive conspiracy, or the milder legalistic argument that it represented a conspiracy in restraint of trade that could be prohibited under antitrust laws.

It is perfectly true that the use of the bargaining power of organized labor to keep up or raise wages or to improve working conditions constitutes a limitation on the working of the free market. Economists normally view labor as simply another commodity whose price should rise and fall with demand. Wages that cannot be cut at will, like a legally stipulated minimum wage, limit the flexibility necessary for such an adjustment between supply and demand to take place, and result in a less-than-optimal distribution of resources, and less than maximum production. The prounion view is that labor is not just another commodity like soybeans or pig iron; the price of labor is also the income a family needs to feed, clothe, and shelter itself, and there are human rights considerations that justify limits on the action of the free market with respect to wages and conditions of employment. Although the state can play a certain role—for example, in setting minimum wage rates—an active union movement is needed, it is argued, to insure that abuses don't occur in specific workplaces.

There is no doubt that, especially in the early years of the development of the industrial economies, horrific exploitation of labor took place. People familiar only with late-twentieth-century conditions in the developed economies may have a hard time understanding the rationale for labor unions because they are not aware of the brutality of the conditions out of which unions grew. Self-interested or corrupt leadership has often given unions a bad name, but it is also true that examples of such abuse are used against unions by people concerned not with abuses of union power but with any union role at all, who would like to return to the days in which there was no restraint on the abuses that could be committed by employers.

In political discourse generally, a proemployer position lies to the right of the political spectrum, one more prounion on the left. Many well-meaning people who are not personally committed to either a management or an employee view of industrial labor relations feel uncomfortable with the antagonism between employer and worker implicit in existing models of labor relations, and are hopeful that there are other ways to approach such relations that would be better for productivity.

Japanese industry has attempted to foster worker enthusiasm and loyalty to the company, in place of antagonistic management-labor relations, through socializing and inspirational techniques. Outsiders often feel uncomfortable with the authoritarianism and conformism of such techniques, although they have been adopted in branches of Japanese businesses operating outside Japan with apparent success. However, it should be noted that other ingredients in the success of Japanese industrial relations are that companies contribute to employee loyalty by more or less guaranteeing life-long employment without danger of layoffs, unlike companies elsewhere, and that Japanese management pays itself much more modest salaries than are common in Europe and America, thus deemphasizing the gap between management and workers.

Another technique for enlisting workers' loyalty to the company and transcending antagonistic labor-management relations is to give workers a stake in the company's performance, in the form of an annual bonus that varies with the company's profitability. This is often combined with expanding workers' sharing in company decision-making, whether at the actual working level or at that of corporate management. Often cited as a model is the system of *codetermination* long established in the Federal Republic of Germany. Introduced in the aftermath of World War II to limit the power given to the lords of industry who had been implicated in the rise of Nazism, workers were given a share in management through their election of a proportion—usually a third—of the members of company boards of directors. In addition, a company's workforce got to choose the company's director for social affairs, who took charge of the quality-of-life aspects of the enterprise's operations: the company's lunchroom, parking facilities, day care center, and so on. These measures had a salutary effect on industrial relations in Germany and have generally been a source of worker satisfaction. In fact, however, workers' participation on boards of directors has had minimal practical effect, as the labor representatives have typically been co-opted or outmaneuvered by the promanagement members of boards.

Nevertheless, there is a great eagerness to find models of industrial relations that minimize class antagonism, especially among centrist political parties such as the Liberal Democrats in Britain, and Christian Democrats elsewhere. Neither management nor labor are particularly keen on workers' participation in management, however. Employers feel that managers should be free to do what they think right without interference from labor representatives, while labor unions generally dislike measures that will compromise union militancy by leading workers to believe that they can be treated fairly without supporting a strong and vigilant union.

THE PUBLIC/PRIVATE MIX

One of the major issues in both developed and undeveloped countries has been the relative share in the economy of privately and publicly owned enterprises. Because Marx identified the private ownership of "the means of production" as the central feature of capitalism, anticapitalist political forces became identified with a socialism defined as public ownership. This reached its final caricature in the monstrous state enterprises of Stalinism, in which unmotivated workers produced inadequate supplies of poor-quality products that were not what the consumers wanted. Identifying socialism with what actually happened in the Soviet Union certainly makes socialism hard to defend. But the collapse of the Soviet Union and the discrediting of its economic model does not necessarily mean that no defense of state-owned enterprises can be made, or that there are no alternatives to the pure capitalist model. Several points should be taken into account:

- There are ways other than by *socializing industry*—such as the progressive income tax and social insurance measures—to try to soften harsh features of capitalism such as poverty and unemployment.

- Some state-run enterprises, especially in the United States and Western Europe, have actually been efficient and well-managed, and provide necessary services at reasonable cost.

- There are some reasons besides ideological opposition to capitalism for establishing industries under state rather than private control.

- Even in capitalist countries, some enterprises are traditionally run by the state, while even in the most socialized country some activities are left in private hands, so that rather than thinking in terms of extreme situations of total public or private ownership, it makes more sense to think of countries as having different mixes of the two.

Postal services, for example, are a typical state enterprise, as are water supply and street lighting. Commonly, in the countries of Western Europe, utilities and railroads are state enterprises, and indeed passenger rail transport is a state enterprise in the United States (Amtrak). Such state enterprises need not be run as government ministries, on the Soviet model, but can be organized as autonomous corporations in which government happens to be the only shareholder.

Why do governments operate industries when ideological factors are not involved? National security is a common rationale. In many countries armaments industries are state enterprises, since they are intimately related to an activity outside the reach of the free market, the provision of national defense, and state control makes it easier to enforce rules of secrecy. In the United States, arms production is carried on in a quasi-private manner, in which privately held companies are closely supervised, manipulated, and subsidized by the Department of Defense, in a way that hardly represents a genuinely free-market situation.

Sometimes industries are taken into public ownership because they provide an essential service but cannot be operated profitably enough for a private company. This was the case with the railroads in the United States and in Great Britain. Using profitability as a criterion, a private company might maintain only high-volume lines, leaving many towns without service.

Sometimes when industries are "nationalized" it is not a question of providing an essential service but rather of keeping jobs going in a politically sensitive area where other sources of employment are not available. While there is no economic justification for such an action within the logic of the free-market system, governments that have no sympathy with socialism still sometimes take over industries under such circumstances for short-term political advantage. A more economically defensible solution is sometimes possible in such situations, where the company breaks even but does not make enough profit for investors as compared to alternative possibilities. In such a case the company can be reorganized as a cooperative, or shares can be sold to workers, who can thus keep their jobs in a functioning enterprise.

Sometimes state enterprises have been established where a service is a natural monopoly and the danger existed that a private company would be able to exploit consumers because it would have no competitor forcing it to maintain its prices low and its quality high. In such a situation—such as the provision of electricity or natural gas to consumers, where the permanent installation of supply lines is necessary and it is not feasible for consumers to switch from one supplier to another week by week in response to price and quality considerations—the European solution is typically for the service to be provided by a public corporation. In the United States, typically a private corporation exists, but is supervised by a regulatory board in the interest of the consumer. At least that is the legislative intent. In practice, the Public Service Commissions that function in the states to supervise monopoly utility providers are frequently brought under the influence of the companies they are supposed to regulate through the political system, sometimes including the provision of campaign contributions and other forms of personal income to political figures.

Despite the fact that some of these reasons for public ownership may have validity in specific situations, it remains in general true that the advantages of a free-market economy usually provide the more powerful arguments. The renewed interest in free-market ideology that has characterized the last quarter of the twentieth century has led to a powerful international movement in the direction of privatizing enterprises that had been taken into public ownership over the years for various reasons, or sometimes for no apparent reason. Often, in Eastern Europe, the solution adopted is simply to close down the public enterprise as not worth saving and let private companies begin business in that field of activity. Often, however, especially in the West, the state corporation may be a going enterprise. In such cases the corporation can be privatized either by being sold to an already existing private company, or by having shares issued that are sold to the general public while the structure of the corporation remains the same. The corporation's board of directors would then eventually come to be chosen by the shareholders, at least nominally, rather than being appointed by the government.

In the rush to privatize, however, sometimes important considerations get overlooked. If, for example, a state corporation engages in various activities, some of which are profitable and others not, there is likely to be pressure from private business to sell separately the profitable components of the corporation's activities. This occurred when British Railways Corporation sold off the hotels it owned. What this can mean is that the public treasury gets left with money-losing activities in perpetuity, whereas before the partial privatization the public corporation may have been breaking even or making a small profit.

A similar result may occur after privatization, when the corporation's new private management may close down loss-making activities, even where these are publicly desirable. For example, some American counties have turned their public hospitals over to profit-making hospital corporations, which may then discontinue offering service to the poor and uninsured who were formerly treated by the county hospitals as charity patients.

What this means is that care should be taken that public interests and purposes are protected, and that if it is mistaken to socialize all possible industry for ideological reasons, it is also mistaken to privatize automatically for ideological reasons. A reasonable person may conclude that individual cases should be treated on their merits and it is probably wisest to let well enough alone and not let ideological commitments overrule common sense.

DEMAND MANAGEMENT

One of the principal activities of modern governments is that of demand management. Even the most laissez-faire government—one that professes to believe that government should leave the operations of the free market strictly alone—finds itself controlling the level of overall economic activity through its policies on budgeting, taxing, and bank regulation. If government spending increases, more money is put into the economy and more jobs are created. If the government runs a budgetary surplus, however, and takes more money out of the economy by way of taxation than it spends through its budget, then the level of economic activity declines. Government also influences the overall level of economic activity through its regulation of banks, by influencing the interest rates that are charged and other rules governing the extension of credit.

Speaking very generally, governments toward the left end of the political spectrum tend to favor an increase in the rate of economic activity, which creates new jobs and reduces unemployment. Governments toward the right end of the spectrum tend to favor lower rates of economic activity, which will maintain the value of money by acting as a restraining influence on the rise of prices, and keeping interest rates high. The right dislikes inflation most; the left, unemployment. The interests of labor weigh more heavily on the left, those of finance on the right. When demand management was the central issue in British politics during the 1950s, one of the best predictors of whether a voter would choose the Labour party over the Conservatives was whether he or she rated unemployment over inflation as the primary problem facing the economy.

In specific cases, the question gets rather more complicated. The most financially restrained of governments may pump money into the economy to get an expansion going in the months before a general election. Even left-wing governments may put on the economic brakes if inflation looks to be getting out of hand.

Some unorthodox theories about demand management have found their way into government policy in recent years, with generally unfortunate results. The basic relationships were laid out by the great British economist John Maynard Keynes between the two World Wars. Prior to Keynes, government budgeting had usually been treated like private budgeting; it was prudent to run a surplus, and the influence of government spending on the economy was ignored. Keynes argued that government finance was significant in its impact on the overall level of economic activity and that governments should rationally not attempt to balance their budgets at the end of the fiscal year—which is after all an artificial period—but over the whole course of the business cycle. That is, governments should run a budgetary surplus when the economy is operating at full blast, unemployment is very low, and prices are rising. This will take money out of the economy and restrain prices. But government should run a deficit during times of recession, to pump money into the economy and get economic activity going again.

In a word, government policies should be countercyclical; they should endeavor to counteract undesirable aspects of the economy's activity, not reinforce them, as they did at the beginning of the Great Depression. What happened then was that as economic activity declined, so did government tax revenues; under pre-Keynesian theories, that meant governments should reduce their expenditures, which is what was done in most countries; government employees were laid off, thus making the depression worse.

After World War II, Keynes's theories became generally accepted. The world experienced dynamic economic growth with only moderate inflation, and a sustained period of prosperity. Politically speaking, however, it is much easier for a government to run a deficit and spend freely than to cut back its expenditures where necessary. The administration of Lyndon Johnson in the United States led the movement away from Keynesianism during the Vietnam War on the premise that government expenditures did not need to be reduced when the economy was operating at full force, because the government budget would be balanced by means of the much larger intake of taxes that would result from the high levels of economic activity.

Ronald Reagan carried this argument a step further by professing to believe that greater military spending could be financed by increased tax revenues, even while tax rates were being cut. Although this policy led to colossal government budgetary deficits, the idea of cutting taxes proved so popular that politicians shrank from proposing to raise taxes again to bring the budget under control. Meanwhile, the impression that the budgetary deficit was permanently out of control led to the revival of the pre-Keynesian belief that a deficit was always wrong. Ironically, renewed ideological hostility to deficits under any circumstances thus coexisted with the reality of colossal deficits fueled partly by the need to pay interest on money borrowed to pay off previous deficits, so that political hypocrisy and public ignorance grew side by side.

This situation has arisen because governments have reduced taxes, which since the era of Franklin D. Roosevelt were designed to fall more heavily on the wealthy. In a masterpiece of public relations, such taxes were called "progressive," in that the rate of tax increased as one "progressed" up the income ladder. The well-to-do understandably counterattacked against such policies, and were finally successful during the Reagan years, with the result that taxes were drastically cut below the level necessary to finance continuing government operations. Ironically, government continued to get the funds necessary for its operations—although those operations were reduced to the point where grave social ills that might have been prevented were allowed to grow huge and apparently insoluble—primarily from the same source, the well-to-do, but in the form of bonds, which required government to pay substantial sums as interest, rather than as taxes.

This shift in economic policy meant the redistribution of income in a regressive direction, for several reasons: (1) income taxes were reduced, especially on the wealthy; (2) the shortfall in government income was partly made up by increasing regressive taxes, such as the sales tax and social security contributions; (3) in the attempt to move closer to balancing the budget, government expenditures were cut; the programs that were easier to cut were those that benefited those politically weaker (and thus normally poorer); (4) the continuing deficit made it impossible to begin or even to propose new social programs, no matter how badly they were needed; (5) the deficit was financed by borrowing (i.e., by issuing government bonds), so that a lot of what revenue could still be raised went into paying interest to the better-off people who invested in government bonds; (6) foreign purchasers of government bonds, whose continued support was necessary, favored the maintenance of high interest rates and a high valuation of the dollar, which tended to restrict economic growth and promote unemployment.

This set of events requires explanation at a more general level: if we start from the premise that in politics people pursue their interests, how did it happen that policies so opposed to the interests of the majority of the public got adopted? Part of the answer is that economic relationships are complicated, and—at least in the United States—politicians gave up conducting political debate on an accurate but complicated level in favor of oversimplifying issues into demagogic slogans. Another part of the answer has to be that it proved that among the things money could buy was public opinion—no news, surely, in the country that invented public relations. It turns out, that is, that voters, at least sometimes, can be beguiled, bedazzled, or befuddled into voting for candidates likely to support policies opposed to their interests. The techniques are no secret: misleading advertising, personal attacks, and the promotion of "social issues" that mobilize various kinds of prejudice and serve to obscure economic issues. Lincoln said you can't fool all the people all the time; but fooling most of them seems to work a lot of the time. In the more abstract terms used in this book, ideologies originally developed to reflect interests may come in specific cases to be opposed to those interests.

PLANNING

Even if governments try to stay aloof from managing the economy on the premise that it will do best if left alone, the acts of government necessarily affect the economy's performance. In addition simply to adjusting the rules of the credit system or the government's own budget so as to influence the overall level of economic activity, governments also engage in planning activities to influence the future direction the economy will take. Of course, the extreme to which planning reaches is the centralized planning that occurred in the Soviet Union, in which five-year plans were announced that set very specific targets for production for the economy as a whole, industry by industry, and factory by factory. In fact a host of things went wrong with the plans. Shortages and bottlenecks developed, managers resorted to expensive and counterproductive expedients to try to meet their planned targets, incentives in the system were often ineffectual or counterproductive, and consumer satisfaction was low.

In the United States and Britain, planning has generally been in bad repute as destructive of the advantages that come with a free competitive market. Some of those favoring some degree of planning in the West, however, have argued that it is possible to plan *with* the market, not, as happened in the Soviet Union, *against* the market. Planning, that is, need not seek to replace the market system, but can introduce new incentives or disincentives so that in making their own free and self-interested decisions, individuals can be influenced to behave in one way or another. That is what happens in any case in the United States and Western Europe, as people change their behavior to take into account new tax laws, tariff rates, or health and safety regulations. Those favoring planning in conjunction with the free market system—what is sometimes called in the United States "industrial policy"—argue that planning takes place in any case, but it is on a piecemeal basis, with the legislature and individual regulatory agencies introducing all kinds of incentives and disincentives into the system with no overall attempt at coordination to see that they do not conflict with each other or that the overall result guides the economy in the desired direction.

Some developed countries have in fact had great success with systems of coordinated economic planning that work with, and not against, the market. The substantial economic growth France has experienced since World War II, for example, owes a great deal to its system of *indicative planning*, under which the expenditures of government itself, and the incentives and disincentives introduced by monetary and fiscal policy, have been designed to steer the economy into the most productive channels, to take advantage of developing opportunities, and to promote industries in which France expects to have a long-term comparative advantage. Japan, similarly, combines a free market with a government planning mechanism, but one that relies on explicit "guidance" communicated to industrialists by government bureaucrats, and not just on anonymous fiscal and monetary incentives alone. Of course the Japanese style in economic planning is consistent with other norms of Japanese society that emphasize cooperation, authority, discipline, and attention to detail. A feature of the Clinton administration was the attempt to move the United States more in the direction of a coordinated economic strategy than had previously been the case.

KEY TERMS

campaign contributions

graduated (progressive) taxation

regressive taxation

codetermination

socialization of industry

Public Service Commission

demand management

countercyclical

indicative planning

III

INTERNATIONAL
POLITICS

CHAPTER 11

International Relations

© ASHLEIGH BRILLIANT 1990.
SANTA BARBARA

POT-SHOTS NO. 5155.

THERE CAN BE NO MEANINGFUL NEGOTIATIONS, UNTIL YOU REMOVE THE PRESSURE WHICH IS FORCING ME TO NEGOTIATE.

Ashleigh Brilliant

THE NATION-STATE

International relations should logically be discussed at this point in our study, since many of the themes dealt with in previous chapters contribute to the understanding of how international relations works. Although the term commonly used is "international relations," the relations we are concerned with are those among states; it would be more correct to speak of "interstate relations." The assumption is normally made that nations and states are the same thing, and this may be commonly true, especially if the state has been in existence for a long time and has been able to develop feelings of a common history and identity among its citizens, together with the use of a common language. Nevertheless, many cases continue to exist where the state and the nation are not identical. Within multinational states different national groups frequently come into conflict; members of a national group left outside the boundaries of a state can be the cause of irredentist agitation. Today, however, identification between *state*, the political unit, and *nation*, approximately the common-language unit, is taken to be the norm, so that states are automatically assumed to be nation-states.

Yet the nation-state has not always been the fundamental unit in international relations. In some periods of its history, the world has been dominated by multinational empires, by transnational churches, or by tribal units without the apparatus of statehood. After the decay of the Roman Empire, medieval Europe saw a patchwork of sovereignties with, until the Reformation, a vague overriding allegiance owed to the Catholic Church and the pope. One by one, relying sometimes on force, on diplomacy, and even on the doctrine of sovereignty, the modern nation-states arose: Britain, France, Spain, and, late in the nineteenth century, Germany and Italy. The pattern was carried to the overseas colonies, to Latin America and Africa, where lines of convenience drawn on the map hardened over time into boundaries between separate sovereignties and national identities.

State boundaries in Asia, similarly, have arisen out of the interaction between ethnic and linguistic demarcations and the lines imposed on the map by successive empires, of both Asian and European origins; with the difference of the extraordinary longevity of the colossal Chinese Empire, which might be conquered—and even temporarily partitioned—but in the long run retained its identity and, approximately, its borders.

Establishing itself as sovereign means that the nation-state monopolizes the legitimate use of force within its territorial boundaries. It asserts its claim to legitimate authority. As a nation as well as a state, it asserts its claim to be the individual's primary focus of loyalty. The nation-state may demand a portion of our property as tax, it may demand that we abandon our families to serve in its armies, or even that we sacrifice our lives in obedience to its laws.

Thus the fundamental problem in interstate relations arises: if states are sovereign and pursue exclusively only those human interests identified with state interests, how are other human interests to be served? If each state is concerned only with its own interests, how are the interests of the whole species and the whole planet to be defended and promoted? If the leaders of any given state take only that state's interests into account, why should they hesitate to inflict suffering on the citizens of states other than their own?

THE NATIONAL INTEREST

The nature of the problem is clear in terms of the framework with which we have been working in this book. Individuals have a variety of identities and therefore of interests. Only one of those identities is as a citizen of the nation-state, yet, according to the absolutist logic of sovereignty, that is the only interest that will be served. The state demands that you serve it, to the extent of participating in its wars as a soldier, even though you may have responsibilities as a spouse and a parent that conflict with the soldier's role. It may require you to enter into combat against subjects of another state who are your coreligionists, even your personal friends. It pursues its interests without regard to the interests, even the lives, of subjects of another state, even though we may fully sympathize with them as fellow human beings. The nation-state represents only one of my multiple identities; yet it lays claim to all of my loyalty and assumes a monopoly of all power.

The leaders of the state, however, can argue that they will be violating their trust if they concern themselves with any loyalties other than that to the state. They cannot take any other interests into account, in the sense that they stand in a *fiduciary relationship* to the political community organized as a state. They are hired by the state to serve its interests, that is, and may not allow themselves to be influenced by other considerations; just as a stockbroker retained by an individual violates his legal responsibilities if he allows himself to be influenced by considerations other than the financial interests of his client.

Let's assume it is prior to 1991 and you tell your stockbroker to invest your funds where they secure the highest short-term rate of return. That may be provided, let us say, by South African government bonds. If he does not invest in those bonds because he feels it would be wrong to provide any support to a government pursuing what he considers to be the immoral policy of apartheid, and instead invests the funds in other bonds that provide a lower rate of return, then your broker has exceeded his responsibilities and violated his trust. Are not leaders of the government of a nation-state in a similar position? Is not their job only to promote the material interests of their constituents?

APARTHEID

Although segregation of blacks from whites had been widely practiced in South Africa previously, when the Nationalist Party came to power in 1948 it imposed a systematic compulsory policy of *apartheid* (pronounced "a-part-haydt"), or "apartness" which not only segregated whites from blacks, but in many respects established separate areas for Asians and "colored" (that is, mulatto) people. The system lacked even the pretense of "separate but equal" facilities that was used as a cover for segregation in the United States at the time, but was based on the clear assumption of white political and economic supremacy. Although blacks constituted at the time over two-thirds of the South African population, only 12 percent of the land area was set aside for black ownership.

The system involved internal passports, heavy penalties for violation of a myriad of rules, many of them petty and illogical even in terms of the system itself, and a prohibition of intermarriage. Apartheid was finally abandoned in principle by the F. W. de Klerk government in 1991, although the intention of the ruling Nationalist Party was clearly to maintain the social and economic position of the Dutch-descended Afrikaner population in more internationally acceptable ways. A principal reason for the change was international economic pressure. The first nonracial elections, held in 1994, saw the African National Congress become the largest party and a black president, Nelson Mandela, elected.

In the classic model of the free-market economy, individuals pursue their own interests but the resultant economic activity "as if guided by an invisible hand" results—given some assumptions—in the greatest material welfare for the greatest number. To be sure, a few government regulations, such as the prohibition of price-fixing, are necessary for the model to work in this manner. Is it possible to organize the world of sovereign states in such a manner that competitive state behavior will nevertheless result in the greatest good for the whole human race, rather than leading to war and destruction?

THE BALANCE OF POWER

In traditional international relations thinking, an affirmative answer to that question is possible. There is a self-regulating model of the world of sovereign states analogous to the self-regulating model of the free-market economy. The mechanism in interstate relations is similar to the one Madison recommended for a national political system: it is that ambition be checked by ambition, interest be balanced against interest. This system of checks and balances in the international arena is known as the balance of power. How it works is that each state, jealous of its autonomy and sovereignty, will be on the lookout against any state that seems to be trying to extend its hegemony. Perhaps individually a state might not be able to withstand an attack or an ultimatum from a state trying to dominate the world; but together, in alliance, states will be able to put together enough military force to be able to defeat the hegemonic state if it should try to invade or annex one of them. Thus, as states rise and fall in power, alliances will shift so that a combination of states will always form a defensive alliance against any one state that threatens to rule the world. During the seventeenth, eighteenth, and nineteenth centuries, politics in Europe was managed along balance-of-power lines, with Britain shifting from one defensive alliance to another to the extent that it became known as "perfidious Albion."

Circumstances make it more feasible for a balance-of-power system to act so as to check aggressive war at some times rather than at others. During the period of superpower confrontation known as the Cold War, the United States and the Soviet Union so far outweighed other states that a balance between them was maintained more by the weapons each could array than by the alliance partners they could enlist.

Balance-of-power politics do not necessarily avoid war all the time. Sometimes the aggressive power is not deterred by the opposing coalition, generally because of the miscalculation or irrationality of the leader of the aggressive power. Of course, it could be said in general that if leaders of states always acted rationally and with adequate information, wars would never be fought, since the state that is going to lose the war would realize that fact and would instead negotiate the best deal it could instead of fighting to defeat.

Nevertheless, the balance of power does have a role to play in moderating interstate politics. Moreover, the balance of power exists not only in the military dimension but also in the economic. A coalition that can arrange an economic boycott of an aggressive state, especially if it can deny it a crucial ingredient of its war effort such as petroleum, can have a potent deterrent effect.

BUREAUCRACY AND DEMOCRACY IN FOREIGN POLICY

Perhaps the phenomenon of bureaucratic behavior mitigates pursuit of national interest. The model of states pursuing their national interest presupposes that officials, elected and appointed, act in the public interest, as their formal roles require. As we know from studying bureaucracy, however, public servants promote not only the interests that their formal roles require, but also those that derive from their other identities—in other words, they promote their individual careers and the interests of their organizations. At the same time, powerful pressure groups are attempting to get the public interest defined in such a way as to reflect their private interests. So in practice countries deviate from what you or I might say were their national interests. This doesn't help in solving the problem, though, because nations continue to pursue competitively and unscrupulously what they *define* as their national interests, even though various deformations reflecting particular individual and group interests have entered into the way those national interests were defined.

Perhaps in a democracy, though, the message that the people have a variety of identities and thus of interests not exhausted by their interest as citizens of the state, transmitted through their legislative representatives, can exercise restraint on the single-minded state-centered logic of the executive branch. Can the independent role of legislatures, as the people's representatives, bring moderation and balance to world politics? A little, perhaps; but the logic of the presumed requirements of the conduct of foreign policy, such as for secrecy, act so as to strengthen the executive in relation to the legislature, the courts, and the institutions of accounting and control.

It is in foreign policy especially that a constitutional system of checks and balances is most likely to break down and the executive branch to be given virtually a free hand, which means that it is all too likely that colossal mistakes will be committed; that actions will be arbitrary, without adequate thought and consultation; that arrogance will be encouraged; and that there will be little check on the substitution of politicians' career interests for the public interest.

A mystique of the necessity for secrecy envelops any discussion of military affairs and foreign intelligence-gathering; but secrecy requirements can be made to apply to other phases of the conduct of international relations as well. This can be taken to mean that members of the legislature cannot be brought fully into participation in the making of foreign policy, and that much policy has to be made in secrecy by executive branch officials. Moreover, any policy involving the moving of troops becomes infused with the rules for discipline, secrecy, and instantaneous decision-making that are the norm in military organizations.

To be sure, some constraints on executive power remain, in the voting of budgets by the legislature and in informal consultation with legislative leaders. In the United States the Constitution requires that treaties be approved by the Senate, which encourages the executive to keep Senate leaders informed in areas where a treaty may eventually result. But constitutional and legislative restraints are frequently evaded by the executive branch. For example, the U.S. Constitution stipulates that only Congress may make a declaration of war. Nevertheless, presidents (most especially during the twentieth century, although the practice was begun by Thomas Jefferson) have fought wars without a congressional declaration, simply using their powers as commanders-in-chief of the armed forces, clearly an evasion of the constitutional mandate. In Jefferson's day, this was merely a question of naval action against North African pirates, while for Theodore Roosevelt and William Howard Taft this meant sending a small contingent of marines into a Caribbean island. Harry Truman fought a major war in Korea, while Presidents Kennedy, Johnson, and Nixon involved the United States in a protracted and unsuccessful war in Vietnam without the Congress ever making a declaration of war. In each of the latter cases, however, Congress supported the president's actions by passing resolutions and voting funds—although on occasion Congress's assent to the president's actions was secured by his misrepresenting the facts to them, as Lyndon Johnson did in the Tonkin Bay incident.

Reluctant to become again bogged down in a military adventure following the failure in Vietnam, Congress has tried to cover similar contingencies by legislation. The War Powers Act requires the president to notify Congress and secure congressional approval when circumstances arise in which he intends to use force, but President Ronald Reagan successfully evaded the provisions of the Act and misrepresented to Congress his administration's thinly disguised undercover wars in Central America.

Woodrow Wilson argued that democracies were less likely to go to war than authoritarian regimes, and believed that by breaking up the old Austro-Hungarian and Ottoman Empires, and by converting Germany from an empire to a republic, when those states were defeated in World War I, he was contributing to the creation of a world without war. Wilson had a good point: dictators are less subject to rational calculation, more intent on personal glory, and less heedful of the human cost of war, than democratic regimes can be expected to be. Certainly World War I had its origins in the rival dynastic ambitions of the German, Austro-Hungarian, and Russian Empires, and in the autocratic incompetence of the German emperor, Wilhelm II. World War II was begun by a dictatorial regime in Germany, allied with dictatorships in Italy and Japan.

> ## THE END OF EMPIRES
>
> World War I was the end of four empires that occupied Eastern and Central Europe: the Russian, German, Ottoman, and Austro-Hungarian. Revolution ended the Russian Empire, and defeat in the war the other three. Each of the empires had been ruling over peoples of nationalities different from that of the ruling group and, in keeping with the doctrines of nationalism and the nation-state that were dominant at the time, those regions were reconstituted as nation-states. Under the leadership of the victorious powers, dominated by the figure of Woodrow Wilson of the United States, the Treaty of Versailles, which put an end to the war, established new states such as Yugoslavia and Czechoslovakia; Latvia, Lithuania, and Estonia were reconstituted, and Albania, Romania, and Hungary were given their independence. Many of these states were to lose their autonomy again under the onslaught of the Nazi advance and the reconstitution of the Russian Empire in the form of the Soviet Union. At the end of World War II, however, the states subjugated by Hitler's Germany were again given their autonomy.
>
> With the breakup of the Soviet Union, another process of fission set in. But this time there was no Versailles conference to supervise the drawing up of boundary lines, and to see that smaller nationalities that had some historic connection were grouped together in federations such as Yugoslavia. In fact, the reverse process took place. In the last decade of the twentieth century, the process of national subdivision seemed to go on and on like the demonstration of a mathematical *reductio ad absurdum*.

Of course, not all democracies are peaceful and not all dictatorships begin wars. Stalin tried desperately to avoid going to war against Hitler; Francisco Franco, the dictator of Spain, stayed out of World War II despite Hitler's attempts to get him involved. Nor should we become complacent about the peacefulness of democracies; democracies can be misled by disingenuous leaders. Lyndon Johnson was not the first president to organize congressional and popular support for belligerent action by misrepresenting the facts. In the 1840s, President James K. Polk set up frontier clashes with Mexican troops that he could blame on the Mexicans and use as an excuse for an aggressive war to conquer Mexican territory (although Congressman Abraham Lincoln opposed the war and Henry David Thoreau went to jail in Concord, Massachusetts, rather than pay a tax that would help finance it). Moreover, public opinion can sometimes be excited and led astray by jingoistic newspaper campaigns, the classical instance being how William Randolph Hearst inflamed the U.S. public by sensationalist and misleading reporting in 1898 so as to provoke war between the United States and Spain over Cuba.

Because of cases like the role of the press and public opinion in bringing on the Spanish-American War, some observers have argued that public opinion in a democracy is necessarily unreliable or warlike; and that public opinion and the representatives of that opinion in Congress should be excluded from the making of foreign policy, which has subtleties that can only be understood by a small elite of practitioners of Realpolitik (a policy based on the cold calculation of national interest, unqualified by constraints of ideology, moral principle, or humanitarian considerations). In fact, in line with these arguments, U.S. foreign policy since the end of World War II has been dominated by an "establishment" of elite foreign policy specialists, characterized ironically by the writer David Halberstam as "the best and the brightest." While this elite had many successes, its arrogance and narrow-mindedness contributed to many failures of U.S. policy, of which Vietnam was only one. True to the dictum of Friedrich Engels (not Hegel, as is usually said) that history repeats itself, with the original tragedy being replayed as farce, the national security institutions and covert operations mechanisms created by this professional establishment of Ivy League foreign policy specialists and Wall Street lawyers in the Truman era ended up in the hands of the clownish operatives of the 1980s—who were certainly anything but the best and the brightest—who blundered their way through such black comedies as providing arms to the Ayatollah Khomeini in Iran, blowing up eighty innocent bystanders in Beirut in a failed attempt to assassinate a terrorist leader, and organizing and financing "anti-Communist" forces in Central America that massacred peasants, stole U.S. funds, and smuggled illegal drugs into the United States. This was covert policymaking carried to the absurdest of extremes. One can only hope that the post–Cold War era will see a diminution in the insistence on secrecy, irresponsibility, and violence. Perhaps what has been principally wrong with U.S. foreign policy in recent years has not been too much democracy but too little.

"REALISM" AND "IDEALISM" IN U.S. FOREIGN POLICY

The theoretical debate over the appropriate foreign policy for the United States has often been expressed as a conflict between "realism" and "idealism." "Realism," a term apparently adapted from the German Realpolitik, presents itself as a hard-headed, unsentimental pursuit of the national interest; "idealism," in this perspective, is a mushy, confused attempt to impose wishful thinking on the world. As the reader will readily appreciate, this model is at odds with the approach taken in this book, which treats ideals as not opposed to interests, but as a generalized statement of interests. The difference between the two perspectives really lies in whose interests are to be given priority. In the realist approach, the priority interest is that of the nation-state, while the approach the realists characterize as idealist puts as its priority the interests of individuals and of the species as a whole. Realism per se is not a factor. Any objective may be pursued more or less realistically; realism should more properly be said to characterize means rather than ends. If we wanted to play word-games, we could argue that the individual and the species are entities in many senses more real than the nation-state, which is a kind of legal fiction. But the point remains that national leaders are hired by the nation-state, so they can be expected to put the national interest first.

However, it is not necessarily clear how the concept of national interest should translate into specific interests in a specific case, and in fact what passes for the national interest is very frequently the interest of the more potent economic pressure groups, such as the oil lobby or the military-industrial complex, which have enough political or bureaucratic influence to get their objectives anointed as national interests. There may be an additional irony involved in incorporating the interests of a corporation into the set of national interests, since often the corporation is in fact multinational in ownership and management. On one occasion, the Nixon administration brought pressure on the Peruvian government to settle a dispute in favor of the International Petroleum Corporation, which turned out to be of Canadian and not U.S. nationality, insofar as a corporation can even be said to have a nationality.

The doctrine of realism, with its single-minded state-centeredness, had a long intellectual tradition in Germany and Austria, and began its career in the United States in the writings of German and Austrian emigré scholars. Realism is essentially an extrapolation from the doctrine of sovereignty, constructed from its basic premises with the logical thoroughness known in German as *Grundlichkeit*. This doctrine was congenial to the circumstances of Prussia, an artificially constructed state with no natural boundaries, whose essential nature was not as a society but as a state—that is, whose characteristic features were its monarch, its ruling class, its military, and its bureaucracy, without which it would have been hard to distinguish from any of the other many German states that existed before a united Germany was created in 1870. Ironically, again, for what is real and what is ideal, the Prussian state and its successor, the German Empire, were highly romanticized and idealized constructs, and the state's "official story"—the monarch, as Frederick the Great put it, was only "the first servant of his people," the Prussian state was humanity's highest form of social development, as Hegel wrote, or even the actualization of Kant's categorical imperative—could give rise to a doctrine that was realist only in a contorted and counterintuitive sense.

The central problem we are dealing with here, however, is not the authenticity or spuriousness of the terms used, nor the intellectual history of a particular concept, but the irreducible facts that still in the world today what power does not lie with multinational corporations and international financial institutions lies in the hands of the leaders of national governments, and that the nation-state commands armies, can impose criminal penalties on those who disobey its laws, and runs educational systems that indoctrinate people with loyalty to itself. If we wish to be realistic in our idealism, so to speak, we have to justify in terms of national interest any purposes we may wish to promote that differ from the self-aggrandizement of the nation-state. Any other interests that are to be served must be shown to be also national interests.

In practice, a certain amount of this goes on by subterfuge—tenderhearted people in positions of influence manage somehow to get it declared in the interest of the nation-state to feed hungry children or to oppose the torturing of political prisoners, no matter what passports the individuals involved may hold, just as the representatives of some corporations manage to get their profitability included as a vital national interest. But for conscientious theorists, this is not good enough. Is there a way in which the interest of humanity in peace, democracy, liberty, and welfare can be shown to be in the interest of the United States, so that the most loyal foreign policy bureaucrat, following national policy guidelines scrupulously, can act so as to promote those objectives? If the answer is yes, this would provide a much more reliable way of promoting such objectives than to accept the view that they are inconsistent with the realistic pursuit of national interest but should be pursued anyway.

In fact, a powerful argument can be made that normally it is indeed in the narrow self-interest of the United States to promote world peace, justice, and welfare. An ideological doctrine that reconciles fundamental U.S. national interests with the interests of people of other countries would feature the following arguments:

1. It makes sense for the United States to promote democratic governments elsewhere in the world, since governments based on the same principles tend to sympathize with each other. Democratic governments sympathize with other democratic governments. This has been true since the Peloponnesian War, when the Athenians established democracies in the city-states they conquered, and the Spartans oligarchies.

2. Governments that do the bidding of the United States only because their leaders are opportunistic or bribed are unreliable, and are likely in the future, or even covertly today, to be pursuing some policies at odds with the interests of the United States. This was seen in extreme form in the case of Manuel Noriega of Panama, removed from power in a U.S. military operation ordered by President George Bush, who was working as a sort of "double agent" for both the United States and Cuba, although his primary loyalty was to his bank account.

3. Democracies are less likely to fight wars and engage in foreign adventures. In fact, when ostensible democracies engage in warlike foreign adventures, it usually happens that their governments have evaded or subverted their own democratic procedures in order to do so. Constitu-

tional democratic procedures are an inhibitor of international mischief-making.

Democracies may intervene abroad out of generous impulses in ways that are not thought through and may have adverse consequences. However, they are much less likely to fight premeditated wars of aggression.

4. The abiding U.S. foreign policy tradition of opposing restrictions on international trade (the "open door" policy) has generally promoted American economic interests, since U.S. businesses were better able to compete in an unrestricted market. (However, exceptions were made in the policy when it seemed clear that specific American interests would be hurt by it.) As a general ideological principle, the "open door" is in the interest of people everywhere because on the whole unimpeded free trade promotes general prosperity, as Adam Smith showed 200 years ago. Moreover, as Josef Schumpeter argued more recently, capitalism promotes world peace, not only because it gives people an economic interest in getting along with each other instead of fighting each other, but also because capitalism replaced the preexisting monarchic and feudal systems, which supported an aristocratic military class that had an interest in fighting wars. However, there are very real human costs imposed in an abrupt transition from protection to free trade, and consideration should always be given to transitory steps to stretch out and cushion adverse effects.

5. There is a U.S. economic interest in supporting higher standards of living abroad. Lower standards of living mean that goods can be produced more cheaply and undersell American products on world markets. For this reason, it was sound U.S. policy in the 1960s and 1970s to finance the American trade union federation, the AFL-CIO, in promoting union organization abroad. Unfortunately, the program was taken over by the Central Intelligence Agency (CIA), which used it as a cover to recruit foreign agents, bribe officials, and subvert leftist governments.

6. Visible support by the United States for policies of welfare and social justice abroad creates a reservoir of goodwill toward the United States. Commenting on the U.S. policy of supporting military dictators in Latin America during the 1950s, Venezuelan president Rómulo Betancourt said "I don't understand why the United States cultivates the dictators who will pass and not the people who will remain."

Betancourt's comment raises another point. Foreign ministries often set their sights on short-term day-to-day objectives tied in with the fate of specific individual political leaders, who are favored or disfavored depending on their attitudes toward current U.S. policy objectives. Governments get punished or rewarded as they go along with the policy *du jour*—to break relations with Cuba, to vote against a U.N. resolution condemning Israel—but lasting solutions demand attention to the fundamental underlying forces of history. Subverting a popular government in Iran in order to reimpose the monarchy, or one in Guatemala in order to impose rule by a military dictator backed by a handful of large landowners, as orchestrated by the CIA for the U.S. government in the 1950s, are examples of policies that try to work against, not with, the direction in which history is moving. Otto von Bismarck once said that one cannot create the forces of history; one can only jump aboard and hope to steer. And former Secretary of State Dean Acheson wrote with great insight that the statesman has to be a gardener, not a mechanic.

7. As the leading world power, the United States is likely to be drawn into fighting in situations of conflict that may start out not involving any obvious U.S. interests. It is less costly and more effective to play a role in promoting just, and therefore long-lasting, settlements of disputes in their early stages, even those in which the United States apparently has no stake, rather than to allow them to escalate and spread until the United States finally gets sucked into an impossible situation The situation that developed in 1994 and 1995 in the former Yugoslavia illustrates this point clearly.

KEY TERMS

national interest

fiduciary relationship

apartheid

balance of power

War Powers Act

Treaty of Versailles

Realpolitik

realism

idealism

CHAPTER 12

Nationalism, Imperialism, and Hegemony

© ASHLEIGH BRILLIANT 1992
SANTA BARBARA

<u>POT-SHOTS</u> NO. 5850.

THE
NATIONAL
FLAG

ALWAYS MAKES
AN
EXCELLENT
BLINDFOLD.

Ashleigh
Brilliant

The world today is organized on the basis of nation-states—that is, states whose populations approximate national communities. The definitions of what constitutes a *nation* vary a great deal, since for every definition offered an exception can be found. For example, if a nation is defined as a set of people bound together by a common language, one can cite the case of Switzerland, where there are four official national languages; if a common territory is the criterion used, an exception must be made for the Jewish people, which lacked a territory until the State of Israel was created in 1948. What this means is that the only necessary defining characteristic of a nation is subjective—a psychological consciousness of national identity.

Although this subjective identification with the nation is the only indispensable defining characteristic, it is not an arbitrary feeling but reflects and grows out of several typical objective facts, the most common of which are use of a common language and a history of common experiences. Thus the set of nations in the world is not fixed; new nations come into existence, and old ones sometimes disappear. An Arab Palestinian nationality has developed over the last half-century, for example, reinforced by the struggle to establish a state free of Israeli domination.

Sometimes, that is, a new *state* can come into being to reflect the existence of a nationality that already exists, as in the case of Israel. Alternatively, however, the nationality may be created out of the common experiences lived through the years by people who happen to be drawn into the boundaries of a specific state quite arbitrarily. Thus German-speaking Austrians were left outside the boundaries of the German Empire when that was formed in 1870. Their separate existence over the years reinforced the concept of Austrian nationality as something distinct from German nationality, despite the attempt by Adolf Hitler, himself born an

Austrian, to erase the distinction by annexing Austria to Germany from 1938 to 1945. If the East German "German Democratic Republic," on the territory occupied by the Red Army in 1945 and converted into a separate state in 1949, had survived, eventually a separate East German nationality would have developed out of those years of separate existence.[1] Mikhail Gorbachev's abandonment of the maintenance by force of Russian control of Eastern Europe, however, left the East Germans free to rejoin the West German Federal Republic.

ADOLF HITLER (1889–1945)

Born in Braunau, Austria, Hitler became chancellor (head of government) of Germany in 1933. He ruled until 1945, committing suicide as Germany faced defeat in World War II, which he had brought about. Appealing through emotional oratory to a population humiliated by defeat in World War I, crushed first by a runaway inflation as the 1920s began and then by a world depression as they ended, Hitler built his National Socialist (Nazi) Party to the largest in popular votes by 1932. It never reached a majority in free elections, however, and Hitler was appointed chancellor by President Paul von Hindenburg, an aging former general, only as a result of the intrigues of right-wing politicians who hoped to use Hitler's popular support to promote their own fortunes.

Hitler used the republic's own constitutional procedures to destroy it, creating a dictatorship bent on a war of revenge against France and Britain and of conquest in Central and Eastern Europe. Early successes in 1939 and 1940 were followed by reverses when a quick conquest of Russia proved impossible and when the United States entered the war in 1941. Hitler's grandiose dreams of a "new order" in Europe based on rule by the Germanic ("Aryan") race over enslaved Slavs and others included the confinement in concentration camps under terrible conditions of political opponents of the regime—leftists, homosexuals, Jews, and Gypsies—and the subsequent organized mass killings of Gypsies and some 6 million Jews in his "final solution" to the Jewish question, which became known as "the Holocaust."

All over Africa nations are in the process of creation, consisting of sets of people that happened to live within the boundary lines drawn arbitrarily on the map of Africa by European colonial powers meeting a hundred years ago at the Congress of Berlin. This process is still in an early stage, however, and most people's primary identification is probably still with their locality and their language group, which causes conflict both within and between states.

The experience of Africa is not unique in this regard. The boundary lines of the early states of Europe did not coincide with the boundaries between

---

MIKHAIL SERGEYEVICH GORBACHEV (1931–   )

The tragic last ruler of the Soviet Union, Gorbachev became secretary general of the Soviet Communist party—the dominant figure in the country's government—with the conviction that the totalitarian system established by Josef Stalin, even in the watered-down version presided over by Stalin's successors, had to end. The stagnation of the era in which Leonid Brezhnev ruled the county (1964–82) was characterized by an economic machine slowly producing less and less, and even that of goods that the consumer did not want, by a wasteful and dangerous military machine, and by a political discourse of pompous lies that nobody believed. Refusing to use military force to repress the Soviet satellites of Eastern Europe, Gorbachev allowed them to recover their autonomy. He closed down the Soviet military adventure in Afghanistan and negotiated far-reaching arms-control agreements with the United States. At home, he moved in the direction of perestroika, the restructuring of Soviet political and economic institutions, and glasnost, openness in politics.

Gorbachev became a tragically doomed figure as his unwillingness to use repression allowed those opposed to his programs to flourish, and the example of the regained autonomy of the East European satellites encouraged minority nationalities within the Soviet Union itself to assert their autonomy; as he attempted to dismantle the command economy without having a clear idea of how to achieve the mixed social market economy he wanted to put in its place; and as his attempt to balance off old-style Soviet politicians and bureaucrats against new liberal and democratic forces while maintaining political control himself succeeded in alienating both sides. The incompetent rightist leaders who attempted a coup against him in 1990 failed to secure power for themselves but they managed to dislodge it from Gorbachev's hands, and he was unable to regain his authority.

---

people of different national identities. Territories were conquered or bartered among rulers without consulting the wishes, or considering the ethnic identities, of their inhabitants, while several early states were collections of dissimilar territories that monarchs had happened to acquire through inheritance or marriage. Moreover, the motivation of rulers in targeting new territories for acquisition was not particularly to unite people of similar language and other characteristics, but often only strategic: to attain defensible boundaries along a river or a range of mountains, for example. Thus the formation of a nationality may follow rather than precede the establishment of a state. The Welsh and the Scots consider themselves quite distinct from the English, even within contemporary Britain. But the English themselves are an amalgam of Angles, Saxons, Jutes, Celts, Danes, and Normans.

THE CREATION OF NATIONAL UNITY

Modern states try to create a strong national consciousness among their citizens through the promotion of symbols such as a national flag and a national anthem, but especially by instituting programs of education in the early grades which glorify national history and constitute a source of national consciousness and pride. Much of this patriotic history taught in the schools has, at least to an outsider, a slightly ridiculous air to it. Children are taught a whitewashed version of history, in which national leaders embodied all the virtues and state policy was always unselfish and noble.

PREJUDICE

Normally, an important component of one's identity is identification with a particular ethnic group, which requires a conceptualization of the boundaries of that group and the identification of other groups as different and alien. In itself, this need not occasion hostility to different sets of people, but that does sometimes follow. Hostility to other ethnic groups may grow out of a sense of historical grievance, passed on in the stories of older people. It may also develop out of personal experience or observation, when one or two instances of unwelcome behavior by members of a particular ethnic, racial, or religious group are taken to reflect a permanent characteristic of all members of that group.

One antidote to prejudice is a sophisticated understanding of what kinds of behavior can be expected generally of human beings in given sets of circumstances (such as discrimination and deprivation), how much attitudes and behaviors reflect cultural patterns, the role that class and education play in behavior, and so on. However, the best single antidote to prejudice and discrimination is an individualist conception of society, in which individuals are not prejudged and opportunities are not denied them on the basis of what someone else of similar identity may or may not have done, but in which each individual is allowed a chance to participate in the full range of the activities of society and the economy and is judged only on the basis of his or her own performance. The same comments apply to prejudice based on gender as to that based on ethnicity.

There is also a sinister side to the state's attempt to foster a common national identity. *Genocide*, the mass killing of people of minority nationalities, often in order to have a single common nationality for all citizens, has occurred many times during the twentieth century. The most notorious case is that of Hitler's slaughter of the Jews and Gypsies of Europe. The most recent is the "ethnic cleansing" conducted by Serbs trying to build a greater Serbia out of the ruins of the former federal state of Yugoslavia by killing Bosnian Muslims and frightening the survivors into fleeing their homes. Less known are the several massacres of Armenians resident in

Turkey that took place over the last century, the most atrocious in 1914. The tyrant of the Dominican Republic, Rafael Trujillo, ordered the massacre of all Haitians living in the Dominican Republic in 1937. Stalin followed the ancient Incas of Peru in trying to create a homogeneous nationality by large-scale transfer of populations from one part of the empire to another, cutting them off from their roots and mixing them with people of other ethnic identities. People of Turkish origin were forced by the Bulgarian government of Todor Zhivkov, ousted in 1989, to adopt Bulgarian names. The Turkish government itself long denied the existence of the Kurdish nationality within Turkey and prohibited the use of the Kurdish language in public.

Even without such compulsion, the passage of time is likely to lead to the greater ascendancy of the majority language and identification with the nation-state rather than with a minority ethnic subculture. The experience of living for some time under a common government, subject to the same laws, exposed to the same messages through the mass communications media, and experiencing the same set of economic ups and downs, provides the basis for a growing national identity.

This point is illustrated negatively by the difficulties of forging a common national identity in Canada. There are two official languages, English and French, which embody different cultures; but an additional inhibitor of the growth of a strong national identity is that the Canadian population is spread out in a vast territory while the main cities are stretched in a line not far north of the border with the United States. As a result, a Canadian city is likely to be closer to an American city than it is to other cities in Canada. Many Canadians are more aware of what is going on in the United States than they are of what is going on elsewhere in Canada.

NATIONALITY AND STATE BOUNDARIES

A host of problems arise where the boundaries of the nation and of the state do not coincide. These problems are of several types. Where one large *ethnic group* coexists with a smaller one, it is all too likely that the majority ethnic group will monopolize positions of power and discriminate against the minority. Where distinct national groups of approximately equal numbers coexist, however, outright conflict and civil war are always a possibility, as the tragic recent history of Lebanon illustrates, unless an agreement is reached by the leaders of the different national groups to share offices. Arend Lijphart has analyzed the circumstances in which such an agreement can prevent conflict, under the name of *consociational democracy*.

Where the minority ethnic group is concentrated in a specific geographic area, it may campaign for *secession* from the national community and the establishment of its own state. Sometimes the demand is made not for secession but only for autonomy—that is, local self-government. Typically, however, the central authorities take the view that autonomy opens the door to eventual secession and are therefore reluctant to concede such autonomy. Where members of the minority nationality occupy territory contiguous to a national border across which lies a state in which their fellow nationals are in the majority, that neighboring state may seek to annex the region in question. This is known as *irredentism,* after the Italian *irredenta* or "unredeemed territories," which was the name given by Italian patriots to Italian-speaking areas of Austria not included in the Italian national state at the time of its unification late in the nineteenth century.

However, if the question of defensible national boundaries is ignored and states are established solely on the basis of the nationality of the people included in them, the resulting state may not have boundaries enabling it to defend itself against the ambitions of its neighbors. This was the fate of the small states of Central and Eastern Europe, established in 1919 by the Treaty of Versailles that ended World War I. Unified national states—Yugoslavia, Czechoslovakia, Poland, Hungary, Romania—were established out of the debris formed from the breakup of the Turkish and Austro-Hungarian Empires. Located between the giant states of Germany and Russia, however, the fate of the small Central European states was to be subjugated first by Germany, then by Russia. Now that the Russians have given up their control of Eastern Europe, these states will no doubt come under the economic influence of a powerful reunited Germany. This time, however, it will surely be a more mature and democratic Germany, itself anchored within the institutions of a European community, which has no need to flatter its vanity by military conquest.

IMPERIALISM AND HEGEMONY

Although legally each state government is sovereign within its jurisdiction, in fact it is quite common that the government of a smaller state is dominated by the government of a larger one. This relationship can take several forms. The most obvious form is imperialism. While it is true that "imperialism" may be used to signify various types of control or influence—for example, economic imperialism or cultural imperialism—the primary meaning of the term is political.

There is a great deal less overt political imperialism in the world today than in that of a hundred years ago, when Britain and France divided between them control of most of Africa, and the British Empire girdled the world so that "the sun never set on the British Empire"—meaning that the sun was always overhead somewhere where the Union Jack was flying from the flagpoles. Political imperialism took two distinct forms: "direct rule" by representatives of the imperial power, with a viceroy or governor-general at the head of the local administration, whose upper reaches were staffed by nationals of the imperial power; and "indirect rule," under which the indigenous political authorities were left in place and the imperial power ruled by having an advisor who would make the wishes of his government known to the local chief. As far as ordinary citizens were concerned, they were subject to rule by the traditional local authority structure, and they may not have been fully aware, under the system of indirect rule, that the chief was acting under orders. This method was generally less expensive for the imperial power, which could also defend itself on the premise that it was not arrogantly changing local practices to conform to foreign models.

An even less obvious and intrusive form of authority is that of hegemony. A major power may have a "sphere of influence," such as the Soviet Union had in Eastern Europe, or France has with respect to its former African colonies, where there is no overt recognition of an imperial relationship. The representative of the hegemonic power is its ambassador. The forms of sovereignty are respected; legally the ambassador is merely one among many ambassadors of foreign countries. He or she does not give orders to the local government, but rather makes suggestions (which are always followed). This kind of situation, in which the power of the metropolitan government is implied rather than being openly acknowledged, is hegemony.

A CASE STUDY IN HEGEMONY: THE UNITED STATES AND THE CARIBBEAN

During the twentieth century the United States has been the hegemonic power as far as Central America and the Caribbean are concerned. The Monroe Doctrine, generally presented in U.S. schools and the public media as an act by which United States government defended Latin American countries from European imperialism, is regarded in Latin America as the announcement of U.S. hegemony in the region, the United States wanting no rival to its preeminence in the hemisphere. In fact the Monroe Doctrine was not imposed in South America, and the British colonized the Falkland Islands subsequent to it. But the Doctrine was fairly well enforced in the "backyard" of the United States—that is, in the Caribbean and Central America.

In the hegemonic relationship, the local government acts on its own so long as it does not transgress the limits acceptable to the hegemonic power. Now different governments of the United States have set those limits rather differently, with some U.S. administrations tending to intervene less in the internal affairs of other countries. Moreover, U.S. presidents vary in the objectives they pursue in the region. Some U.S. governments stress the achievement of democracy and the respecting of human rights, while others have only strategic or economic concerns. In general, how-

---

THE MONROE DOCTRINE

The Monroe Doctrine was the work of Secretary of State John Quincy Adams, but was announced by President James Monroe in 1823. It stipulated that the United States regarded the Western Hemisphere as no longer a suitable place for European powers to establish colonies: the European powers should not interfere with the affairs of the Western Hemisphere just as the United States had no intention of interfering with the affairs of Europe. The original occasion of the announcement of the Doctrine was to deter Russia and Britain from encroaching in the Pacific Northwest, but for most of its lifetime it has been applied especially to Latin America.

Latin Americans regard the Doctrine with profound skepticism, as a declaration by the United States that it intends to exploit the hemisphere for its own benefit; this is at variance with the feeling of most Americans who have learned about the doctrine in school, that it is designed to promote democracy and national self-determination in the Western Hemisphere.

Although applying in principle to all of the Western Hemisphere, the Doctrine has been enforced consistently only with respect to the areas closest to the United States, in the Caribbean and the surrounding area, where the United States has tended to intervene, with armed force or by other means, to remove governments from power, or to prevent political movements from coming to power, it they were thought to be potentially sympathetic to major states that were rivals of the United States in international politics.

---

ever, the boundaries within which the local government can operate autonomously appear to be that countries are expected to follow the lead of the United States in international relations, or, as a minimum, not to side with the rivals of the United States in world politics; and they are not to limit the freedom of U.S. business interests to operate within the country, own property, and repatriate profits. Since the hegemonic relationship respects the forms of sovereignty, it is more acceptable in today's world, and is certainly more consistent with the democratic ideology of most Americans, than a straightforward imperial relationship would be.

There are a variety of methods by which the hegemonic relationship is enforced, some being more obvious and violent than others. Let us take these up in turn, starting with the most obvious and violent techniques and going on to the milder and less obvious.

1. The most obvious method used, if the dependent government gets out of line, if it oversteps the limits of what is acceptable to the United States, is to send in the marines. This is a crass technique whose obituary is often pronounced, but which rises from its grave whenever other methods seem unpromising. Most recently, President Reagan sent in the marines to overthrow the government of Grenada, President Bush sent in

troops to seize the ruler of Panama, and President Clinton used soldiers to restore the elected president of Haiti. This method is not preferred by the U.S. government, and is usually resorted to only when other methods have failed or when no time seems available to practice other, more subtle, methods. Direct military intervention is too open, too public; it provokes hostility to the United States on the part of countries in Latin America and elsewhere. It may be unpopular at home, especially if U.S. personnel get killed.

Since a naked act of force of this kind can be embarrassing for U.S. governments, if possible they use the fig leaf of sponsorship by an international organization. When the Johnson administration sent the marines into the Dominican Republic in 1965, it managed *ex post facto* to get a supporting resolution from the Organization of American States, some nominal contingents of troops from other countries, and a Brazilian general to act, in name at least, as overall commander of the military operations. For the Grenadan invasion, President Reagan managed to unearth the obscure Organization of Eastern Caribbean States to give its blessing, since no other international organization would do so.

THE ORGANIZATION OF AMERICAN STATES

There had been intermittent attempts at continuing organization of the Western Hemisphere countries for over a hundred years before the Organization of American States (OAS) was established in March 1948. The OAS took over the Pan-American Union, which had been the organizational focus of periodic Pan-American conferences. The secretariat of the Organization is located in Washington and the OAS has generally been controlled by the United States, although it has shown some independence when strong governments in the major Latin American countries happened to coincide with governments of the United States that pursued policies that were unpopular both within the United States and outside it. Canada joined the OAS recently, and the former British and Dutch colonies in the Caribbean region were admitted as they became independent during the second half of the twentieth century. The OAS is a regional organization under the definition of the United Nations charter and works closely with the UN organization in some areas, particularly health.

2. Less obtrusive than the marine expedition is the exile invasion; the United States does not invade with its own forces, but sponsors an invasion of exiled nationals of the target country. The disguise of the exile invasion, that this is a spontaneous form of activity in which the United States has no hand, is always thin and was impossible to maintain, for example, in the case of the Nicaraguan *contras,* who were organized, trained, and equipped by the Central Intelligence Agency for the purpose

of overthrowing the Sandinista government of Nicaragua. U.S. sponsor-ship of the exile invasion of Cuba in 1961, at first denied, later became a matter of common knowledge. The exile invasion of Guatemala in 1954, whose sponsorship by the United States was still being officially denied by Vice-President Richard Nixon when he debated with John F. Kennedy in the first televised presidential debates in 1960, was apparently success-ful in overthrowing the mildly leftist government of Jacobo Arbenz Guzmán; actually the exiles themselves were quite ineffectual, but the Guatemalan army refused to fight against them, and the U.S. ambassador used a great deal of pressure to get the Guatemalan military to accept the leader of the exiles, Carlos Castillo Armas, as president of the country.

Thus the record on exile invasions is not very promising—failure in Cuba and Nicaragua[2] and success due to luck in Guatemala. Apart from the innocents who are made to suffer in the fighting and the decline of the prestige of the United States as U.S. complicity in the exile invasion be-comes known, however, there is also a fundamental political problem with the exile invasion scenario. In Nicaragua and Cuba the invasion was di-rected against a revolutionary government that had defeated and dis-banded the army of the dictator. This was necessarily the case, since if the old army had still been in place it would have been simpler, more effective, and less obvious to solicit a military coup from the soldiers rather than to bother with the exile invasion.

In Guatemala, where the old army was intact and predisposed against Arbenz, it is not clear why an exile invasion was thought necessary in any case. Where the old army has been abolished and replaced by a revolution-ary army, and where the masses have been given ground to hope for im-

---

THE CENTRAL INTELLIGENCE AGENCY

Episodic and only semiserious efforts of the United States at spying and secret operations abroad outside the normal intelligence-gathering activities of the State Department culminated in the establishment of the Office of Strategic Services (OSS), which was formed and operated during World War II. The OSS provided the nucleus for the Central Intelligence Agency, established by the National Se-curity Act of 1947. Not the only intelligence-gathering arm of the U.S. govern-ment, which also funds a National Security Agency, a Defense Intelligence Agency, a Drug Enforcement Administration, and others, the CIA is nevertheless the largest agency and the one with the most general mandate. The director of the CIA is supposed to be coordinator of all government intelligence activities and the president's chief advisor on intelligence matters—which did not prevent the Rea-gan administration from establishing its own covert operations run out of the White House itself in order to try to avoid even the minimum supervision and compliance with the legal mandates of Congress that apply to the CIA.

provement in their material well-being, it is unrealistic to expect that the population will rally to the flag of the exile invasion, in whose ranks people recognize some of the notorious figures of the previous dictatorship. So the exile invasion is little used, which is just as well for the sponsoring power. If the exile invasion is successful and the head of it becomes president, then, as in Guatemala since 1954, the new regime, in trying to put back the clock of revolution and root out support for a popular government, commits all kinds of atrocities for which the United States, as sponsor of the new government, must accept its share of the blame. If the exile invasion is unsuccessful, then the problem arises of what to do with the unsavory characters recruited by the CIA to form the invasion force. Presumably many will end up in Miami, smuggling dope, hiring out as hit men, and in general polluting the moral atmosphere of that unfortunate city.

3. Less overt, and implicating the U.S. government to a lesser extent, is the sponsored military coup. The U.S. government takes particular care to be on friendly terms with the ranking officers of the armies of Latin America. Military officers are brought to the United States for short courses or familiarization visits. Military attachés at U.S. embassies make it their business to be on good terms with their local counterparts, and no fuss is made when ranking officers deal themselves in for "commissions" on arms purchases. Not all military coups occur in Latin America because of the sponsorship of the United States, but some do, and it is quite common that even if a conspiracy to seize power is formed among the military independent of U.S. prompting, it will then be "cleared" with the embassy to find out what the attitude of the U.S. government would be to a new government originating from a coup, and specifically whether military assistance will continue at the same level—which it normally does.

4. Usually, however, these violent methods of overthrowing governments are not necessary. Usually the objectives of the United States can be realized through nonviolent methods, principally economic and financial pressures. There are many avenues through which these pressures can be made effective. The United States is the principal trading partner of countries in the Caribbean and Central America and the implicit threat to reduce or discontinue purchases on the part of the United States has far-reaching implications for the small countries of the region. For most countries, moreover, access to credit is crucial in financing their investment and foreign trade programs, and the government of the United States is in a key position to bring pressure on the international lending agencies, as much as on private U.S. banks. In fact it is usually not even necessary for overt economic pressures of this kind to be used. Political leaders in the region are well enough aware of the economic and financial power of the United States that they take care not to transgress the limits of policies that are acceptable to the United States. This is what Carl J. Friedrich called "the rule of anticipated reactions"—the probable reaction

of the hegemonic power is a factor built into the calculations of the government of the dependent country, so that U.S. wishes are generally followed without their even being expressed.

5. As well as these carrots and sticks that apply to the behavior of national governments, similar kinds of influence are brought to bear on key individuals in the political life of the dependent country. Various illicit incentives and disincentives are used, with some form of bribery being not uncommon.

6. Finally, there are techniques used just to promote general goodwill toward the United States on the part of elites in the dependent country. The State Department operates exchange programs that bring foreign students, journalists, academics, and politicians to the United States. The U.S. Information Service operates libraries and reading rooms, sponsors lectures and cultural performances, and attempts to maintain good relations with the cultural elites in the dependent countries. Of course, pro-U.S. attitudes are generated, quite without the intervention of the State Department, by the extraordinary volume and range of North American cultural products—movies, television, and the dominance of the Latin American media by reports from U.S.-owned news agencies.

Political power comes in many forms, and can be used to different degrees. The character of a government is expressed in what kinds of power it uses, and to what ends.

NOTE

1. Marc Howard has in fact made a plausible case that East Germans now have to be considered a distinct ethnic group within united Germany. "An East German Ethnicity? Understanding the New Division of Unified Germany," *German Politics and Society*, vol. 13, no. 4 (Winter 1995).

2. Although the exiles were not successful in overthrowing the Nicaraguan government, it might be argued that their activities contributed to the pressure to hold elections in which the Sandinista regime was defeated.

KEY TERMS

nation	secession
state	*irredenta*
genocide	Monroe Doctrine
ethnic group	Organization of American States
consociational democracy	Central Intelligence Agency

CHAPTER 13

International Law, International Organization, and Diplomacy

© ASHLEIGH BRILLIANT 1988.

POT-SHOTS NO. 4677.

WHY ARE LITTLE GENTLE CHANGES

NEARLY ALWAYS PREFERABLE TO BIG SUDDEN ONES?

Ashleigh Brilliant

In the world of international relations, which is the world of competing state sovereignties, from time to time the governments of some states have decided to pursue their objectives by force and begun wars against their neighbors. Because of the possibility that this can occur, almost all states equip themselves with armed forces and lethal weapons, fearful that they could be subdued, forced to surrender territory, or even enslaved by an aggressive power. In Chapter 14 we will examine military policies of states.

However, unilaterally establishing a military force to defend themselves from foreign attack is not the only way in which states have tried to deal with the problem of military threat. In addition, attempts have been made to civilize the conduct of international relations by establishing a system of international law and by founding international organizations to achieve purposes individual states cannot realize on their own.

INTERNATIONAL LAW

International law is law of a very particular kind. It is not made by a legislature whose majority votes bind all members of the political community, although some rules of international law are agreed by assemblies of national delegates. Nor is it enforced by a police force with powers of compulsion over individuals. Since the individual state is still sovereign, there are no enforcement powers belonging to a world government that can compel individual states or the citizens of individual states to observe the precepts of international law. And certainly states do not always obey international law; but most of the time they do. Why? Because it is in their interest to do so.

Generally states follow international law because sometimes a predictable and fair body of rules is necessary to regulate international trade, transportation, and diplomacy. If they become known as habitual violators of the rules, other states will be reluctant to trade and do business with them. Moreover, in specific cases, violation of the rules may bring on *retaliation* by the injured state or a coalition of states. In having as its ultimate negative sanction retaliation by the injured party against the offender, international law resembles other systems of decentralized law that exist in the absence of state authority——like the revenge killings and feuds that were traditional in Appalachia or still occur today in the highlands of Papua New Guinea.

Retaliation occurs when the rules of *reciprocity* are not followed. Reciprocity means that a state is obliged to extend to another state any privileges which that state has given it. Under an international agreement that forms part of international law, for example, a formally accredited diplomat is given immunity against arrest and prosecution for breaches of ordinary domestic law. If I am the French ambassador in the United States, for example, I can park my car illegally and refuse to pay parking tickets. France reciprocates by allowing the U.S. ambassador to France to have similar immunity from parking regulations. Now a good ambassador will try not to accumulate parking tickets; but this immunity is intended to prevent a government from using personal threats against ambassadors to force them to accept agreements on less favorable terms than they would otherwise demand or to deviate in other ways from the faithful performance of their duty.

The practices of reciprocity and retaliation can sometimes seem silly; if the Soviet Union restricted U.S. diplomatic personnel to a radius of only fifty kilometers from Moscow, for example, then the United States would prohibit Soviet diplomats from traveling more than fifty kilometers out of Washington, D.C. This tit-for-tat practice may seem childish, but it is designed to uphold the dignity of the state, defend its autonomy, and encourage states to behave appropriately in the hope of receiving the same treatment themselves.

Cases arising under international law can be heard in the courts of individual countries, or in international courts, although the judgment of such courts is not self-enforcing if one of the parties refuses to abide by the result. The United States, for example, refused in the 1980s to abide by a decision of the International Court of Justice requiring it to cease committing acts of war against Nicaragua and to compensate Nicaragua for such acts already committed. Most of the time, however, decisions are accepted by the parties.

The sources of international law, as it is followed by states and applied by courts, are primarily agreements among states, either in the form of particular treaties between two or a small number of states, or general conventions that have been subscribed to by most of the world's countries. It is clear that the principle of sovereignty is not violated by the existence of international law, since sovereign states have agreed to abide by these rules. Formal written agreements can be supplemented by less formal sources the court can look to for guidance: customary practices that states seem to accept even without their being embodied in treaties; general principles of law and equity that seem to be recognized throughout the civilized world; principles reflected in previous judicial decisions; or the teachings of the most highly regarded specialists in the field.

Clearly, while international law can be of great assistance in running the everyday affairs of states and individuals in trading, traveling, or signing contracts, it is not the kind of instrument that can settle major political questions. Moreover, it helps to bring order to things as they are, safeguarding existing property rights, for example, and cannot readily serve as an instrument for promoting change or redistributing the world's wealth. Nevertheless, in facilitating the conduct of the world's business, in enabling states to deal with each other smoothly, in providing mechanisms for the settlement of disputes, international law does help to reduce the likelihood of conflict.

INTERNATIONAL ORGANIZATIONS

International organizations are of various kinds. There are very many private international organizations, which range from the dedicated and courageous Amnesty International, which attempts to secure freedom for political prisoners and universal respect for human rights, to powerful multinational business corporations. Most of the time, however, what are generally referred to as international organizations are those that have national states as members. These public international organizations are most helpfully classified in terms of their membership and their purposes, each of which can be limited or general (see Table 13.1).

AMNESTY INTERNATIONAL

Founded in 1961 in London, Amnesty International campaigns for the freedom of "prisoners of conscience" all over the world. Taking up the cause of those imprisoned for the mere expression of their views or for peaceful political activity, Amnesty campaigns by publicizing the facts of individual cases and by organizing letter-writing, usually to those responsible for their imprisonment or ill-treatment. Individual Amnesty chapters "adopt" individual prisoners of conscience and sometimes have success in organizing pressure on behalf of those persecuted for their political views. In 1977 Amnesty was awarded the Nobel Peace Prize for its work.

Table 13.1
Examples of Public International Organizations

Membership		
	General	*Limited*
Purpose: General	United Nations	Arab League; Organization of American States
Limited	Universal Postal Union; World Health Organization	Organization of Petroleum Exporting Countries; European Coal and Steel Community

An example of an organization with limited membership would be the Arab League, each of whose member states has a majority of its population that is ethnically Arab; however, the League is not limited in its purposes, which can extend to anything its members wish to do. The Universal Postal Union, on the other hand, is general, or unlimited, in its membership, but is limited in its purposes. All states that wish to participate in the world system of mail delivery are members, but the organization concerns itself only with delivery of mail and nothing else.

Some organizations are limited both in membership and in purpose: the Organization of Petroleum Exporting Countries has a limited membership and also limited purposes: to attempt to maintain high prices for oil exports by regulating oil production and export. There is, however, one organization that is unlimited in both membership and purpose: the United Nations Organization. Today it includes virtually all independent states in the world, except for some that are too tiny to shoulder the burden of maintaining a delegation at UN Headquarters, like San Marino; not united, like North and South Korea; or, like Switzerland, afraid that membership would compromise their absolute neutrality. The organization's purposes are, likewise, universal and the United Nations can get itself involved in anything that happens on the planet.

The United Nations Organization was established by treaty in 1945, growing out of the wartime alliance of the states that opposed Nazi Germany. Although at first membership was not universal, the readmission of the defeated countries of World War II into the international community, and the decision by the United States and the Soviet Union in the middle 1950s not to block the admission of states sponsored by the rival superpower, has led to the current situation in which membership is virtually universal. In fact, membership in the world organization has become something of the ultimate badge of statehood, so that the final act in the series of events that occurs when an ex-colony becomes independent is the hoisting of the new nation's flag at the United Nations Plaza in New York.

The United Nations has only intermittently performed the military peacekeeping function its founders intended. On occasion, the United Nations has borrowed small contingents of soldiers from member states to police borders, maintain internal order, or supervise elections. The United Nations has thus far not been able to maintain military forces of its own, among other reasons because it cannot know in advance whether the nationality of the troops being used would itself create problems in a particular situation. UN troops have twice fought in actual wars. In Korea from 1950 to 1955, a largely U.S. force fought under the UN banner to try to repel a North Korean invasion of the South; and a UN force was involved in attempting to prevent the secession of Katanga province from Zaire in 1960–63. Rivalry between the United States and the Soviet Union limited the situations in which the use of military force by the United Nations was feasible—approval of the action in Korea was made possible only because of a boycott of the UN Security Council by the Soviet delegate at the time—but the end of the Cold War has led to a dramatic expansion of the UN's role as an armed peacemaker or peace maintainer.

All member states have seats in the General Assembly of the United Nations, and one vote each in the passage of its resolutions, which do not have a binding character. Of course, giving each state the same single vote does not recognize the vast inequality among them; an attempt to do that, however, is made in the membership and voting arrangements of the Security Council, whose votes are supposed to be legally binding on the UN membership. Five of the members of the Security Council are permanent—the major powers of the victorious World War II alliance: the United States, the Soviet Union, Great Britain, France, and China. The other nine members of the Council are elected for two-year terms by the General Assembly. The custom has developed for these nonpermanent seats to be allocated among regional groupings, with two each for Latin America, Africa, and Asia, and one each for the Middle East, Western Europe, and Eastern Europe.

A resolution requires a two-thirds vote to pass the Security Council, including the affirmative vote of all the permanent members; that is, each permanent member has a veto. The granting of the veto power represented at the same time the hope that the World War II allies would remain united in the management of world affairs, and also the realization that it would be imprudent to try to impose some policy against the wishes of a major power. Of course, the major powers of 1945 are not those of the 1990s; Germany and Japan would certainly have to be included in any set of major powers today, and indeed a case is building for them to become permanent members of the Security Council.

In addition to its policing functions on behalf of world peace, the United Nations serves as an arena for the development of a consensus on world issues and a convenient meeting place for the informal discussion of questions involving more than two countries.

In addition, the vote of an overwhelming majority of the General Assembly in favor of a resolution may exercise strong moral pressure on a deviant state and arouse world opinion. Sometimes, it is true—especially in the opinion of the outvoted governments—this represents no more than the mobilizing of prejudices by governments without any immediate interest or knowledge of the subject, and sometimes United Nations debates may inflame a dispute instead of calming it. On balance, however, most observers of the organization would probably conclude that its role in the mobilizing of world opinion has been a positive one.

The chief official of the United Nations organization is its secretary-general, elected by the General Assembly for a five-year term and eligible for reelection. Different secretaries-general have conceived of their role differently. Some aspire to play a major role in the solution of international problems, others are preoccupied more with the management of the organization itself. They have typically been diplomats, sometimes with a political background, more often career civil servants, from countries regarded as hostile by neither the United States nor the Soviet Union.

In addition to its principal political organs, the United Nations consists also of a vast network of specialized agencies within whose framework states band together to take action on scientific and cultural matters, the environment, and a host of other matters of common concern. Regrettably, as in any bureaucratic organization, many of these agencies provide a home for time-serving careerists, politically well-connected loafers, and egoistic empire-builders. Salary and perquisites are extremely good, so that many seeking jobs with the United Nations are motivated by concerns other than promoting the welfare of mankind. Nevertheless, many dedicated public servants work for the specialized agencies and a great deal of good is done by them.

Other international organizations are not directly connected with the UN structure. Preeminent among these are the World Bank and the International Monetary Fund (IMF). The World Bank takes an active role in providing finance for development projects, especially in the Third World. It takes a slightly more generous and risk-taking approach than commercial banks are supposed to, but is still a bank and not a charity. The IMF has as its mission the maintenance of currency convertibility. It is a powerful organization that acts as a sort of policeman of the international capitalist economy, providing loans for states that are running out of hard currency to finance their imports, usually on condition that they take a series of drastic measures designed—at least in principle—to restore the health of their currencies by severe cuts in government spending, and to promote free market economies. These programs are invariably hugely unpopular, and are often met by strikes and riots. It has not been unknown for IMF stabilization programs to cost more in policing and clearing up the damage from riots than the amount they were intended to save.

In addition to public international organizations of this kind, there are very many private, or nongovernmental, international organizations to promote all kinds of causes and interests.

REGIONAL AND FUNCTIONAL ORGANIZATIONS

Not all organizations are of global scope; the world is filled with regional organizations, some of them with ties to the UN structure, some not. The oldest of the regional organizations, the Organization of American States, founded in 1948 but growing out of a preexisting structure that is now one hundred years old, has a specialized public health organization, the Panamerican Health Organization (PAHO), which serves at the same time as the regional division for Latin America of the World Health Organization in the UN structure.

The most successful regional organization is, like PAHO, also a functional one: the European Economic Community, as it is often still known, although its official name was changed in 1993 to the European Union. This interesting organization, which now includes most of the states of Western Europe, grew out of the political vision of the French public servant Jean Monnet and secured the political sponsorship of French Prime Minister Robert Schuman and West German Chancellor Konrad Adenauer. Its fundamental impulse was to unite France and Germany so firmly that they could never again go to war, as they had three times between 1870 and 1940. The mechanism used was to create a common market, which would enlist powerful forces of economic self-interest to work for reconciliation and unification. The common market has been extremely successful, not only economically in raising standards of living in Western Europe, but also politically in that institutions in Western Europe are now so scrambled together that it would be difficult for the West European countries to wage war on each other even if they wanted to.

The success of the European Economic Community has strengthened the views of those who argue that the way to achieve lasting world peace is to create long-term common interests and habits of working together among the countries of the world so that the incentives to maintain peace become stronger than any incentive to go to war. This emphasis on the creating of collaborative mechanisms to pursue concrete common interests as a road to world peace is sometimes called "functionalism." There seems to be merit in the idea. Those who advocate a single world government often take the view that the way to proceed is to persuade everyone of the desirability of such an arrangement and then summon a world constitutional convention to draft the appropriate document.[1] If a world government ever arrives, however, it is much more likely to originate in the steady accretion of international organizations forming a web of interrelations that gradually limits the autonomy of sovereign states in the interest of the performance of a multiplicity of worthwhile functions.

DIPLOMACY

The truth of the matter, regrettable or not, is that for the foreseeable future we have to live in a world of sovereign states in which most of the key actors will be concerned primarily with the welfare of the national populations to which they are responsible and only secondarily, if at all, with the welfare of populations living outside the borders of their states. The pursuit of national interests need not, however, always be conducted at the expense of the interests of other states. In fact, professionals in conducting international relations appreciate that the particular matter in hand is only one in a continuing series of problems that need to be dealt with, most of which will entail consultations, and often agreement, with the representatives of other states. A ruthless disregard of the interests of other states in the pursuit of national interest with respect to one issue will only make more difficult the pursuit of national interest with respect to other problems that arise.

Another way of putting this is to realize that there is not only a national interest in attaining a specific objective at a given time, but there is also a continuing national interest in maintaining good relations with representatives of other states; and to achieve that it is necessary to recognize the legitimacy of their aspirations and thus to reach mutually satisfactory arrangements as much as possible. Sometimes national interests are in direct conflict, and what is given to one country must be taken from another. But most of the time, if the issue is worked on carefully and assiduously, solutions can be found that satisfy more of the national interests that are at stake than would be possible in a simple winner/loser model.

This is the approach usually taken by those professionally concerned with the practice of international relations. Their profession is that of diplomat and the continuing management of relations among states is called *diplomacy*. Like any professional calling, that of diplomacy breeds certain habits of thought and behavior appropriate to its successful practice, and it may sometimes appear to someone who is committed to a particular objective that the professional diplomats are too concerned with maintaining good relations with their counterparts from other countries to pursue the desired objective with sufficient seriousness or vigor.

This writer has often felt that American and British diplomats have failed to make strong representations on behalf of people deprived of their rights, in order to maintain good relations with the government of some dictatorship; and the maintenance of good relations among the diplomats of different countries can become a means pursued for its own sake, with the ends it was to serve being lost sight of. Nevertheless, at its best, diplomacy not only balances pursuit of immediate purposes against the maintenance of good relations required in future negotiations, but also against the realization that the current government of a particular country will not be in power forever, and that one may be called to account by a future government whose political complexion is different for actions which will seem to that government irresponsible or undesirable.

At its best, diplomacy becomes *statesmanship*: the willingness to sustain some loss in the present gratification of an obvious interest for the greater gratification of some larger interest in the future. It is to the successful practice of statesmanlike diplomacy that we must look for the foreseeable future as the best hope for the alleviation of the dangerous situations in which the world so frequently finds itself.

NOTE

1. The former senator from Alaska, Mike Gravel, leads an organization, Philadelphia II, that follows this approach.

KEY TERMS

retaliation	General Assembly
reciprocity	Security Council
Arab League	International Monetary Fund
Universal Postal Union	World Bank
Organization of Petroleum Exporting States	European Economic Community (European Union)
Amnesty International	diplomacy
United Nations	statesmanship

CHAPTER 14

Military Security

POT-SHOTS NO. 5455. ©ASHLEIGH BRILLIANT 1991.

REASON
SHOULD NOT
BE
RESORTED TO
UNTIL
ALL ATTEMPTS
AT A
SOLUTION
BY FORCE
HAVE BEEN
EXHAUSTED.

Ashleigh Brilliant
SANTA BARBARA

THE USE OF MILITARY FORCE

In a world of self-interested sovereign states that contains no effective world government, violence may occur as one state attempts to impose its will on another. States try to avoid such contingencies by developing a body of international law to regulate disputes among them; they construct organizations to deal with international problems; but they also prepare themselves to use armed force if the need should arise.

Armies are always presented as though their purpose was entirely defensive, to protect the territory and resources of the nation-state, to repel invasions and resist having to make concessions out of weakness. Of course, if the opportunity presents itself, armed forces can also be used aggressively, to take territory and resources from a neighbor, especially under the guise of "liberating" people residing in the disputed area. Even where excuses of this type do not exist, aggressive wars have been fought simply to add to the glory of the nation and especially of its leader. The campaigns of the great imperialists—Alexander, Napoleon, and Hitler—seem to have had as their real purpose the psychological gratification of the ruler's will to dominate.

Nevertheless, almost all governments feel that they have to maintain armed forces, which involves not only colossal expense but, for a majority of countries, the possibility, which all too often becomes an actuality, of military interference in politics. The armed forces may be organized and equipped for purposes of national defense; but once such a force is in existence it subserves other purposes, including that of defending and promoting its own interests, which may entail exercising a veto power over government policies or even seizing power itself. Because of the continual problem created for Latin American countries by the proclivity of their military forces to intervene in politics, Costa Rica decided, after a 1948 revolution in which an armed popular movement defeated the armed forces of a dictatorial regime, to abolish its armed forces. Costa Rica gets along perfectly well with only a small police force, despite the fact that the United States has tried to get Costa Rican governments to maintain an army to defend themselves against the supposed danger of invasion or guerrilla war. In 1994 and 1995, Panama and Haiti also abolished their armed forces.

Some states are clearly more ready to use force than others. The Kingdom of Prussia was developed along military lines and the Prussian military tradition was inherited by the German state after Germany was unified in 1870. Defeat in two World Wars in the twentieth century seems to have eliminated any German predilection to war, however. The American democracy, slow to enter both World Wars, became transformed thereafter to a state of continuous mobilization, ready to go to war at any time.

AGGRESSION AND BALANCE OF POWER

The rationale for the U.S. global system of alliances, foreign military bases, and overseas intelligence operations developed during the second half of the twentieth century was to thwart Soviet attempts at world domination. But long before the Russian Revolution, when Lenin was an obscure exile writing pamphlets in Switzerland, Theodore Roosevelt assumed for the United States the role of policeman of the Western Hemisphere, sending marines to occupy small countries in Central America and the Caribbean whose governments behaved in ways of which he did not approve. The fundamental principle here may simply be that enunciated by Thucydides in his *History of the Peloponnesian War*, "Of the gods we believe, and of men we know, that by a necessary law of their nature they seek to dominate wherever they can." It seems to be true, in other words, that a state that realizes itself to be much stronger than its neighbors will always find one good reason or another to throw its weight around. The United States took up its burden of defending the free world from Communism because after World War II it was the strongest non-Communist state. How much a state will try to extend its influence and control, in other words, may simply be determined by the power it has at its disposal.

This is certainly what states assume most of the time in their relations with each other. Each state tries to extend its influence, using the means it has at its control, at the same time jealously guarding itself against being dominated by other states.

One of a state's chief traditional means of defending itself is to form mutual support alliances, so that an aggressive state that might feel strong enough to conquer a defensive state by itself will be deterred by having to face the combined strength of the alliance. As a generalized system for

---

THUCYDIDES

Author of the classic history of the Peloponnesian War, in which he fought, the fifth-century B.C. Athenian is generally regarded as the first modern historian. Leaving the supernatural out of his story, and trying to explain events by strict standards of logical causality, Thucydides wrote an elegant history that set a standard for his successors. He did, however, take liberties in reconstructing conversations as he believed they must have taken place, without having eyewitness evidence. He is particularly well-known for his description of the dynamics of power politics.

---

keeping the peace, this method is what we have discussed previously as the *balance of power*. In Europe from the seventeenth to the twentieth centuries, a shifting system of alliances tried with mixed success to insure that no state or combination of states would feel itself strong enough to embark on a policy of conquering the others.

One of the ways of avoiding conflict is for major powers not to involve themselves in the affairs of some small countries that they acknowledge to be in another power's *sphere of influence*. At some times the British and the Russians have agreed, for example, that northern Afghanistan should be in the Russian sphere of influence and southern Afghanistan in the British sphere (the British at the time were in control of present-day India and Pakistan). Most commonly, a major country will have a sphere of influence close to its own borders which provides a security zone for it, so that it can be confident that it need fear no threat to its security from its immediate neighbors.

The Soviet sphere of influence in Eastern Europe was intended to provide just such a security zone; the United States has had the same attitude toward Central America and the Caribbean (the Monroe Doctrine). U.S. governments have intervened repeatedly in the affairs of countries in the region if it looked as though they might produce governments that would be not amenable to U.S. influence. Although a rival major power may complain bitterly about the denial of freedom to the peoples in its rival's security zone—which the maintenance of such a sphere of influence implies—it usually accepts such a zone as legitimate.

Thus, although the United States had been calling on the people of Eastern Europe to rise and throw off the Soviet yoke in the late 1940s and early 1950s, when the people of Hungary actually did rise in 1956 and produce a nationalist government that wanted to leave the Soviet bloc, Secretary of State John Foster Dulles hastened to reassure the Russians that the United States would not interfere in Hungary, and the Red Army was able to reassert Soviet control. When Prime Minister Nikita Khrushchev emplaced Soviet missiles in Cuba, President John F. Kennedy forced him to withdraw them.

THE CUBAN MISSILE CRISIS

In 1963 a confrontation between the United States and the Soviet Union that might have led to actual nuclear war took place over the emplacement of Soviet missiles in Cuba. Nikita Khrushchev, then the leader of the Soviet Union, believed he could offset the fact that the United States had missiles that could strike the Soviet Union from U.S. territory—whereas the Soviet Union could not retaliate because it had only short-range missiles—by placing short-range nuclear-armed missiles in Cuba, from where they could reach the United States. There was also some thought that the presence of missiles in Cuba would help deter a U.S. attack to overthrow the government of Fidel Castro.

When U.S. surveillance planes uncovered the existence of the Soviet missiles, President John F. Kennedy chose to interpret their presence as a violation of implicit Cold War ground rules that each superpower would respect the immediate security zone of the other. After considering several possible courses of action, including a military strike against the missiles, Kennedy established a naval blockade (which he called "a quarantine," since a blockade is technically an act of war under international law) around the island.

Although great international concern arose about the possibility of a nuclear war between the superpowers originating from this situation, it was assumed that the Soviet Union would back down from actual military conflict, which it had no interest in starting and no prospect in winning, especially not a conflict beginning in the backyard of the United States, where all the logistic advantages were on the American side.

However, it subsequently transpired—to the shock and amazement of U.S. observers—that the Soviet Union had given its local commanders on the ground authority to fire the missiles if they were to come under attack without further authorization from Moscow, so apparently the danger of nuclear war existed despite the calculations of U.S. strategists who assumed rational and well-informed behavior on both sides. Khrushchev capitulated to the American ultimatum to remove the missiles—without consulting with a resentful Fidel Castro—and his "adventurism" in placing the missiles in Cuba in the first place became one of the counts cited against him when he was subsequently removed from his position as Soviet leader.

Traditionally, a policy of balance of power rested on *both* the maintenance of armed forces *and* the organization of alliances to deter any would-be conqueror. This was also the case during the Cold War. However, the great disparity in military might between the Soviet Union and the United States on the one hand, and everyone else on the other, together with the very rapid development of military technology, made the maintenance of a balance of power between the United States and the Soviet Union predominantly a matter of competition in weapons. We will examine the development of that competition in Chapter 15.

PREPAREDNESS AND DETERRENCE

Most states have believed that since a military attack is always possible they must always be in condition to repel such an attack. As transportation has become more rapid and weapons more powerful, the time that could be allowed to prepare a response has shrunk. To most governments, it does not seem reasonable to wait for an attack to occur before beginning to organize and train an army to respond to it. Accordingly, *military preparedness* is generally thought necessary. And yet such preparedness immediately confronts a series of paradoxes that makes its adequacy quite problematic. The first of these is that the structure of the state's armed force—its weapons, training, and disposition—depends on the threat it is to meet. Yet it is impossible to know ahead of time the exact nature of any threat. There may be one or a combination of enemies, attacking by air, sea, or land, in a massive surprise attack, or a long war of economic attrition. Yet it is not physically or financially possible to prepare for all possible contingencies. As a result, one prepares for the contingencies thought most likely to occur.

It is only too common, however, that the contingencies thought most probable prove not to be those that arise, so that one is caught with an inappropriate and ineffective response when the crisis actually comes. In 1982, for example, the British were well armed and prepared to meet the threat of a Soviet nuclear attack in Europe; they were quite inadequately prepared to meet what actually occurred: an Argentine seizure of the Falkland Islands in the South Atlantic. The United States was overprepared, one might say, to meet a Soviet attack anywhere in the world; it did not have the appropriate trained troops, weapons, or tactical doctrines needed to rescue U.S. hostages held in the Middle East.

One of the characteristic errors in military preparedness arises from what would seem the prudent thing to do, to learn from experience—which has given rise to the adage "The generals are always fighting the last war." The most notorious example is that of the *Maginot Line*, the series of fortifications erected by the French in the 1920s to prevent the kind of infantry attack the Germans had used in World War I, but which proved inadequate to counter Hitler's *Blitzkrieg* (lightning war) tank advances in 1940.

And yet the attempt to imagine what a war of the future, fought with new technology, would look like, may make a better science fiction scenario than it does a guide to military planning. This was clearly demonstrated by the book *Nuclear Weapons and Foreign Policy*, which established Henry Kissinger's reputation. The book envisioned a war of the future in which tactical nuclear weapons would be used in a limited war. Weapons of that magnitude would have to be used against large targets, but seeing that the war was to remain limited they would somehow have not to destroy any cities. Pure nonsense, of course; but it provided the basis for U.S. strategic doctrine, and for the training and equipment of U.S. troops in Europe.

The final paradox of preparedness is that the expense involved in the continuous maintenance of troops and the building of weapons constitutes a substantial economic drain that may prove in the long run as damaging as defeat in a war might have done. The huge economic burden of maintaining superpower levels of military preparedness was in fact a key factor, if not the key factor, that led to the collapse of the Soviet Union.

Preparedness, however, is not designed merely to fight and win wars that occur; it is also designed to *deter* a potential attacker by making it clear that an attack would not be successful. Unfortunately, further paradoxes are lurking in the concept and the practice of deterrence, the discouraging of a potential aggressor by the display of military force. The first of these paradoxes is that effective deterrence requires that the potential adversary be aware of one's military strength. Yet information concerning troop strength, organization and disposition, and weapons is usually treated as secret.

This ambiguous situation leads to such practices as the institution of the military attaché, a military officer attached to the embassy one state has in the capital of another, whose job it is to find out everything he can about the armed forces of the host country. That is his role, and the host country knows it perfectly well; if he is diligent in his mission, however, and exceeds the bounds of propriety, he might find himself expelled for "activities inconsistent with his diplomatic status," that is, for spying—even though everyone knows that his role is that of a sort of licensed spy.

A more significant problem is that effective deterrence assumes that a potential adversary will calculate the relative strength of forces correctly, and will then act rationally, not starting a war he is not sure he can win. And yet history is full of examples of leaders who acted less than rationally, or on the basis of miscalculation. Hitler thought England and France wouldn't fight; he thought he could conquer Russia, even with the example before him of Napoleon, who made a similar miscalculation. If the rulers of Japan had calculated the balance of forces correctly, according to the theory of deterrence, they would hardly have attacked the United States in 1941—yet, in fact, those Japanese military experts who had made the appropriate assessments knew that Japan would lose the war, but were ignored by the commanding officers who started it.

But miscalculations can apply to the evaluation of intentions as well as of capabilities. That is, preparations for defense and deterrence may appear to a neighboring country to be preparations for an aggressive attack.

THE SCHLIEFFEN PLAN

After the German triumph in the Franco-Prussian War of 1870, German Chancellor Otto von Bismarck assumed that the French would try to take their revenge and reconquer the province of Alsace-Lorraine, which they had lost to Germany in the war. He was not concerned that the French army by itself could prove superior to that of Germany; but he was afraid that Germany would be defeated if it had to divide its army in order to fight on two fronts at once, in the east as well as in the west, which he should have to do if Russia were to enter a war as an ally of France. The object of his diplomatic policy was thus to maintain an alliance with Russia and also to attempt to neutralize Britain, so that Britain would not ally itself with France.

After young Kaiser Wilhelm II removed Bismarck from office and took over the management of German policy himself, Bismarck's carefully managed diplomatic alliances were allowed to decay, while Wilhelm followed a policy of bravado and bluster. Russia was alienated when Wilhelm backed up the ambitions in Southeast Europe, the Balkans, of the "fellow-Germanic" Austrian Empire; while Britain became alienated as Germany competed with it for colonies in Africa, a policy Bismarck had never followed.

As a result, German military strategists had to prepare a contingency plan for the possibility of a war that Germany would have to fight on two fronts, against a France that would be allied with Russia and possibly backed by Britain. Starting with the premise that the German army could not emerge victorious if it had to be divided into two, they reasoned that the army could first defeat the French in the west and then turn to meet the Russians in the east, allowing for the fact that, because the Russian army was spread over such a large territory, it would take four weeks before troops could be collected and brought to the front by train.

Because time was thus of the essence, the contingency plan drafted by General Alfred von Schlieffen called for a lightning war against France, the rapid defeat of the French, and the subsequent transfer of the troops to the east. This concentration on speed made the German response a hair-trigger one; so that when the Austrians became embroiled with the Russians in a dispute over Serbia, the Germans did not wait for actual fighting between the two to break out before they ordered their troops on the most rapid route to Paris—which unfortunately lay through neutral Belgium. To Germany, it was a question of necessary self-defense. To the public elsewhere, who were not privy to Germany's strategic plans, what seemed to happen is that the Germans had taken advantage of confusion in the Balkans to launch a wanton aggression against poor Belgium.

This was the interpretation written into Clause I, the "war-guilt" clause of the Versailles Treaty, which was made the basis for the German obligation to pay reparations to the victorious powers of World War I. To the Germans, this always seemed unjust; their resentment at the treaty, and especially at the war-guilt clause, helped to provide Hitler with one of the planks in the platform on which he subsequently came to power.

This may induce it to build up its own forces in response, so that the original intention of the state that initiated the process, to have a superiority in weapons that would deter an aggressor, becomes more difficult to achieve. In fact, the situation may develop into a perpetual arms race, to the ruin of both countries. Moreover, such a competitive arms race, even if begun with defensive intentions on the part of both states, may itself provide the occasion for war, of the so-called *preventive* kind, if one state achieves military superiority but is afraid it will lose it to the other state, whose intentions it believes to be aggressive. It may then be tempted into launching an attack in order for the war to be fought sooner rather than later, while it still has the military advantage.

The term *preemptive* has been used when one state launches an attack because it believes its rival is preparing to attack very soon and it wishes to retain the advantage of striking the first blow. World War I originated with a preemptive attack of this kind, Germany attacking France in anticipation of being faced with an eventual joint attack by France and Russia.

The logic of military preparedness and deterrence, based on the building up of forces and weapons superior to those available to a potential adversary, is in its purest form too one-sided to serve as an effective guide to national policy. Because the goals of national security policy are conceived of in apocalyptic terms, like "national survival," the demands of military preparedness are normally given priority over other demands on the national budget—very often to excess, since there is no limit to the possible hypothetical circumstances for which one can be prepared. All too often this leads, in the modern industrial state, to a severe imbalance, with vast quantities of money spent in preparation for highly unlikely contingencies, while crying nonmilitary needs go unattended.

Even so, the total military might possessed by a state is not the same as the actual military force it can bring to bear in specific circumstances—in little-known mountainous terrain a long way from home, for example. And what can be bought with a military budget may not include the elements that may be crucial in determining the outcome of a war—the psychological and moral factors that go into creating the will to fight: the belief that one's cause is just, the willingness to make extreme sacrifices indefinitely rather than to surrender, belief in the extreme importance of what is at stake. It was in this moral and psychological dimension, not in funds and weapons, that the United States lost in Vietnam.

VIETNAM AND THE LIMITS OF MILITARY LOGIC

Many lessons can be learned from the U.S. experience in the Vietnam War about the limitations of purely military logic, or at least about the importance in military situations of factors other than numbers of troops and weapons. The critical will to fight is less among soldiers fighting a long way from home for some principle related to the international balance of power than for soldiers fighting on their home ground to expel a foreign force. And of course local troops are more at home, more familiar with the terrain and the local circumstances, better able to understand and blend in with the local civilian population, better able to function with the food and supplies available locally.

It seems bizarre and illogical to Americans that in Vietnam the strongest military power in the world could not defeat a minor power. But what is important in any concrete situation is not the total military resources in troops and weapons a country possesses, but the actual military force that can be brought to bear at a specific point and at a specific time, and in that context the massive destructive power of American arms was simply not relevant. This is especially true when a war is being fought to occupy a specific populated territory. In this sense, force can destroy, but it cannot necessarily conquer.

In the moral and psychological dimension there are six relevant populations: one's own soldiers, the opposing army, the civilian inhabitants of the territory fought over, one's own population back home, the enemy's home population; and the populations of noncombatant countries—"world opinion." There is a moral and psychological balance of forces working in each of these populations, just as much as there is a physical balance of forces in combat on the ground.

The United States finally lost in Vietnam, just as the Russians were forced to withdraw from Afghanistan, because of defeat in the moral and psychological dimensions, not the physical dimension. In this respect, the legitimacy of one's cause in a war is like the legitimacy of a government: it depends on both origins and performance.

Some of those who later turned against the war accepted the initial engagement of the United States in Vietnam as legitimate. It could plausibly be presented as resistance to the forcible attempt of an outside power to dominate a peace-loving one, if North and South Vietnam were considered two separate countries (which was, however, an open question with a controverted history). But the United States lost legitimacy—inevitably, perhaps—by the way the war was fought. Civilians were killed, human rights were violated, facts were misrepresented, predictions were proved incorrect, covert activities ran riot. And finally there seemed no end to the war, whose human costs had far exceeded what the U.S. public had been led to expect: 509 Americans killed in action by July 1963, when Kennedy considered withdrawing; by December 1967, after Johnson had escalated the war, 15,979; by 1973, after Kissinger had said peace was at hand, 58,191.[1]

Yet even apart from the terrible costs inflicted on the country of Vietnam itself by the war, and the direct costs to the United States of fighting it, the secondary costs to the United States were great enough to have called the balance sheet into question even if the United States had gained a clear victory. The inflationary factors set loose by Lyndon Johnson's financing of the war contributed to the weakening of the U.S. economy; the ending of two decades of economic growth of the world as a whole, with all of the economic, political, and social problems that that entailed; and the beginnings of the out-of-control U.S. budget and trade deficits, with all their consequences for the fate of the level of social welfare that had been achieved in the United States. The war gave an impetus to the use of drugs by Americans, and the CIA promoted the drug trade as a way of financing the mountain tribes that were U.S. allies in the fighting.

The war destroyed political consensus in the United States and led to polarization, violence, even acts of terrorism. U.S. persistence in a clearly doomed struggle, and the eventual destruction of the South Vietnamese ally, alienated U.S. allies. As a by-product of the war, the United States invaded Cambodia, upsetting the country's delicate political balance and beginning the escalation of hostilities there that led to the Khmer Rouge massacres.

While nothing can serve to make the Vietnam experience profitable, some value might be gained from it in the form of lessons that would serve to avoid similar disasters in the future. The difficulty is that everyone drew their own lesson from Vietnam, very often the wrong one. Hard-line anti-Communists simply thought that the lesson of Vietnam was the necessity to be even more ruthless, even more unscrupulous, to begin fighting sooner, and the like; and the Carter and Reagan administrations gave many of the same government officials that had been involved in the Southeast Asian debacle the chance to test their theories all over again in Central America—in Nicaragua and El Salvador. All they achieved there, along with the loss of as many as a quarter-million Central American lives, was more division of the American people, more violation of the U.S. Constitution, more alienation of U.S. allies, and more corruption of the American political process. The compromise solutions finally achieved in Nicaragua and El Salvador by the end of the Bush administration were more or less what could have been peacefully negotiated twelve or fifteen years before.

NOTE

1. Sidney Blumenthal, "McNamara's Peace," *The New Yorker*, May 8, 1995, pp. 69–70.

KEY TERMS

Prussia	preventive war
sphere of influence	preemptive war
military preparedness	Schlieffen Plan
Maginot Line	Vietnam War

CHAPTER 15

The Rise and Fall
of the Cold War

© ASHLEIGH BRILLIANT 1988. POT-SHOTS NO. 4752.

HOW CAN WE LOVE
OUR COUNTRY,

Ashleigh
Brilliant

UNLESS
IT HAS
THE POWER
TO DESTROY
THE WHOLE
WORLD?

$\mathbf{F}$or almost half a century, American foreign policy was dominated by the Cold War with the Soviet Union. It molded the way U.S. policymakers thought about international relations, causing every situation to be viewed in the perspective of how it affected the overall rivalry of the two superpowers—even when, in fact, any such effects were negligible or even imaginary.

THE ORIGINS OF THE COLD WAR: SOVIET FOREIGN POLICY

The Cold War had its ultimate origins in the policies of national aggrandizement and noncooperation with the West followed by the Soviet dictator, Josef Stalin, in the aftermath of World War II. The U.S. response to Stalin's policies then became institutionalized, embodied in bureaucratic structures, political rhetoric, and popular attitudes. Stalin's successors continued, more or less, to follow the dictator's policies, so that it appeared that both sides were doomed to be locked forever into postures of mutual hostility that became increasingly counterproductive as both subordinated their prosperity and that of the rest of the world, their other interests in international relations, and the harmony of their domestic societies to the winning of marginal gains in the Cold War. Although the best minds on both sides had long perceived the futility and self-defeating character of the struggle, it took the audacious statesmanship of Mikhail Gorbachev to thaw the ice.

Although the origins of the Cold War lay in the altogether understandable reaction of the United States and its Western allies to the self-aggrandizing moves made by Stalin in Europe, traditional attitudes on both sides to problems of foreign policy helped to reinforce the mutual hostility that then developed. The Soviet Union emerged from World War II with the most powerful land army in the world. Germany and Austria, which had traditionally provided a check in Europe to Russian expansionist ambitions, lay in ruins, so that there was no effective counterpoise to Russian power in Eastern Europe.

For the Russians, who had just been invaded for the fifth time in 130 years and had sustained colossal losses, it seemed eminently desirable to strengthen national security by building up a belt of pro-Soviet regimes in Eastern Europe that would provide an in-depth defense against any future attack. To be sure, Soviet domination of Eastern Europe was not presented to the peoples of Eastern Europe themselves or to the world in general in these terms of strategic defense, but was instead rationalized in terms of Communist ideology as the revolutionary establishment of socialist regimes representing a more advanced form of society and working in the popular interest. Nevertheless, the ideological rationale was no more than a cover for a policy of regional hegemony on the part of the Soviet Union.

For those abroad, including those in the United States, who took Stalin's rhetoric seriously, the slogans about liberation of the oppressed masses, of the Soviet Union leading the proletariat in its overthrow of capitalism, and the like, implied that Eastern Europe was just the first installment in a Soviet policy of world conquest. In fact, however, the Soviet Union aimed at world conquest only in its rhetoric and its daydreams. Although the Soviet Union later settled into the Cold War game of trying to line up allies and score points over the United States, embarking on a reckless program of world conquest was far too risky for Stalin. He was even dubious about enrolling new countries in the "socialist camp," outside of those conquered by the Red Army. Such countries would need Soviet aid and support, diverting resources that were needed at home. Moreover, staking a Soviet claim to countries outside of the immediate range of the Red Army would be likely to provoke the Western powers and lead to dangerous confrontations.

After all, Stalin had reached the Soviet leadership not as a heroic leader and orator, but as a consummate bureaucrat, a backstage manipulator who was cautious rather than bold, careful rather than risk-taking, calculating rather than emotional. (These are the characteristics that also distinguish him clearly from Adolf Hitler, and make it misleading to equate the systems founded by the two men.)

Stalin had defeated his arch-rival for leadership, Leon Trotsky, precisely over the question of world revolution, with Stalin opposing Trotsky's global ambitions with the program, much more acceptable to members of the party apparatus, of concentrating on building socialism within the Soviet Union rather than frittering away effort on wild adventures abroad.

Although this was in fact the substance of Soviet foreign policy, Stalin provided evidence for those who believed that his goal was instead a general world revolution, by insisting that Communist parties everywhere follow the lead of Moscow. In fact, however, in their pronouncements and political activities related to international affairs, those parties were required to support, not the requirements of world revolution, but instead the immediate foreign policy objectives of the Soviet Union.

The safety of the Soviet Union, the world's first socialist state, came first, and Communist parties everywhere were asked to subordinate not only the interests of their own countries, but also the prospect of revolutions within their own countries, and even their own reputations, to the immediate needs of Soviet policy, as Stalin saw them. This he called *proletarian internationalism*.

When it seemed to him that Britain and France were not going to stand up to Hitler but were instead going to appease him, Stalin feared that the Soviet Union would be left to stand against Hitler alone, and so he concluded his 1940 nonaggression pact with Hitler, expecting foreign Communist parties to abandon their anti-Fascism and fall into line. Most of their leaders did. Of course, this set back any possibilities they might otherwise have had of ever coming to power, as far as most countries were concerned. When Hitler violated the pact in 1941, and recklessly invaded the Soviet Union, however, the party line changed; Communists loyal to the Soviet Union everywhere became leaders in the anti-Fascist struggle and the most committed underground fighters against Nazism in the countries that Hitler had occupied.

U.S. PERCEPTIONS OF THE SOVIET THREAT

By contrast with the Russian experience of having been frequently invaded, the United States, bordered by much weaker neighbors and protected by an ocean on either side, has become accustomed to a high level of national security. The experience of living with the threat of war during the Cold War period thus led to a higher level of emotional tension among Americans than it did, for example, among Europeans to whom the possibility of war with neighboring powers was a routine fact of everyday life.

Moreover, the quarrels of the rest of the world seemed so remote to Americans that when their governments decided to embark on war they thought it insufficient to present the case as that of contributing to a balance of power or securing some minor territorial advantage. If Americans were to fight, it could only be on behalf of a great and transcendental principle. A great deal of manufactured crisis and misrepresentation of the facts thus went into getting the United States involved in Mexican-American and Spanish-American Wars, while Woodrow Wilson launched a crusade to end all wars in order to persuade Americans to enter World War I.

With this mind-set and this tradition, perhaps it was inevitable that the United States would interpret its rivalry with the Soviet Union as an ideological crusade, a quasi-religious struggle for the soul of the world. In doing so it was not only responding to its own predilections but also to the Russians' rhetoric. And yet ironically the launching of the Cold War, in the form of the *Truman Doctrine*, grew out of a simple balance of power problem, when the British government informed the Americans that the worsening of their economic situation made it impossible for them to continue to maintain a sphere of influence in the Balkans that would impede the spread of Russian influence to Greece and Turkey.

Believing that the Congress would not vote the necessary funds for aid to the governments of Greece and Turkey if he cast the issue in simple balance-of-power terms, Secretary of State Dean Acheson instead opted for an alarmist sensationalizing of the issue as one of resistance to Communist plans for world conquest. His message was only too effective, and the balance-of-power problem became instead a crusade that profoundly affected not only foreign policy but every corner of life within the United States.

It was ironic that the conflict became interpreted in ideological terms. Long before Lenin was born, in the early nineteenth century, Alexis de Tocqueville had written that the territorial expansion of Russia and the United States made it inevitable that the two countries would some day come into conflict with each other.

The United States sought to counter the outward thrust of Soviet expansionism on various levels. At one level, the threat was that of Soviet military power, of the movement of armies across frontiers, and the effort was made to form alliances and produce armaments to counter that threat. The threat was also political, in the sense of Communism's winning of adherents in the domestic political struggles of countries in Western Europe and elsewhere. To meet that threat, the United States embarked on a program of economic aid to strengthen the institutions of those societies, so that the public would be generally satisfied with a non-Communist state of affairs.

A covert program was also begun, which grew eventually to vast proportions, for funneling financial assistance to non-Communist politicians and parties, strengthening non-Communist labor unions, conducting propaganda operations, bribing politicians and journalists, and infiltrating and manipulating left-wing parties.

On a third level, the threat was regarded as that of Communist infiltration of U.S. society and government with the multiple aims of manipulating American popular attitudes, influencing government policy, and stealing military secrets. Although there was a basis of truth to these perceptions, they were inflated out of all proportion to the actual scope of the threat. Much of American policy became a self-destructive obsession with imaginary dangers.

CONTAINMENT AND ITS CRITICS

At the military level, the U.S. policy of blocking possible Soviet expansion was given theoretical definition by George F. Kennan, then head of the Policy Planning Staff in the State Department, under the name of *con-*

tainment. Although containment also had economic and ideological aspects, its primary character was military. The policy sought, in effect, to create all the way around the periphery of the Soviet Union and its contiguous dependent states a barrier of counterforce, a set of alliances and armed forces that would be able to block any Soviet attempt at military expansion with a superior combination of forces. In keeping with this policy, the United States created a network of alliances, and encouraged and sometimes financed the arming of governments around the world.

Interestingly, the containment policy was criticized from all points of the political compass. On the right, containment was faulted for proposing only to check further Soviet advances, not to push back Soviet power from the point to which it had already expanded. Policies proposed to achieve the reversal of Soviet advances were called "liberation" or "rollback" and were featured heavily in Republican criticisms of the Truman administration, which had adopted containment as its official strategy. However, when the Republicans came to power with Dwight David Eisenhower in 1952 and with the apostle of liberation, Secretary of State John Foster Dulles, it soon became clear that any attempt at "liberating" areas already under Soviet control posed an unacceptable risk of general warfare. When the Hungarians rose in revolt against Russian domination in 1956, expecting from Dulles's rhetoric that the United States would send armed forces to back them up, the U.S. administration made clear that nothing of the kind was going to happen, and liberation was dead as a strategy. It survived only in the form of covert harassment of governments allied with the Soviet Union, orchestrated by the Central Intelligence Agency.

From the left, represented for example by Henry Wallace's candidacy for president in 1948 on the Progressive ticket, containment was criticized for ascribing aggressive rather than merely defensive intentions to the Rus-

---

THE LOYALTY-SECURITY PROGRAM

Established by President Harry S. Truman in a 1947 executive order, the loyalty-security program was based on the premise that the Soviet Union sponsored both espionage agents and "agents of influence," who would try to shape U.S. policy in directions favorable to the Communist cause. Instead of succeeding in its objectives, however—any actual Soviet spies and agents of influence, if they existed, were too few and too well-concealed to be identified by an effort as clumsy—the loyalty-security program became a vehicle for the dismissal and persecution of a great number of people who had socialist or progressive views, organizational memberships, or even family members. The vagueness of the criteria applied, the numerous cases of mistaken identity, and the general hysteria to which the program gave rise made it ineffective; but it created a climate that helped to legitimize the McCarthyism of the 1950s.

sians, and for abandoning all hope of attempting to work cooperatively with them through such international institutions as the United Nations.

From the moderate right, represented by the conservative wing of the Republican party then led by Senator Robert Taft of Ohio, *isolationist* objections were raised to the great cost of the containment strategy and to its unwonted concern for the people of other countries. The business of the United States government, it was said, was to defend the United States, and this could be done quite effectively and at low cost without the United States having to defend half of the countries of the world besides.

Perhaps the most interesting and prophetic criticism of containment came from a more centrist position, from the political commentator, Walter Lippmann, who wrote that containment would cause the United States to overextend its resources; it would place the United States in the position of supporting every vicious and corrupt dictator who claimed to be anti-Communist; it overestimated Soviet control of the satellite countries— Russian armies were not in fact available to threaten additional countries because they had trouble maintaining control of the population of the East European satellites; and, by assuming that it was up to the United States to undertake the defense of the countries along the periphery of the Soviet empire, it underestimated the strength of the local will to resist.

Many of the problems and difficulties foreseen by Walter Lippmann in his critique of the containment policy at its inception indeed came to pass. The Cold War with the Soviet Union, necessary as it may have seemed at the time, provided ample evidence of the disastrous consequences of an obsessive search for perfect security. The three witches expressed the thought when they plotted the downfall of Macbeth: "For you all know, security / Is mortal's chiefest enemy."

HOW THE COLD WAR WAS FOUGHT

The world has been dominated by the logic of the opposition between East and West, both of which got themselves onto the treadmill of the military model of reality, the belief that survival was at stake and that all other considerations had to yield to the requirements of a security defined exclusively in military terms.

Standard military doctrine teaches that military preparedness should be based not on the *intentions* of a potential enemy, which are difficult to know, and may change, but on the enemy state's *capabilities*. This can mean that preparedness has to be massive, with potential demands that are almost infinite. The potential enemy has to be deterred from an attack by the possession of overwhelming military power which he cannot hope to match.

Seeing that the Soviet Union had no way of knowing for sure that the weapons accumulated by the United States were really intended only for defensive purposes—they also based their military posture on their rival's capabilities rather than his intentions—they felt themselves constrained to build up an array of force sufficient to deter the United States from an attack. Thus the two sides engaged in an arms race.

As was written in Chapter 14, an arms race, even if it starts out with defensive intentions, may itself precipitate a war. Fortunately, the Cold War arms race did not lead to a preventive war—if it had I would probably not be around to write this, nor you to read it.

But the arms race has had deleterious effects in other ways. Of course, the tremendous expense involved in building today's high-technology weapons has contributed to the distortion of the U.S. budget, as military spending gets first priority and needed social programs are starved of funds. But the arms race has distorted the economy, as well as the budget. Most of the money spent on technical research and development in the United States was spent on weapons, and most engineers worked in arms-related industries. This is one of the reasons why the United States dropped behind its international competition, especially Japan, in the manufacture and marketing of durable consumer goods—if engineers are working on missiles, they can't be perfecting VCRs and television sets; while the arms production companies, and the federal deficit due partly to military spending, provided ways to absorb capital that was thus not available to help the United States to compete in civilian consumer goods.

As early critics of containment policy predicted, the dynamics of the Cold War led the United States to become the hegemonic power for all the world outside the sphere of Soviet influence, to prop up or even to impose nasty dictatorial regimes that oppressed their own people, that tortured and stole money, so long as they were reliably anti-Communist; and conversely to crush revolutionary or reformist movements that might tend to the Soviet side in the Cold War, or even that might be neutral, or even that might merely try to resist U.S. domination and control. Thus, for example, the Central Intelligence Agency managed the overthrow of the moderate social democratic government of Mohammed Mossadegh in Iran and organized the return to power of the shah, whose extravagance and repressive policies only prepared the way for the fundamentalist Islamic revolution of Ayatollah Khomeini. The mildly reformist Guatemalan government of Jacobo Arbenz was overthrown by CIA skullduggery in 1954, being replaced by a ferociously right-wing military regime which, with its successors, have ruled by terror and assassination. The moderate left-wing revolutionary movement of the Sandinistas in Nicaragua, which tolerated opposition parties and an opposition press, an active Roman Catholic Church, and a mixed economy primarily in private hands, was persecuted by a counterrevolutionary war organized and financed by the CIA that contributed only to needless death and suffering.

During the Cold War, U.S. policymakers focused overwhelmingly on the Soviet Union, magnifying the presumed threat it presented out of proportion to reality, and giving defense against that threat a priority over all other considerations. Most foreign policy questions were reduced to questions of anti-Communism, while some related domestic political problems were ignored and allowed to become intractable, or were simply swept under the rug. The very serious dangers involved in the production of nuclear weapons, for example, were minimized. Nuclear accidents were hushed up, so as not to give ammunition to those who opposed the production of nuclear weapons, even when this meant that people living near nuclear plants who had been irradiated were not informed, so that they did not seek proper medical attention.

One of the great achievements of the United States has been its democratic system, with its free press and lively opposition, its balancing of power among different agencies of government to prevent authoritarianism and oppression, its democratic accountability through the legislature to the people. Sadly, that great American achievement was subverted by the practices developed to fight the Cold War. The Constitution says that only Congress can declare war; but the CIA fought its secret wars, responsible only to itself and to a president who sometimes knew only as much as the agency chose to tell him. Inconvenient foreign politicians were assassinated. Huge amounts of funds were used without responsible accounting and applied to improper purposes. The American public, along with that in other countries, was misinformed by fraudulent news stories concocted by the secret agencies and fed to gullible or bribed journalists. On occasion, drug smuggling was encouraged to provide sources of income for the secret armies being operated in Southeast Asia and Central America. Political processes in other countries were subverted through bribery, manipulation of the electoral process, and the sponsoring of military seizures of power. It is a sorry record.

THE END OF THE COLD WAR

Nevertheless, during Mikhail Gorbachev's leadership of the Soviet Union, the world was presented with an extraordinary opportunity. The Soviet Union was being transformed so that it no longer resembled the totalitarian monolith of the Stalin years. The East European countries recovered their freedom of action, as Gorbachev pledged that Soviet troops would not intervene in their internal affairs, and they used it to move toward open political systems and open economies. The Cold War could now be liquidated. The principles of political and economic freedom had won; in a sense the West had won, although in another sense the reformers and indeed most people in the Soviet Union and Eastern Europe had certainly won, too.

At first the more frozen cold warriors in the West refused to believe the evidence of their senses. By definition, totalitarianism could not change. Soviet propaganda was designed to mislead; perhaps *glasnost* (openness; transparency) and *perestroika* (restructuring) were simply fraudulent elements in a new Soviet disinformation program.[1] But finally the genuineness of the changes in the East became too obvious to be denied and the government of the United States confronted a challenge. Had too much inertia built up behind the old routines? Could the secret agencies be made accountable? Had it become too comfortable for presidents to pose as gladiators rather than to deal with real problems? Instead of a genuine adjustment to reality, it might be easier to keep the apparatus of the national security state intact and merely direct it against a new target: Iraq, perhaps, or North Korea; a war on terrorism perhaps, or a war on drugs—which could be kept going indefinitely because it would be impossible to know they were ever finally won.

The ending of the Cold War and the coming of democracy to Eastern Europe presented the world with a bright moment of hope and opportunity. But it also provided an occasion for remembering that the problems that the classical political philosophers had been concerned with, and the dangers the framers of the U.S. Constitution had tried to guard against—the various ways in which power can be abused—did not begin with the Cold War and have not ended with it.

NOTE

1. Caspar Weinberger, Reagan's secretary of defense, was quoted as late as October 1993 saying, "I've never been an admirer of Gorbachev. He's a phony. He took in the West. He never actually repudiated communism." *Image* magazine, *San Francisco Examiner*, October 24, 1993, p. 4.

KEY TERMS

Cold War   isolationism

proletarian internationalism   glasnost

Truman Doctrine   perestroika

containment

Conclusion:
Past, Present, Future

CHEER UP!

THINGS MAY BE
GETTING WORSE
AT A SLOWER RATE.

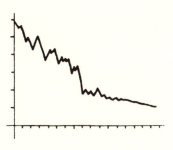

Ashleigh Brilliant

Man is a part of nature, which means he has been programmed to survive, to assert himself, to procreate, and to protect his young; to achieve those purposes he has had to develop techniques of combat, of conflict and cooperation, of competition and the establishment of consensus. Much of his behavior is rationally designed to achieve these goals, even when its rationality is not known to the conscious mind but is only instinctive. Just as an ideology that was based on the achievement of interests may become functionally autonomous, however, and indicate behavior that is actually contrary to one's interests in a particular case, so some fundamental drive, or even a culturally learned pattern of behavior whose implicit purpose aims at the furtherance of nature's intentions, may become functionally autonomous. That is, it may not in fact be productive of the intended purpose in this specific case. For the person in question, the behavior may have an "expressive" rather than an "instrumental" function—that is, it may make him or her feel better to act in that way, but it will not achieve their goals and may in fact defeat their achievement of those goals.

People may have successful political careers because they are lucky, but they have probably also been behaving instrumentally, with a lively sense of the best way to achieve their purposes. Those purposes represent some combination of the promotion of one's own career and the pursuit of goals in the interest of the political community, or of some partial community the politician represents. Some politicians seem to have hardly any goal beyond self-promotion. To be sure, without a certain amount of self-promotion, a politician cannot survive and prosper; but the judgment of history, and ours as students of politics in general, cannot be kind to the political figure who has no ambitions beyond personal power and wealth.

The best-drawn constitutions, like those of the United States and the Federal Republic of Germany, try to create institutions so constructed that the efforts of even the most opportunistic and narrow-minded of politicians will work for the general good, because that is how election and re-election are won and bureaucratic turf defended. Nevertheless, it is not possible for optimum or even satisfactory solutions of many problems to be achieved simply on the basis of the automatic functioning of cleverly designed institutions. For the satisfactory resolution of some problems it is necessary to take into account interests that may not increase one's vote total in the next elections: the interest of future generations, for example, or even the long-range interests of existing populations. For this reason, we have learned to honor statesmen, who can see beyond the immediate and the short-range, who have the courage to sacrifice some immediate short-term element of interest, perhaps to risk their careers, in order to achieve lasting solutions, solutions of greater value for more people over a longer time.

PROBLEM-SOLVING AND CONSENSUS-BUILDING

In situations of conflict, people's positions are usually stated in terms of ideological principle. One faculty member may announce that a greater stress should be put on research, while another will argue that teaching has not received enough emphasis. The government of one country may proclaim its devotion to the freedom of the seas, while another may appeal to the rights of national self-determination.

As we have already noted, however, ideology is normally a generalized statement of interests. The first step in resolving a dispute is to find out what specific interest each of the contenders is concerned to defend or promote. It is altogether likely that an insistence on different principles will lead to nothing but conflict, whereas it may be possible to reach an accommodation with respect to the specific interests at stake. In his work as a university administrator, the author has found that if apparently irreconcilable conflicts of principle are set aside, a reasonable compromise settlement of the underlying differences about specific interests can usually be found that is acceptable to all parties.

In fact, disagreements about principle are so often rationalizations of competing claims for allocation of resources that it is amusing to see how often presentations to decision-making bodies—for example, testimony before congressional committees—can be quite adequately translated as "Please give us money."

As has been pointed out, an individual's political attitudes and behavior grow out of a particular conception of identity, leading to the specification of interests and to an ideological formulation that serves as a guide to attitudes and action in cases where interests are not obvious. The same can be said for countries. The principles of a country's foreign policy, seen in this light, are an ideologization of its interests, as these are derived from a concept of national identity.

Thus Mexico, for example, although a country of substantial population and area, thinks of itself as small and weak because it is next to the powerful United States, and because it has historically been the victim of annexation of its lands by the United States and the involvement of the United States in its political affairs, usually on behalf of U.S. economic interests operating in Mexico. As a result, Mexico identifies its interest as being able to manage its own affairs while still receiving foreign investments and being involved in international trade. The ideology of Mexico's foreign policy, therefore, as announced on many occasions over the years, stresses the juridical equality of states, no matter their size; state sovereignty and the denial of any right of foreign intervention; and the solution of disputes by peaceful means only. Sometimes, in fact, those principles are at variance with what it is in Mexico's interests to do in a specific case. In that case, interests and not principles are followed, but the principles are nevertheless firmly reasserted on the next possible occasion, and serve to guide Mexico's policies when no countervailing interest seems at stake.

The process in the United States is similar. Americans conceive of their country as democratic and capitalist (although "free-market" terminology is more common, as "capitalist" has a flavor of Marxism about it, and some negative connotations). Because of its capitalist character, the economic interests that U.S. foreign policy defends are often those of large corporations, normally but not always "domiciled" in the United States.

The transformation of the global situation that followed on the end of the Cold War has been called the "New World Order." A new world order is indeed taking shape, its salient characteristics being the triumph of "free-market" economic norms, and the general acceptance of at least the rhetoric, if not always the practice, of constitutional democracy. This is an occasion for rejoicing, but only in part. As one set of problems seems to have been solved, another set has taken its place.

The triumph of capitalism has not only been the victory of certain principles of economic organization; it has meant the strengthening of the power of international corporations and financial institutions, and the corresponding weakening of attempts by national governments to regulate them. Much of that regulation was uneconomic, counterproductive, and wasteful; but it also had a purpose, which was to avoid the concentration of power, to promote a more equal distribution of income, and to ensure that the general interests of the community would be protected. Although the ideology of capitalism is now generally dominant in the world, those regulatory functions still need to be performed. The danger is always present that governments will come to represent only the rich and powerful.

In other words, the power of the institutions of international capitalism needs to be counterbalanced—as excessive power, as James Madison taught us, must always be counterbalanced. In general, this can occur in two ways: by a revival of the consciousness of governments of their responsibility to those who happen not to be rich and powerful, through a reinvigoration of the institutions of democratic control, such as political parties and public education; or by the strengthening of the interests and organizations of people other than the owners of wealth—that is, of labor and consumers.

The power of labor has grown weaker as changes in the processes of production have continuously replaced labor by investment in new technology or new forms of organization, which is, after all, the nature of a dynamic capitalism. It may be, however, that the role of labor will become more important again in a different form, at the level of the individual company or productive unit, as more complicated technologically sophisticated processes require the involvement of workers in decision-making to a greater extent, so that workers may have a participatory role, although perhaps locally rather than at the level of nationally organized labor organizations. Additionally, more businesses that do better than break even, but not enough better to produce a satisfactory rate of return for investors, may come to be owned by their workers.

Consumer organizations are likely to grow in importance, as voting blocs or pressure organizations, or even in the form of environmentally conscious or "green" political parties. The environmental movement is one form in which the interests of consumers, present and future, are brought to bear to limit, or balance, the narrower interests promoted by the owners and managers of corporations.

At all events, there is room for optimism. In human affairs, there seem to be cycles, as situations that have developed too far in one direction swing back in the other. Surely Hegel had it right: history moves dialectically, in pendular movements; as contradictions develop, each thesis produces its own antithesis. Or to vary the metaphor, in the environmentalist language we are learning to speak: like other parts of nature, human society has the ability to heal itself, to recover and regenerate its well-being. What could be more appropriate than to face a new millennium in a hopeful mood?

Suggested for
Further Reading

GENERAL

Butz, Otto. *Of Man and Politics: An Introduction to Political Science*. New York: Holt, Rinehart & Winston, 1960.

Lipson, Leslie. *The Democratic Civilization*. New York: Oxford University Press, 1964.

Needler, Martin C. *The Concepts of Comparative Politics*. New York: Praeger, 1991.

Sabine, George H. *A History of Political Theory*. New York: Henry Holt, 1937.

Shively, W. Phillips. *Power and Choice: An Introduction to Political Science*. New York: Random House, 1987.

CHAPTER 1

All available in various editions:

Aristotle. *Politics*.
Hobbes, Thomas. *Leviathan*.
Locke, John. *Second Treatise on Government*.
Plato. *The Republic*.
Rousseau, Jean-Jacques. *The Social Contract*.

CHAPTER 2

Almond, Gabriel and Sidney Verba. *The Civic Culture*. Princeton: Princeton University Press, 1963.

Cassinelli, C. W. *The Politics of Freedom. An Analysis of the Modern Democratic State*. Seattle: University of Washington Press, 1961.

Dahl, Robert. *A Preface to Democratic Theory*. Chicago: University of Chicago Press, 1956.

Franklin, Daniel and Michael Baun. *Political Culture and Constitutionalism: A Comparative Approach*. New York: M. E. Sharpe, 1995.

Friedrich, Carl J. *The New Image of the Common Man*. Boston: Little, Brown, 1950.
Needler, Martin C. *The Problem of Democracy in Latin America*. Lexington, MA: Heath-Lexington, 1987.

CHAPTER 3

Burke, Edmund. *Reflections on the Revolution in France* (various editions).
Hayek, Friedrich. *The Road to Serfdom*. Chicago: University of Chicago Press, 1944.
Marx, Karl and Friedrich Engels, *The Communist Manifesto* (various editions).
Mill, John Stuart. *On Liberty* (various editions).
Smith, Adam. *The Wealth of Nations* (various editions).

CHAPTER 4

Bickel, Alexander M. *The Morality of Consent*. New Haven: Yale University Press, 1975.
Calvert, Peter. *Revolution*. London: Macmillan, 1970.
Cohen, Carl. *Civil Disobedience: Conscience, Tactics and the Law*. New York: Columbia University Press, 1971.
Hook, Sidney. *Heresy, Yes—Conspiracy, No*. New York: John Day, 1953.
Weber, Max. *Economy and Society*. New York: Bedminster Press, 1968.
Wolfe, Alan. *The Seamy Side of Democracy*. New York: David McKay, 1973.

CHAPTER 5

Black, Cyril E. *The Dynamics of Modernization*. New York: Harper & Row, 1966.
Black, Jan Knippers. *Development in Theory and Practice: Bridging the Gap*. Boulder: Westview, 1991.
Huntington, Samuel P. *Political Order in Changing Societies*. New Haven: Yale University Press, 1968.
Needler, Martin C. *Political Development in Latin America: Instability, Violence, and Evolutionary Change*. New York: Random House, 1968.
Seligson, Mitchell, ed. *The Gap Between Rich and Poor*. Boulder: Westview, 1984.
Sharkansky, Ira. *The United States: A Study of a Developing Country*. New York: David McKay, 1975.

CHAPTER 6

Berger, Suzanne, ed. *Organizing Interests in Western Europe: Pluralism, Corporatism, and the Transformation of Politics*. Cambridge: Cambridge University Press, 1981.
Burnham, Walter Dean. *Critical Elections and the Mainsprings of American Politics*. New York: Norton, 1970.
Campbell, Angus, Philip Converse, Warren Miller, and Donald Stokes. *The American Voter*. New York: Wiley, 1960.
Downs, Anthony. *An Economic Theory of Democracy*. New York: Harper & Row, 1957.

Duverger, Maurice. *Political Parties*. New York: Wiley, 1954.

Rae, Douglas W. *The Political Consequences of Electoral Laws*. New Haven: Yale University Press, 1967.

CHAPTER 7

Farrand, Max. *The Framing of the Constitution of the United States*. New Haven: Yale University Press, 1976.

Fustel de Coulanges, Numa Denis. *The Ancient City*. Garden City, NY: Doubleday Anchor, 1955 (first published 1864).

Friedrich, Carl J. *Constitutional Government and Democracy*. Boston: Ginn & Co., 1950.

Hamilton, Alexander, James Madison, and John Jay. *The Federalist Papers* (various editions).

Riker, William H. *Federalism: Origin, Operation, Significance*. Boston: Little, Brown, 1964.

CHAPTER 8

Allen, Graham. *Reinventing Democracy*. London: Features Unlimited, 1995.

Linz, Juan and Arturo Valenzuela, eds. *The Failure of Presidential Democracy*. Baltimore: Johns Hopkins University Press, 1994.

Neustadt, Richard. *Presidential Power*. New York: Wiley, 1960.

Norton, Philip. *The British Polity*, 2nd. ed. New York: Longman, 1990.

Rose, Richard and Ezra N. Suleiman, eds. *Presidents and Prime Ministers*. Washington, DC: American Enterprise Institute, 1980.

CHAPTER 9

Allison, Graham T. *Essence of Decision: Explaining the Cuban Missile Crisis*. Boston: Little, Brown, 1971.

Crozier, Michel. *The Bureaucratic Phenomenon*. Chicago: University of Chicago Press, 1963.

Goodsell, Charles T. *The Case for Bureaucracy*. 2nd ed. Chatham, NJ: Chatham House, 1985.

Krislov, Samuel. *Representative Bureaucracy*. Englewood Cliffs, NJ: Prentice-Hall, 1974.

CHAPTER 10

Blair, John M. *The Control of Oil*. New York: Random House, 1976.

Daly, Herman, ed. *Economics, Ecology, Ethics*. San Francisco: W. H. Freeman, 1980.

Eisner, Robert. *How Real Is the Federal Deficit?* New York: Free Press, 1986.

Heidenheimer, Arnold J, Hugh Heclo, and Carolyn Adams. *Comparative Public Policy*, 2nd ed. New York: St. Martin's Press, 1983.

Kymlicka, B. B. and Jean V. Matthews. *The Reagan Revolution*. Chicago: Dorsey, 1988.

Shonfield, Andrew. *Modern Capitalism*. Oxford: Oxford University Press, 1965.

CHAPTER 11

Claude, Inis L., Jr. *Power and International Relations*. New York: Random House, 1962.
Fozouni, Bahman. "Confutation of Political Realism." *International Studies Quarterly*, vol. 39, no. 4 (December 1995).
Kennan, George F. *American Diplomacy, 1900–1950*. New York: Mentor Books, 1952.
Morgenthau, Hans. *Politics Among Nations*, 5th ed. New York: Knopf, 1978.
Wolfers, Arnold. *Discord and Collaboration*. Baltimore: Johns Hopkins University Press, 1962.

CHAPTER 12

Deutsch, Karl W. *Nationalism and Its Alternatives*. New York: Knopf, 1969.
Emerson, Rupert. *From Empire to Nation: The Rise to Self-Assertion of Asian and African Peoples*. Cambridge, MA: Harvard University Press, 1967.
Hobson, J.A. *Imperialism*. London: Allen and Unwin, 1938.
Needler, Martin C. *The United States and the Latin American Revolution*, 2nd. ed. Los Angeles: UCLA Latin American Center, 1977.

CHAPTER 13

Clark, Grenville and Louis B. Sohn. *World Peace Through World Law*, 3rd ed. Cambridge, MA: Harvard University Press, 1966.
Claude, Inis L., Jr. *Swords into Plowshares: The Problems and Progress of International Organization*, 4th ed. New York: Random House, 1971.
George, Stephen. *Politics and Policy in the European Community*. New York: Oxford University Press, 1985.
Weiss, Thomas, David Forsythe, and Roger Coate. *The United Nations and Changing World Politics*. Boulder, CO: Westview, 1994.

CHAPTER 14

Gansler, Jacques S. *The Defense Industry*. Cambridge, MA: MIT Press, 1990.
Garthoff, Raymond. *Soviet Strategy in the Nuclear Age*, 2nd ed. New York: Praeger, 1962.
Kissinger, Henry. *Nuclear Weapons and Foreign Policy*. New York: Harper & Row, 1957.
Stares, Paul B. *The Militarization of Space: U.S. Policy 1945–1984*. Ithaca, NY: Cornell University Press, 1985.

CHAPTER 15

Agee, Philip. *Inside the Company: CIA Diary*. London: Penguin Books, 1974.
Dallek, Robert. *The American Style of Foreign Policy*. New York: Knopf, 1983.

Eldridge, Albert F. *Images of Conflict*. New York: St. Martin's Press, 1979.
Needler, Martin C. *Understanding Foreign Policy*. New York: Holt, Rinehart, and Winston, 1966.

Index

ABOUT THE AUTHOR

MARTIN C. NEEDLER is Dean of the School of International Studies at the University of the Pacific. He has taught at Harvard, Dartmouth, the University of Michigan, and the University of New Mexico, where he also directed the Latin American Studies program and the doctoral program in political science. Formerly a senior associate member of St. Antony's College, Oxford, a research associate at the Harvard Center for International Affairs, and a senior research fellow at the University of Southampton, he is also a Fellow of the Mountbatten Centre for Strategic Studies.

ISBN 0-275-95440-4

EAN

90000>

9 780275 954406

HARDCOVER BAR CODE